The Coming
China Wars

FT Press
FINANCIAL TIMES

In an increasingly competitive world, it is quality
of thinking that gives an edge—an idea that opens new
doors, a technique that solves a problem, or an insight
that simply helps make sense of it all.

We work with leading authors in the various arenas
of business and finance to bring cutting-edge thinking
and best-learning practices to a global market.

It is our goal to create world-class print publications
and electronic products that give readers
knowledge and understanding that can then be
applied, whether studying or at work.

To find out more about our business
products, you can visit us at www.ftpress.com.

The Coming China Wars

Where They Will Be Fought and How They Can Be Won

Peter Navarro

Upper Saddle River, NJ • Boston • Indianapolis • San Francisco
New York • Toronto • Montreal • London • Munich • Paris • Madrid
Cape Town • Sydney • Tokyo • Singapore • Mexico City

www.ftpress.com

Vice President and Editor-in-Chief: Tim Moore
Executive Editor: Jim Boyd
Editorial Assistant: Susie Abraham
Development Editors: Russ Hall and Dr. Cynthia J. Smith
Associate Editor-in-Chief and Director of Marketing: Amy Neidlinger
Cover Designer: Chuti Prasertsith
Managing Editor: Gina Kanouse
Senior Project Editor: Kristy Hart
Copy Editor: Keith Cline
Senior Indexer: Cheryl Lenser
Compositor: Interactive Composition Corporation
Manufacturing Buyer: Dan Uhrig

FT Press

FINANCIAL TIMES

© 2007 by Pearson Education, Inc.
Published by Financial Times
Upper Saddle River, New Jersey 07458

FT Press offers excellent discounts on this book when ordered in quantity for bulk purchases or special sales. For more information, please contact U.S. Corporate and Government Sales, 1-800-382-3419, corpsales@pearsontechgroup.com. For sales outside the U.S., please contact International Sales, 1-317-581-3793, international@pearsontechgroup.com.

Company and product names mentioned herein are the trademarks or registered trademarks of their respective owners.

Printed in the United States of America

First Printing October, 2006

ISBN 0-13-228128-7

Pearson Education LTD.
Pearson Education Australia PTY, Limited.
Pearson Education Singapore, Pte. Ltd.
Pearson Education North Asia, Ltd.
Pearson Education Canada, Ltd.
Pearson Educatión de Mexico, S.A. de C.V.
Pearson Education—Japan
Pearson Education Malaysia, Pte. Ltd.

Library of Congress Cataloging-in-Publication Data

Navarro, Peter.
    The coming China wars : where they will be fought and how they will be won / Peter Navarro.

        p. cm.

    Includes bibliographical references and index.
    ISBN 0-13-228128-7 (hardback : alk. paper) 1. China—Foreign economic relations.
2. China—Foreign relations—Forecasting. 3. China—Commercial policy.
4. Globalization—Economic aspects—China. 5. China—Economic policy—2000- 6.
China—Politics and government—2002- 7. International economic relations. I. Title.

    HF1604.N38 2006

    337.51—dc22

                                                                        2006014209

DEDICATION

One of the consequences of raising children in this world is that they make you think a lot more about the future. Because of the storms brewing in China, the future our children now face appears to be, at best, highly uncertain. At worst, it could be one that the philosopher Thomas Hobbes might describe as "nasty" and "brutish"—if no longer short.

Threats of terrorism and some nuclear or biological cataclysm are not at the epicenter of my concern about the future. Although these threats are all too real, as a professional economist, I must leave them to be pondered and parsed and, I hope, countered by qualified political and military strategists.

Rather, as a professional economist, what deeply concerns me is a single country—China. China has put itself on a collision course with the rest of the world. The Coming China Wars will be fought over everything from decent jobs, livable wages, and leading edge technologies to strategic resources such as oil, copper, and steel, and eventually to our most basic of all needs—bread, water, and air. Unless all of the nations of this world—including China—immediately address these impending conflicts, the results will be catastrophic.

This book is dedicated to preventing that catastrophe—and to the children. May they not be engulfed by the maelstrom.

The art of war is of vital importance to the State. It is a matter of life and death, a road either to safety or to ruin. Hence it is a subject of inquiry which can on no account be neglected.

—Sun Tzu, *The Art of War*

CONTENTS

ABOUT THE AUTHOR

Peter Navarro is a business professor at the University of California-Irvine. He is the author of the path-breaking management book, *The Well-Timed Strategy,* and the bestselling investment book *If It's Raining in Brazil, Buy Starbucks.* His unique and internationally recognized expertise lies in his "big picture" application of a highly sophisticated but easily accessible macroeconomic analysis of the business environment and financial markets for investors and corporate executives.

Navarro's articles have appeared in a wide range of publications, from *Business Week,* the *Los Angeles Times, New York Times,* and *Wall Street Journal* to the *Harvard Business Review,* the *Sloan Management Review,* and the *Journal of Business.* Professor Navarro is a widely sought after and gifted public speaker. He has appeared frequently on Bloomberg TV and radio, CNN, CNBC, and NPR, as well as on all three major network news shows.

His free weekly investment newsletter is published at www.peternavarro.com.

Other Books by Peter Navarro

The Well-Timed Strategy: Managing the Business Cycle for Competitive Advantage (2006)

What the Best MBA's Know: How to Apply the Greatest Ideas Taught in the Best Business Schools (2005)

When the Market Moves, Will You Be Ready?: How to Profit From Major Market Events (2004)

If It's Raining in Brazil, Buy Starbucks: The Investor's Guide to Profiting From News and Other Market-Moving Events (2001)

The Policy Game: How Special Interests and Idealogues Are Stealing America (1984)

The Dimming of America: The Real Costs of Electric Utility Regulatory Failure (1984)

INTRODUCTION

News Release, October 25, 2012

U.S.-China Chill Melts Down World Markets

NEW YORK—Global stock exchanges were devastated this week by the worst collapse in history as a wave of panic selling followed the sun from Asia through Europe and back to Wall Street. The pandemonium was triggered by a Chinese government announcement that it would no longer finance the mounting budget and trade deficits of a "profligate United States" that "refuses to live within its means" and that "insists on scapegoating China for its own internal economic problems." Nor would China continue to try to prop up "an increasingly worthless dollar."

As the Chinese began dumping U.S. assets on Wall Street, both stock and bond prices plummeted. The panic soon spread to other exchanges around the world as gold soared to more than $1,000 an ounce and fear of a global depression deepened.

China's actions have been widely interpreted as harsh retaliation for U.S. congressional passage of stiff protectionist tariffs on a wide range of manufactured goods. With the presidential election less than a month away, both houses of Congress up for electoral grabs, and the U.S. economy stuck in reverse, Republicans and Democrats alike are pushing additional legislation addressing everything from the growing trade in Chinese counterfeit goods, illegal drugs, and ballistic missiles to the international spillover from China's mounting environmental pollution.

It's been a tough year for Sino-U.S. relations. In January, the U.S. ambassador to the United Nations stormed out in protest over "the repeated crass commercial use" by China of its U.N. veto to "shield terrorist regimes such as Iran from diplomatic sanctions in exchange for oil." In March, China's president abruptly cancelled a state visit after the U.S. Treasury Department branded China a "currency manipulator." During an unusually hot August that raised collateral fears of global warming, the U.S. Pacific Fleet engaged in a tense, week-long standoff over Taiwan with China's recently acquired, and nuclear missile-equipped, blue water navy.

Meanwhile, domestic unrest in China continues to escalate as an increasingly restive population seeks greater income equality, more worker rights, improved health care, a cleaner environment, a halt to widespread government corruption, and an end to massive public works projects such as the Three Gorges Dam that have displaced millions of people without adequately compensating them. A recent report released by the U.S. Central Intelligence Agency has warned that should such domestic unrest reach a boiling point in China, the result may be "sharper military conflicts with the United States, Taiwan, and possibly even Japan as Chinese leaders seek to unify the now increasingly fractured nation against a 'common enemy.'"

The best of economic times for China are fast becoming the worst of times for the rest of us. China's "cowboy capitalism" and amoral foreign policies are triggering a whole range of economic, financial, environmental, political, and military tsunamis that threaten to engulf us—as well as the Chinese people. The ever-growing dangers lay in a model of rapid, unsustainable economic growth, coupled with a wanton disregard for both human life and intellectual property. The myriad dangers from the Coming China Wars are real—and increasingly personal. Consider these scenarios based on actual events:

- Your father almost dies from a massive heart attack because the "Lipitor" prescription he filled on the Internet was laced with

Chinese fakes. Your mother breaks her hip because the phony "Evista" medication she took for osteoporosis was nothing more than molded Chinese chalk. Your house gets robbed by a drug addict high on methamphetamines made from ephedra grass grown on Chinese state-run farms and transported to New York via Panama by Triad gangs.

- You walk out of a Wal-Mart with a big smile and a large basket laden with cheap Chinese goods ranging from a fancy new laser printer and plasma TV to shirts, socks, and running shoes. Your smile quickly turns to a frown as your eyes begin to sting and lungs burn from the Asian "brown cloud" now visible on the horizon. It is 90-proof "Chinese chog"—a particularly toxic atmospheric smog that has hitchhiked on the jet stream all the way from China's industrial heartland where everything in your basket was first manufactured.

- Your bank balance drops precipitously as rising interest rates drive your adjustable rate monthly mortgage payment off the charts and as you shell out more than you ever dreamed to fill your gas tank. Your mortgage payments are being held hostage to China's currency-manipulation policies. You pay dearly at the pump because of the price-shocking effects of China's rapidly rising thirst for oil.

The Coming China Wars is not just a story about how China's emergence as the world's "factory floor" is affecting you and your pocketbook. The story is far larger than any one of us or any single country. This book takes a tough, hard look at the eight major China Wars already well underway:

1. The Not-So-Swashbuckling Piracy Wars

Following a centuries-old tradition of skullduggery in the South China Seas, China has become the world's largest pirate nation. China's modern buccaneers, with the strong support of their government, are not just stealing software and Hollywood movies on DVDs. They are blatantly counterfeiting virtually the entire alphabet of goods—from air conditioners, automobiles, and brake pads to razors, refrigerators, and the world's most recognizable pharmaceuticals such as Lipitor, Norvasc, and Viagra.

In the process, these pirates are posing grave health risks to hundreds of millions of people. They are also destroying all semblance of global intellectual property law protections vitally needed to spur innovation.

2. The 21ˢᵗ Century Opium Wars

With an unholy triangle of Triad gangsters, international smugglers, and corrupt Communist Party officials as cartel kingpins, China has emerged as one of the world's biggest dope dealers. Most despicably, China is not just the world's "factory floor" for legitimate goods but also for the so-called precursor chemicals used to produce all four of the world's major hard drugs: cocaine, heroin, methamphetamine, and Ecstasy.

China has also retained its historical role as a major transit area for opium from the Golden Triangle, and it is rapidly emerging as a highly efficient production center for Ecstasy and speed. Not coincidentally, Chinese criminal syndicates are awash in illicit cash, and China's banking system is becoming an important hub for global money laundering.

3. The Air Pollution and Global Warming Wars

With claim to 16 of the world's 20 dirtiest cities in the World Bank's environmental Hall of Shame, China has been dubiously crowned as the most polluted nation on Earth. As a result of its rapid industrialization and lax environmental controls, China's prodigious toxic emissions are now spewing well beyond its environmentally porous borders.

Storms regularly rise up from China's Inner Mongolian desert steppes and blanket Korea and Japan with tons upon tons of toxics-laden dust. Chinese chog regularly hitchhikes along the jet stream, only to descend thousands of miles away in big cities such as Los Angeles and Vancouver and to despoil visibility in pristine towns such as Aspen. With its belching coal plants and rapidly multiplying automobile fleet, China will soon eclipse the United States as the single largest contributor to global warming.

4. The "Blood for Oil" Wars

With its economy rocketing, China has emerged as the world's second largest petroleum consumer behind only the United States. Astonishingly, China now accounts for almost *half* the growth in global oil demand and is the primary catalyst for an oil market hurtling toward $100 a barrel.

To lock down its petroleum supplies—and lock the rest of the world out—China has adopted a reprehensible foreign policy based on President Hu Jintao's amoral mantra of "just business, no political conditions." It has shipped ballistic missiles and transferred nuclear weapons technologies to the radical Iranian regime, used its diplomatic veto in the United Nations to sanction genocide in the Sudan, and facilitated the looting of public treasuries by dictators in oil- and mineral-rich African countries from Angola to Zimbabwe.

This unconscionable blood for oil diplomacy has resulted in the slaughter of millions, the impoverishment of millions more, and a rapid spike in nuclear proliferation in both the Middle East and Asia.

5. The New Imperialist Wars

In a supreme historical irony, one of imperialism's worst former victims has become the 21st century's most relentlessly imperialistic nation. From Brazil, Cuba, and Venezuela to Equatorial Guinea and the Ivory Coast, China dangles lavish, low-interest loans and sophisticated weapons systems as bait. It then uses its "weapons of mass construction"—a huge army of engineers and laborers—to build everything from roads and dams to parliament buildings and palaces.

After these unwitting countries are driven ever deeper into China's debt, China's imperialistic quid pro quo is the rapid extraction of the country's raw materials—Bolivian tin, Chilean copper, Cuban nickel, Congolese cobalt, gold from Sierra Leone, Rwandan tungsten, and the vast mineral wealth of South Africa.

As the despotic puppets running China's "new colonies" transfer billions in bribes to their Swiss bank accounts, the peasants these despots rule over slide ever deeper into poverty.

6. The Damnable Dam and Water Wars

China is the dam-happiest place on Earth. With far too little water, far too much of that water horribly polluted, and the once-mighty Yellow River running dry for more than 200 days a year, China is facing a severe water crisis that already pits angry farmers against encroaching industrialists, millions of displaced "peasants with pitchforks" against corrupt government officials, and downstream versus upstream provinces.

This is also a fierce diplomatic battle being waged between upstream and downstream *countries.* Upstream, China is constructing a phalanx of mega-dams on the Mekong River despite the strong protests of the downstream countries of Cambodia, Laos, Thailand, and Vietnam. These dams—including one that will be more than 100 stories tall and the tallest in the world— now threaten the food supply, transit routes, and livelihoods of more than 50 million people living in the Lower Mekong River Basin. Already, the Mekong has recorded its lowest levels ever and has flowed close to rock bottom near the end of its journey in Vietnam.

Precisely because of these many and varied economically driven conflicts, we and our children are destined to fight a complex and highly interrelated series of wars with China on many, many fronts. As you will see in the chapters that follow, a reckless and ruthless Chinese government is directly to blame for many of these Coming China Wars. However, it is also disturbingly true that China's hyper-growth is causing the world's most populous nation to spin out of the control of its leaders.

As China's economy continues to grow at unprecedented rates, the "strange bedfellow" combination of a totally unrestrained free market capitalism operating under a harshly repressive totalitarian umbrella is becoming more and more like a political and social Molotov cocktail rather than an exemplary economic model for the rest of the world. That is precisely why the greatest danger to the world community may be China's coming "wars from within." These wars from within may be triggered by any number of internal ticking economic and demographic time bombs that threaten to bring on that which the Chinese people fear most—"chaos" or *luan*.

7. China's Wars from Within

Over the past decade, the number of protests and riots in China has risen to nearly 100,000 annually. This is hardly surprising to any astute China watcher. People are being pushed beyond tolerance as the Chinese countryside becomes a slave labor camp and dumping ground for every imaginable pollutant.

The rural peasantry is being sucked dry by wastrel government tax collectors. Corrupt local government officials seize land on behalf of developers, pocket the monies that are supposed to compensate villagers, and then enlist local gangsters to quell protests.

In the big cities, unpaid construction workers leap to their deaths in protest of wages that go callously unpaid. Meanwhile, on China's Western prairies, ethnic separatist tensions continue to smolder over the ongoing "Hanification" of the mostly Muslim population on the Western frontier.

8. China's Ticking Time Bombs

China is rapidly graying—getting old faster than it is getting rich. China is now facing a pension crisis that will make solving the unfunded social security liabilities of equally graying countries such as the United States, Japan, and Germany look like strolls through the park.

China is also a nation getting increasingly sick. Environmental pollution serves as a deadly catalyst for an explosion of myriad cancers and an epidemic of respiratory and heart diseases. This rapid rise in ill health is coming precisely when China's once-vaunted public health-care system has totally unraveled.

Adding to these extreme pressures is an HIV/AIDS epidemic that may soon become the worst in the world. This epidemic began with *the* most scurrilous HIV/AIDS blood donor scandal on the planet. It is being rapidly fueled by rampant intravenous drug use, a late-blooming 1960s-style sexual revolution, and the explosive reemergence of China's once-infamous flesh trade.

The radical remedies and reforms that will be required to avoid the chaos, casualties, and hardships of the Coming China Wars—both within China and beyond its borders—will never occur unless we gain a much better understanding of the basic economic forces driving these political, financial, social, energy, and environmental conflicts. My abiding hope, particularly for the children, is that a better understanding of the complexities of the economic origins of the Coming China Wars will help lead to their peaceful resolution. Cultivating such an understanding—and calling China and the rest of the world to action—are the ultimate goals of this book. The fictional News Release from the year 2012 leading off this Introduction is just one glimpse of a future that we all should urgently seek to avoid.

1

THE "CHINA PRICE" AND WEAPONS OF MASS PRODUCTION

The China Price. They are the three scariest words in U.S. industry. Cut your price at least 30% or lose your customers. Nearly every manufacturer is vulnerable—from furniture to networking gear. The result: a massive shift in economic power is underway.

—Business Week[1]

China has an official policy for the economy to grow at 7%–8% per year, the rate which the ruling mandarins calculate is needed to create about 15 million new jobs a year, to absorb new entrants into the labor market and discards from the shrinking state sector. Every policy, from the value of the Chinese currency to the delay in closing an unsafe coal mine, is calibrated to ensure that economic output continues to expand at this rapid pace.

—Financial Mail[2]

Since 1980, China's Adam Smith-on-steroids economy has grown by almost 10% a year—doubling an astonishing three times. During its ascent, China has far outperformed Japan's 1980s "economic miracle." It has also run circles around the vaunted "Four Dragons"—Hong Kong, Korea, Taiwan, and Singapore—even in their economic heydays.

Any complete understanding of the Coming China Wars must begin with this observation: China's hyper-rate of economic growth is export driven; and the ability of the Chinese to conquer one export market after another, often in blitzkrieg fashion, derives from their ability to set the so-called China Price.

The China Price refers to the fact that Chinese manufacturers can undercut significantly the prices offered by foreign competitors over a mind-bogglingly wide range of products and services. Today, as a result of the China Price, China produces more than 70% of the world's DVDs and toys; more than half of its bikes, cameras, shoes, and telephones; and more than a third of its air conditioners, color TVs, computer monitors, luggage, and microwave ovens. The country also has established dominant market positions in everything from furniture, refrigerators, and washing machines to jeans and underwear (yes, boxers *and* briefs).

Given China's demonstrated ability to conquer one export market after another, the obvious question is this: How has China been able to emerge as the world's "factory floor"? The answer lies in China's primary "weapon of mass production"—the China Price. The nine major economic "drivers" of the China Price are as follows:

- Low-wage, high-quality work by a highly disciplined, educated, and nonunion work force
- Minimal worker health and safety regulations
- Lax environmental regulations and enforcement
- The supercharging, catalytic role of *foreign direct investment* (FDI)

- A highly efficient form of industrial organization known as "network clustering"
- An elaborate, government-sanctioned system of counterfeiting and piracy
- A chronically undervalued, "beggar thy neighbor" currency
- Massive government subsidies to numerous targeted industries
- "Great Wall" protectionist trade barriers, particularly for "infant industries"

In analyzing the nine key economic drivers, I show you that *only one*—network clustering—is truly legitimate from the perspective of a global economic system that is supposed to be based on free and fair trade. Each of the other eight China Price drivers violate one or more of the many "rules of the trading road" that have been established by organizations such as the World Trade Organization and treaties such as the General Agreement on Tariffs and Trade or that are embodied in international labor and environmental standards.

The broader point that should emerge from the foundation chapter is that by engaging in a comprehensive set of unfair trade policies and by wielding its primary "weapon of mass production," the China Price, China is enjoying unprecedented rates of export-driven economic growth—and thereby trouncing the competition in global markets. In the process, China is effectively sowing the economic seeds of the Coming China Wars with the rest of the world. And, in the worst "wars from within" scenario, China is also setting itself up for its own environmental, political, and social destruction.

Low Wages for High-Quality Work

What is stunning about China is that for the first time we have a huge, poor country that can compete both with very low wages and in high tech. Combine the two, and America has a problem.

—Professor Richard Friedman, Harvard University[3]

It is difficult to estimate accurately wage levels in China because much of the data is of poor quality. In addition, the government wants to hide the fact that numerous companies illegally pay their workers far less than the stated minimum wage.

Estimates that do exist put the average hourly earnings well below a dollar. Interesting, however, is that in many other countries, wages are as low or even substantially lower than in China. These countries, scattered all over the world, range from the Dominican Republic and Nicaragua in Latin America and Bangladesh and Pakistan on the Indian subcontinent to Burma, Cambodia, and Vietnam in Southeast Asia. Despite their lower wages and often equally wretched working conditions, none of these countries can compete effectively with China. One important reason is simply that manufacturers in China get a lot more *productivity* bang out of the wage buck. Chinese workers are relatively better educated and, more important, far more disciplined than the workers found in the poor barrios of Caracas or Rio de Janeiro or the slums of Soweto or Lesotho. This means that dollar for dollar and yuan for yuan, China can provide higher-quality, more-disciplined workers; on a productivity-adjusted basis, their workers are highly competitive with virtually every other country in the world.

There is, however, a far more subtle part of this wage story —one that seeks to answer the question: How is it that year after year, indeed decade after decade of record economic growth, Chinese wages do not really rise much? Or to put it another way, how can Chinese manufacturers continue to pay such low wages for a high-quality work force in the face of rapid growth that in other countries would quickly tighten the labor market and cause wages to spike?

At least part of the answer lies in one of the great ideological, economic, and darkly comic ironies of our time. In a country that was built on a foundation of Marxist doctrine, there exists the largest "reserve army of the unemployed" ever created in human history. In this regard, one of the central tenets of Marxist theory is that the exploitation of workers by capitalists is made possible because capitalism will always generate significant unemployment. The inevitable presence of this "reserve army" of unemployed workers will always depress wages and allow the capitalists to exploit their workers in other ways, too (for example, poor working conditions).

On this count, and at least at this time in China's history, Karl Marx got it absolutely right. The size of China's reserve army is breathtaking and, at least on first hearing, almost unbelievable. This reserve army of surplus labor numbers significantly more than a hundred million workers. To put this in perspective, this means that China has almost as many unemployed and underemployed workers as America employs in total.[4]

Now, here is what is perhaps most interesting about this surplus labor: Despite two decades of double-digit GDP growth, *China's reserve army continues to grow, not shrink.* The next question is how this huge pool of surplus labor that so effectively depresses wages and benefits in China got to be so large—and why it continues to grow. The answer may be found in four important elements that explain China's labor market advantage: continued population growth in the world's most populous country; a massive privatization of the work force that has cast off tens of millions of industrial workers from the security of the "iron rice bowl" system; a government-decreed, rapid urbanization that is moving hundreds of millions of farmers into Chinese factories; and a system, in many cases, of quasi-slave labor facilitated by the outlawing of labor unions.

Population Growth and Privatization

Mao Zedong would shudder at the vibrant free-market energy of Chinese city centres, their rush-hour gridlock, packed restaurants, glitzy shopping malls and young fashionistas chattering on the mobiles they change more often than their shoes. But they are ringed with rusting "iron rice bowls"—the unviable, revenue-draining state-owned enterprises (SOEs) whose progressive closure is a key to market reform. China has shed 41 million SOE jobs and 21 million more from co-operatives; no wonder it regards America's 6.1 percent unemployment rate dry-eyed. These iron rice bowls provided not just jobs for life, but housing, healthcare . . . , education and pensions.

—*The Times* (London)[5]

As you might suspect, population growth in China has played a critical role in generating surplus labor. In truth, however, two other elements are much more important in creating China's reserve army of the unemployed. The first is the *privatization of industry* as part of China's economic reform process. The second is a rapid rise in *urbanization* of the population—a rise driven in large part by chronic rural poverty.

It is beyond the scope of this book to provide a detailed history of China's economic reforms. Suffice it to say here that prior to these reforms, which began in the late 1970s, the Chinese economy was organized along the lines of an "iron rice bowl." In this Marxist system, all *state-owned enterprises* (SOEs) guaranteed workers not just a livable wage, but also housing, health care, pensions, and other benefits. The system was modeled on the Soviet-style collectivization of industry and embraced by Mao Zedong and the Communist Party shortly after their rise to power in 1949. The big problem with the iron rice bowl system, however, was that it was marked by extreme levels of inefficiency and waste; with their wages and pensions guaranteed, employees in SOEs had little incentive to produce.

Beginning in the 1990s, the Chinese government accelerated dismantling its iron rice bowl system in favor of free market enterprises fueled largely by foreign direct investment (more about FDI later in this chapter). The purpose of what was a rapid and dramatic privatization of much of China's work force was to make Chinese industry competitive with the rest of the world. The practical effect of these reforms, however, has been to help create the largest "floating population" (*liudong renkou*) of unemployed and underemployed workers ever seen.

Almost all estimates of this vast migration population exceed one hundred million and comprises the largest part of the core of China's "reserve army of the unemployed." The reforms are not the only contributor to this army. In fact, prospectively, it will be the Chinese government's decision to rapidly urbanize its population that will keep this surplus army growing ever larger—and always behind even the most rapid pace of economic growth.

China Urbanizing Imperative

Some say they want to be a driver, a scientist or a teacher. But nobody wants to go on being a farmer.

—Du Nengwei, teacher, Shuanghu, China[6]

Even a wretched job is better than no job . . . Most rural workers find their life in cities bearable because they have hopes and dreams: a color TV, a brother with a college degree, a new house to live in, or even a new apartment in one of the cities.

—Professor Qumei She, Wanli University[7]

Demographer estimates indicate China's urbanization rate will reach 50 percent by 2030, when China's total population is expected to jump to 1.6 billion. Factoring in such a calculation, approximately 15 to 16 million itinerant farm workers will annually head to the cities in the next 30 years.

—*The China Daily*[8]

China's urbanizing imperative is one of the most critical components of the Coming China Wars. It is the result of a huge, fundamental, and ever-growing disparity between the income levels and prospects of China's massive rural peasantry and the much more affluent and upwardly mobile young urban professional "Chuppies" or Chinese yuppies.

China has so many farmers and so little land that most Chinese farmers have very small plots—often less than an acre or two. This land constraint makes it a virtual certainty that the best most peasants can do is to simply eke out a subsistence living.

Moreover, from a big-picture point of view, the extreme decentralization of Chinese agricultural makes it difficult for Chinese farmers to operate efficiently and create large economies of scale. To understand the problem, consider that in the U.S., less than 2% of the population is engaged in farming, whereas in China more than half the population works in the agricultural sector.[9] Despite this difference, the grain production in the two countries in any given year is roughly comparable.[10]

From the perspective of the Chinese central government, rural poverty is a ticking time bomb, both economically and politically. Economically, a poor and aging peasant population will put tremendous strains on the government's social welfare budget—as these farmers' health and welfare needs must be addressed. Politically, as income disparities grow between the rural and urban areas, so, too, grows peasant discontent. In this regard, the Chinese government is all too aware of Mao's warning that "a single spark can start a prairie fire" and that it was Mao himself who rode into power on a wave of rural discontent.

The broader point is that as a matter of policy, *China has embraced rapid urbanization as a panacea for all its rural ills.* Over the next several decades, the goal of the Chinese government is to move 300 million or more peasants off their small farms and into China's teeming cities and factories. To put this migration in perspective, the number is equal to the entire current population of the United States and *double* the size of the current U.S. work force.

Now here's the rub: *Even if China continues to grow at a rate of close to 10% a year, China's reserve army of the unemployed is not likely to shrink significantly and may even swell.* Moreover, if the Chinese economy slows down, unemployment—and political discontent—will skyrocket. Is it any wonder that the Chinese government is so intent on fueling rapid economic growth?

The Final Piece of the Low-Wage Puzzle: Nonunion Labor

Each eyelash was assembled from 464 inch-long strands of human hair, delicately placed in a crisscross pattern on a thin strip of transparent glue. Completing a pair often took an hour. Even with 14-hour shifts most girls could not produce enough for a modest bonus. "When we started to work, we realized there was no way to make money," said Ma Pinghui, 16. "They were trying to cheat us."

She and her friend Wei Qi, also 16 and also a Chinese farm girl barely out of junior high school, had been lured here by a South Korean boss who said he was prepared to pay $120 a month, a princely sum for unskilled peasants, to make false eyelashes. . . . Two months later, bitter that the pay turned out to be much lower, exhausted by eye-straining and wrist-wrenching work, and too poor to pay the exit fee the boss demanded of anyone who wanted out, they decided to escape. But that was not easy. The metal doors of their third-floor factory were kept locked and its windows—all but one—were enclosed in iron cages. . . . Said Ms. Wei, "What they called a company was really a prison."

—*The New York Times*[11]

Any complete discussion of China's low-wage contribution to the China Price must necessarily include the observation that labor unions are banned in China.[12] On the surface, this may seem to be a good thing to many people. After all, labor unions have earned a bad name in many developed countries—particularly because many unions have used their bargaining power to lock employers into contracts and pension plans that eventually render them unable to compete.

That said, it is equally true from a broader historical perspective of the union movement that when individual workers lack representation on the most basic issues of health and safety, exploitation cannot be far behind. This is certainly true in China, where any form of worker dissent or attempt to organize are certain to be met with beatings, demotions, dismissals (referred to as becoming "fried squid"), and even torture.

In the absence of any union representation, many Chinese workers are forced to endure some of the most dangerous, repetitive, and oppressive working conditions in the world. Part of the problem is a form of corporate organization that has its roots in the commune structure and a culture in which many Chinese have grown up under Communist rule.

In the new capitalist variation, many workers are housed in dormitories, are forced to work 12- to 18-hour days, and are steeply fined if they attempt to take unauthorized vacation time or quit. Predictably, some have likened such dormitories to "slave camps." It is not, however, locks on the doors or bars on windows that make many Chinese factories "prisons." In many cases, the chains that bind workers to these factories are real economic needs in the face of a seemingly paradoxical massive unemployment problem and grinding rural poverty.

Lax Health, Safety, and Environmental Regulations

Yongkang, in prosperous Zhejiang Providence just south of Shanghai, is the hardware capital of China. Its 7,000 metalworking factories—all privately owned—make hinges, hubcaps, pots and pans, power drills, security doors, tool boxes, thermoses, electric razors, headphones, plugs, fans and just about anything else with metallic innards.

Yongkang, which means "eternal health" in Chinese, is also the dismemberment capital of China. At least once a day someone . . . is rushed to one of the dozen clinics that specialize in treating hand, arm and finger injuries, according to local government statistics. . . . The reality, all over China, is that workplace casualties had become endemic. Nationally, 140,000 people died in work-related accidents last year—up from about 109,000 in 2000, according to the State Administration of Work Safety. Hundreds of thousands more were injured.

—The New York Times[13]

The Chinese government imposes few health and safety or environmental regulations on its corporations or remaining state-run enterprises. What rules do exist are only weakly enforced, evaded, or simply ignored.

Not surprisingly, the lack of a basic regulatory and legal system is viewed as a great virtue by foreign corporations that want to evade much harsher regulatory and legal regimes in their own countries. Indeed, as China has flapped its *laissez faire* butterfly wings, foreign capital and foreign companies have flocked to its shores—*often bringing their own lobbyists to ensure that the rules do not change.* In this way, countries as near as Korea, Japan, and Taiwan and countries as far away as the United States have been able to "export" effectively their pollution and workplace risks to China.

Today's Chinese production facilities are not unlike the Dickensian sweatshops of nineteenth-century industrializing England or the dangerous American factories at the turn of the century that were exposed by the "muckrakers."

In China's factories, if the blades or presses do not sever a limb or take a life, the dirt and dust in the lungs or chemicals that seep in through the skin provide a much slower death. According even to China's own under-reported statistics, China is one of the most dangerous places to work in the world.

For those workers who do lose a limb or fall prey to a work-related disease, no functioning legal system exists to protect them. Upon being injured or maimed, they simply become the detritus of a ruthless manufacturing machine. Because the workers do not receive health care from the state and are unable to extract adequate compensation from their employers, the Chinese (and multinational) companies that grind up and spit out these workers enjoy a cost advantage over countries where workers are better protected.

The Catalytic Role of Foreign Direct Investment

[A] major driver of Chinese productivity gains has been the rapid growth of foreign and foreign-invested firms. These ventures represent foreign direct investment—long-term investments in the Chinese economy that are directly managed by a foreign entity. Close oversight of these operations by experienced foreign managers provides for the transfer of modern technical and managerial techniques, leading to higher productivity levels. In fact, joint ventures of foreign companies with Chinese firms are seven times as productive as state-owned operations and over four times as productive as domestically run private enterprises.

—The U.S. Conference Board[14]

[A]s capital floods in and modern plants are built in China, efficiencies improve dramatically. The productivity of private industry in China has grown an astounding 17% annually for five years.

—*Business Week*[15]

Cheap labor and lax health, safety, and environmental laws are giving China a direct competitive edge over many other nations, particularly in the developed world. However, these elements of the China Price also have indirectly helped attract a massive inflow of catalytic *foreign direct investment* (FDI). Since 1983, FDI has grown from less than $1 billion a year to more than $60 billion, and it is projected to soon reach $100 billion annually. The lion's share of these funds comes from five main sources: Hong Kong, the United States, Japan, Korea, and Taiwan.

The FDI influx provides Chinese companies with two incredibly powerful catalysts for honing their competitive edge. First, this FDI is being spent on the most sophisticated and technically advanced manufacturing processes available. Such technology transfer means that China is getting much better equipment and machinery much sooner than other developing countries, which allows Chinese manufacturers to always produce more efficiently on the cutting edge. These FDI efficiencies are reflected in dramatic double-digit rates of productivity growth over the past decade.

Second, the catalytic FDI has brought with it some of the best managerial talent and managerial "best practices" from around the world. The result has been a winning combination: cheap Chinese labor on the production lines and local Chinese "scouts" who use their connections (known as *quanxi*) to grease the bureaucratic wheels coupled with the crème de la crème of foreign managerial talent in the middle and upper ranks.

Network Industrial Clustering in China's Ultimate Pin Factories

National and regional economies tend to develop, not in the isolated industries, but in clusters of industries related by buyer-supplier links, common technologies, common channels or common customers. The economies of the Pearl River Delta region are no exceptions. The region has developed a broad range of clusters in garments and textiles, footwear, plastic products, electrical goods, electronics, printing, transportation, logistics, and financial services. The Pearl River Delta region's electronics and electrical cluster is particularly strong and accounts for the vast majority of Chinese production in a wide range of industries.

—*Regional Powerhouse*[16]

The world can rightly howl about the unfairness and illegality of many aspects of the China Price—whether it be lax pollution controls or the many and various mercantilist trade policies discussed shortly. However, what no one can legitimately complain about—and what every business executive and bureaucrat can learn from—is China's incredible "industrial network clustering."

For the production of a wide range of China's export goods, companies located in close physical proximity to one another have formed highly synergistic networks and clusters of activity that yield significant economies of both scale and scope. In doing so, these industrial network clusters have become the modern embodiment of Adam Smith's famous pin factory, where an extreme division of labor and hyper-economic efficiency both rule.

To understand the nature of these network clusters, take a look at the figure on the following page from the book *Regional Powerhouse*. It illustrates the famous toy cluster in Guangdong Province. This province, located in the Pearl River Delta along with Hong Kong and Macao, has effectively cornered the world market on toy production.

You can see in this figure that every single factor needed for toy production is produced in close proximity to the major toy manufacturers. These factors of production range from packaging, plastic parts, paint, and label printing to springs, screws and nuts, soft filling, and synthetic hair.

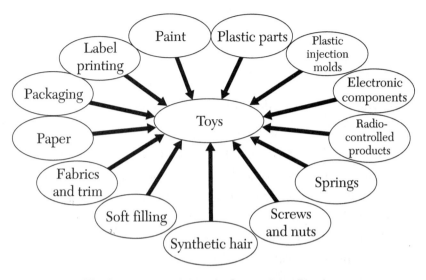

The famous toy cluster in Guangdong Province

Perhaps what is most impressive about the clustering is that it is often done by whole townships or cities. In an extreme and extremely efficient modern version of Adam Smith's specialization of labor, China features *entire cities or towns* that specialize in particular industries or industry segments.

For example, in Guangdong Province, the city of Huizou is the world's largest producer of laser diodes and a leading DVD producer. Foshan and Shunde are major hubs for appliances such as washing machines, microwave ovens, and refrigerators. Dongguan's Qingxi Township is one of the largest computer production bases in China. Hongmei focuses on textile- and leather-related products, Leilu on bicycles, Chencun on flowers, Yanbun is the underwear capital, and so on.[17]

The result of industrial network clustering is the generation of tremendous synergies and economies of scope along the supply chain. In this regard, it is worth noting how similar—yet so different— this form of industrial organization is to the kind that triggered the vaunted Japanese miracle of this past century.

During the 1980s, Japanese industry made famous the use of "just-in-time" systems in which the various parts necessary for production arrive from all over the world just in time for assembly and manufacturing. This type of uniquely Japanese manufacturing, borne of geographic necessity, dramatically cut inventory costs.

The Chinese have taken this system one level higher because it has been able to transform quickly whole cities and towns and tens of thousands of acres of "green field" farmland into industrial production sites. In their industrial network clustering model, Chinese manufacturers do not have to rely on an elaborate and globally dispersed supply chain as the Japanese do to bring in all the various parts to produce the whole. Instead, most of the various factors of production are located in close proximity in any given industrial network cluster, providing great savings in transportation and transactions costs and accelerating the spread of knowledge sharing.

Rampant Piracy and Counterfeiting

China is the epicenter of the counterfeits boom . . . Just a few years ago, counterfeiting was all Gucci bags and fake perfume. Now it's everything. It has just exploded. It is many times larger a problem than it was only a few years ago. The counterfeit inventory ranges from cigarette lighters to automobiles to pharmaceutical fakes that can endanger a life. I would bet that there are companies in this country [the U.S.] that don't even know they're getting screwed around the world.

—Frank Vargo, VP of International Economic Affairs National Association of Manufacturers[18]

Chapter 6, "The 21st Century Opium Wars—The World's Emperor of 'Precursor Chemicals,'" describes in detail the breathtaking scope of China's government-sanctioned counterfeiting and piracy.

However, two brief points related to the China Price are worth noting here.

The first is obvious: To the extent that China's entrepreneurs use counterfeit or pirated factors of production—such as pirated software on their computers—they are able to cut significantly their costs relative to countries where intellectual property rights are respected.

The second point is equally important. The piracy and counterfeiting that exists in China is largely the result of a tacit government policy to allow such practices to flourish. China has a relatively comprehensive set of antipiracy statutes on its books. However, little or no enforcement exists, and what fines and punishments do exist serve as only weak deterrents.

The reason for China's tacit sanctioning of widespread counterfeiting and piracy is that the Chinese government is well aware of two things. Counterfeit and pirated goods sold domestically help keep inflation low, and selling these goods internationally creates jobs and export revenues.

Beggaring Thy Neighbors with a Chronically Undervalued Currency

China's undervalued currency encourages undervalued Chinese exports to the U.S. and discourages U.S. exports because U.S. exports are artificially overvalued. As a result, undervalued Chinese exports have been highly disruptive to the U.S. and to other countries as well, as evidenced by trade remedy statistics.

—U.S.-China Economic and Security Review Commission[19]

On the one hand, countries such as the United States and Japan as well as the European Union abide by "floating exchange rates" in which the values of the dollar, yen, and euro are determined in the free market. Thus, when a country such as the United States sees its trade deficit rising with either Japan or Europe, the value of the dollar will tend to fall relative to the yen and euro as dollars pile up in foreign banks.[20] This weakening of the dollar makes imports into the United States more expensive and U.S. exports more competitive. In this way, free-market forces in the world's currency markets help bring global trade flows back into balance.

China, on the other hand, has adopted a "fixed exchange rate system" in which it pegs the value of its currency, the *yuan*, to the value of the U.S. dollar.[21] The result, as Chinese imports have flooded into the United States, has been a large undervaluation of the yuan relative to the dollar. The most reliable estimates put the size of this currency undervaluation at anywhere from 15% to 40%.

As a practical matter, China's "fixed-peg" system means that *no matter how big a trade deficit the United States runs with China, the dollar cannot fall relative to the yuan.* This fixed peg also gives China a big advantage over much of the rest of the world—from Europe and Asia to Latin America—when it comes to accessing lucrative U.S. markets. Accordingly, China's "beggar thy neighbor" currency policy is an important engine of its export-driven growth.

Massive Subsidies and the Great Protectionist Walls of China

Under state control, many Chinese state-owned manufacturers are operating with the benefit of state-sponsored subsidies, including: rent, utilities, raw materials, transportation, and telecommunications services. That is not how we define a level playing field.

—U.S. Department of Commerce Secretary Donald Evans[22]

China's state-run banks have routinely extended loans to state-owned-enterprises that are not expected to be repaid.

And right now, the big four state banks in China are, for all practical purposes, insolvent.

—U.S.-China Economic and Security Review Commission[23]

As part of its broader mercantilist trade strategy, China has constructed a "Great Wall of Protectionism" around both its agricultural and industrial sectors. One of its two-pronged protectionist strategy involves a complex web of direct and indirect subsidies, particularly to promote key "pillar industries." The second involves an equally complex set of trade barriers that provide shelter to some of China's most vulnerable domestic industries and agricultural sectors.

In this regard, both energy and water are heavily subsidized, and cheap electricity is a significant cost advantage for China's steel plants and heavy industry. At the same time, its state-owned enterprises, which still control key sectors of the economy such as oil and steel, benefit from free land; other enterprises are given preferential access to land by local and regional governments.

In addition, China's state-run banks provide heavily subsidized capital and credit to Chinese enterprises. These banks currently and collectively have on their books tens of billions of dollars in loans without any expectation of repayment—essentially free money! Finally, on the subsidy side, many industries in both high-tech sectors such as biotech, electronics, and computers and middle-tech sectors such as autos and aircraft receive direct and substantial R&D support from the government.

It is not enough that China's government seeks to provide its export industries with every possible advantage. Its government seeks to protect many of its domestic sectors. Such protectionism is achieved through a labyrinthine set of tariff and nontariff barriers.

For example, on the agricultural side, China has imposed so-called tariff-rate quotas on a wide variety of bulk commodities such as wheat, corn, cotton, and vegetable oil. Such tariff-rate quotas involve tariffs that rise with the level of imports.

On the industrial side, China has similarly used unjustifiable and idiosyncratic technology standards to build walls around its software, mobile phone, DVD, wireless networking, and other industries. In addition, it has used preferential tax treatment to promote and protect key industries such as semiconductors, limited access to domestic market channels, and imposed excessive capitalization requirements on foreign financial services.

Of course, in the wake of China's entry into the World Trade Organization in 2001, these subsidies and protectionist measures were supposed to melt away. However, China's compliance with both the letter and spirit of the WTO has turned out to be as big a farce and fiction as much of what appears in the heavily censored and, for the most part, state-controlled Chinese press. China is the reigning emperor of antidumping complaints against its industries, while China's Great Wall of Protectionism provides significant cost advantages to numerous Chinese industries.

Summing It All Up

In this foundation chapter, we have examined the nine key drivers of the China Price. Clearly, the ability of Chinese entrepreneurs to offer the China Price across an incredibly diverse array of industries is China's premier weapon of mass production—one that is at the root of China's conquest of one export market after another.

The remaining chapters demonstrate how China's export-led hyper-growth is, in turn, spawning a thousand different points of conflict in the Coming China Wars. And no conflict may be more sharp and bloody than the one examined in the next chapter.

2

CHINA'S COUNTERFEIT ECONOMY AND NOT-SO-SWASHBUCKLING PIRATES

The larger truth is that the Chinese economy has staked a great deal on its counterfeiters. They provide people with affordable goods. Often, as in the case of medicines and medical devices, some foods, school textbooks, and clothing, counterfeit goods are essential goods, meaning that any government crackdown, in effect, taxes China's needy consumers. Counterfeiters also serve their country by usurping foreign technology China desperately needs to meet its industrial goals. The counterfeiters give China's growing number of globally competitive companies the means to compete with powerful foreign rivals who are forced to pay full fare for proprietary technologies. And in a broader geopolitical context, China's counterfeiters deny the world's advanced economies, America's and Japan's in particular, the wherewithal to sell to China the valuable designs, trademarked goods, advanced technology, and the world-beating entertainment products that the Chinese urgently desire but cannot yet produce on their own.

—Ted Fishman, *China, Inc.*[1]

You might find it hard to feel sorry for Gucci or Nike or Microsoft or Disney when Chinese pirates and counterfeiters knock off their luxury handbags or fancy running shoes or steal software and first-run movies and then offer them to the world at affordable prices. After all, these big, fat-cat corporations can afford it. Right?

That is certainly one way of looking at the whole phenomenon of Chinese piracy and counterfeiting—and it is a perspective that appears to be wholeheartedly embraced both by most Chinese and many Americans, Europeans, and others around the globe. However, something big is missing in this Robin Hood attitude: Counterfeiting and piracy can be dangerous. Consider these fictional scenarios—which are *all* are based on real-world events:

- Your scalp develops a severe rash because your knock-off "Head and Shoulders" shampoo contains toxic chemical residue.

- You complain to your optometrist about headaches and a recent deterioration in your vision, and she determines that the lenses in your counterfeit Oakley sunglasses are causing the problem.

- In the dead of night, the counterfeit power strip that you bought in the bargain bin of the local hardware store starts an electrical fire. Your smoke detector does not work because your fake "Duracell" batteries leaked acid all over the alarm system. Did you get out of the house before it burned down?

- You are hospitalized with a bad case of the flu two weeks after taking a flu shot. Turns out your "vaccine" was bacteria-laden tap water—which also explains why you felt so lousy for several days after the shot.

- A small pebble shoots up from the tire of a truck in front of you and hits your windshield. The "safety" glass does not crack but shatters and shards of glass fly everywhere. You escape serious injury but wind up with small cuts on your forearms, hands, and face.

- You get a postcard from a friend visiting China who tells you about his own wounds from flying glass. Seems he bought a six-pack of phony "Budweiser" at a Shanghai supermarket and one of the bottles exploded in his hand just as he was about to open it.

- On the way home from school, your child's school bus driver hits the brakes to stop for a red light. The knock-off brakes fail, and the bus is hit broadside by a Toyota Corolla. Fortunately, none of the children are badly hurt, but the driver of the Corolla winds up in the morgue.

- Your father almost dies because neither the "Norvasc" he was taking for high blood pressure nor the "Lipitor" that he was taking for high cholesterol had any active ingredients. Days later, your mother winds up in the hospital with a broken hip because her phony "Evista" medication for osteoporosis was nothing more than molded chalk.

- Your brother orders Viagra over the Internet because he is too embarrassed to ask his doctor for a regular prescription. After a nice candlelight dinner with his spouse, he winds up in a hospital bed with a wild heartbeat. The next week your prized Himalayan "lap cat" succumbs to liver failure because the tick medicine she was taking turned out to contain poison.

- A mental patient is administered a regimen of the antipsychotic drug Zyprexa and after several weeks of ingesting an unintentional placebo, he goes berserk in your local supermarket and injures one of your best friends.

- On a sultry summer night, two of your co-workers—a 22-year old gay man and a 24-year old heterosexual woman—buy fake "Durex Extra Safe" condoms at the same pharmacy. Later that night, in separate encounters, the condoms burst. The gay man gets HIV, and the woman contracts chlamydia (which renders her sterile).

The Buccaneer Nation and Counterfeit Kings

"Harry doesn't know how long it will take to wash the sticky cream cake off his face," begins the latest Harry Potter *blockbuster. "For a civilized young man it is disgusting to have dirt on any part of his body. He lies on the high-quality china bathtub, keeps wiping his face, and thinks about Dali's face, which is as fat as the bottom of Aunt Penny."*

If you're familiar with the Harry Potter *novels of J. K. Rowling, you will sense already that this novel isn't up to her usual standard, which makes it surprising that she allowed her picture to be used on the cover of "Harry Potter and Leopard Walk up to Dragon," published for an enthusiastic public in China. . . . That's because she didn't write it. Apparently it's a ripping yarn. Harry gets turned into a fat hairy dwarf, which for those of us who never cared much for the little wizard anyway isn't such a bad result. But the book is a knockoff, written by a Chinese author to cash in on Chinese Pottermania.*

—Tim Phillips, *Knockoff* [2]

Piracy refers to the unauthorized production, distribution, or use of a good or service. The goal of a pirate is to create a look-alike "knock-off" that can be sold to a customer as such.

Counterfeiting ups the piracy ante by pawning off pirated products as that of the real, branding corporation. Thus, a golf club that looks just like a Callaway driver but has a name like "Hallaway" is a pirated knock-off, whereas as knock-off sold as a "Callaway" club is a counterfeit.

The World Customs Organization estimates that counterfeiting accounts for fully 5% to 7% of global merchandise trade and represents the equivalent in lost sales of around $500 billion. Such counterfeiting costs the pharmaceutical industry alone close to $50 billion a year, the auto industry more than $10 billion annually, and the software and entertainment industries billions more.

Of course, China is hardly the only country engaged in this half-trillion-dollar trade. Other hotbeds include Russia, India, Vietnam, South Africa, and even tiny Paraguay on the notorious Triple Frontier region bordering Argentina and Brazil. China is, however, hands down, the largest pirate nation on the planet—with its *de facto* nationalist banner no longer Mao's five-star red flag but the infamous Jolly Roger. The statistics speak loudly and clearly for themselves. As worldwide production of counterfeit goods has leaped by 1,700% since 1993,[3] China accounts for two thirds of all the world's pirated and counterfeited goods and fully 80% of all counterfeit goods seized at U.S. borders.

The Economic Logic of China's State-Sanctioned Piracy

No problem of this size and scope could exist without the direct or indirect involvement of the state. In China, the national government in Beijing appears to be sincere in its recognition of the importance of protecting intellectual-property rights, but national-level authorities are policy and lawmaking bodies, whereas enforcement occurs on the ground at the local level. At this level, local governments are either directly or indirectly involved in supporting the trade in counterfeit goods.

—Professor Daniel C. K. Chow, Ohio State University[4]

The obvious question arises: Why does the Chinese government allow piracy and counterfeiting to flourish? This is a particularly interesting question because, at least at the federal level, the Chinese central government has made a big show of cracking down on counterfeiting and piracy.

The answer may be found in an intertwining set of economic piracy drivers and cultural norms. From an economic perspective, Chinese state-sanctioned piracy and counterfeiting is a vital *de facto* "policy tool" that allows all layers of the Chinese government to control inflation, create jobs, expand its tax base, and raise the standard of living for the Chinese people. As noted by Oded Shenkar:

> *Today, local authorities are dependent on revenues from enterprises that use knocked-off designs, such as China's 100 plus car manufacturers, most of which would be out of business if they had to pay for development costs. Some local jurisdictions are dependent on lucrative trade and distribution centers for bogus goods for much of their income and are reluctant to relinquish those benefits, especially when they find a central government willing to look the other way. With unemployment already a serious economic, social, and political threat, the central authorities are reluctant to take action against an industry that employs millions of people; the unrest that might result is the nightmare of a regime billing itself as a guardian of order and stability.*[5]

Because of the positive and powerful effects that counterfeiting and piracy have on the Chinese economy, there exists a virulent form of "local protectionism" from government officials for counterfeiters and pirates. In fact, it is the same kind of local protectionism that one observes for both private and state-run businesses that may pollute the air or water or maim their workers but that provide an important source of employment and tax revenues for the local economy. As Li Guorong, the general manager of a security firm in China, put it well:

> *[C]ounterfeiting is now so huge in China that radical action would crash the economy overnight, ruining Deng Xiaoping's 27-year-old economic strategy. It would ruin local economies in the poor south of the country, and even destabilize a government where counterfeit factories and warehouses are often*

owned by local military and political grandees. If the knockoff economy is 7% of world trade and China is responsible for two-thirds of that, then, using the most conservative estimates, China's counterfeiters are responsible for about 5% of world trade. It wouldn't just be China's small businesses that would be out of business if the supply of product was cut off.[6]

As a final overarching driver of the China Piracy Wars, there is the problem of a set of cultural norms that flow from an arguably amoral fusion of a 60-year old Maoism and a centuries-old Confucianism. The government of the People's Republic of China was founded in 1949 on the bedrock principle of the abolition of private property and the communitarian idea that all should share. Thus, there exists several generations of Chinese executives who grew up being taught that property rights simply do not exist outside the collective. As noted by the former U.S. ambassador to China James Lilley, "We would come up against party cadres who told us that any technology in the world is the property of the masses."[7]

When one adds to this Maoist version of property a large dose of Chinese culture and tradition in the form of Confucianism, the counterfeiting and piracy picture comes much more sharply into focus. Since ancient times, Confucianism has revered, rather than reviled, imitation. The result is the perfect cultural laboratory for a counterfeiting boom—one wholeheartedly embraced by a large segment of the Chinese population.

You Can Have Anything You Want at Mao's Restaurant

It's a busy September afternoon at the Zhiyou Automotive Parts Market in this southern port city [of Guangzhou, China]. Messengers zoom in and out of the square on motorcycles carrying orders. Vans pull up to load and unload. Buyers and vendors haggle over prices at stalls that display parts from every single major automaker and parts maker in the world. Fram filters. Ford accessories. Champion spark plugs. Philips and Bose audio systems. BMW wheels. All at discount prices and all in their original packaging. But most, if not all, are fake.

The Zhiyou bazaar is the heart of the counterfeit parts business in this region of China. It has been raided and closed many times but always springs back to life. By its very openness and refusal to stay closed, it underscores how deeply ingrained the culture of auto-parts counterfeiting is in China.

—Automotive News[8]

Although more and more people are becoming aware of China's status as the world's pirate nation, many people still believe that such intellectual property theft is limited to luxury items such as Prada purses and Rolex watches and software such as the Windows operating system. Nothing could be further from the truth—as the following sidebar indicates.

A Small Sampling of China's Counterfeit Universe

- Baby food, soft drinks, and hard liquor
- Batteries and film
- Cigarettes and Zippo lighters
- Mobile phones and watches
- Makeup and perfume
- Shampoo and razors
- Air conditioners and refrigerators
- Automobiles and motorcycles
- Chemicals, including flame-retardant chemicals
- Elevators and toilet seats

- Power strips and extension cords
- Blank CDs and tapes
- Circuit boards and connectors
- DRAM modules
- Hard drives, network interface cards, and printer cartridges
- Resistors and potentiometers
- Servers, laptops, and monitors

One of the biggest and most lucrative sectors of China's knock-off economy is that of replacement auto parts. Chinese pirates account for 70% of all counterfeit auto parts in the world,[9] and more than half of all Chinese vehicles contain counterfeit components.

The highly organized market includes everything from brake pads, oil filters, and fan belts to fenders, engine blocks, windshields, and windshield wipers. Given that the selling of new cars is often a "loss leader" to establish a lucrative aftermarket in replacement parts, such counterfeiting represents a particularly crippling form of economic "cream skimming" that cuts deeply into the bottom line of the legitimate auto industry. As has been noted in *Forbes,* "Replacement parts are to car companies what popcorn is to movie theaters. It's how they pay the rent."[10]

There are also significant safety issues for an industry (in which several tons of metal travel at high speeds) that depends on equipment reliability. In some cases, the quality and appearance of the fake auto parts is so good that is difficult to distinguish between a fake and original product. In many other cases, the parts are of such poor quality, they are doomed to early and often dangerous failure. As reported in *Automotive News,* some of the "many horror stories" include "brake linings made of compressed grass, sawdust or cardboard; transmission fluid made of cheap oil that is dyed; and oil filters that use rags for the filter element."[11]

The dangers (and company liabilities!) inherent in the fake auto parts market have been rhetorically noted by an executive from the heavy-duty truck industry: "How would you like to have fake brakes with your brand name on them installed on a heavy truck, which happens to be bearing down on a stalled school bus?"[12] However, it is not just auto parts that the Chinese steal. They also are fond of stealing entire automobile and motorcycle designs.

Months before General Motors began selling its $7,500 Chevrolet Spark in China in December, a $6,000 knockoff version, the Chery QQ, with the same grinning front end but missing some subtle details (like an air bag), was cruising Chinese streets. Even more galling: The manufacturer of the pirated version was partially owned by GM's Chinese business partner.[13]

The Chinese version of "Grand Theft Auto" similarly includes purloined Hondas. Its workhouse CR-V design was stolen, and the counterfeit cars are being sold as the "SR-V" by the Hebei Shuanghuan Auto company. It is not just autos: eight out of every ten "Yamaha" motorcycles in China are knock-offs.

A second and equally lucrative counterfeit sector in China is that of cigarette production and distribution. Rivaling any one of the big multinational producers, China churns out 65% of the world's counterfeit cigarettes. Of the more than 35 billion cigarette sticks it produces each year, almost 30 billion of them are exported.[14]

In contrast to the counterfeit auto sector, which is highly organized and largely visible, many of China's cigarette pirates operate in a much more decentralized cottage industry structure. Many of the small production facilities are quite literally underground in basements or in subterranean rooms accessible only by tunnels.

In these hidden dens, "counterfeiters will hire workers for just a few days or even hours to produce a batch of counterfeit cigarettes using old machines and hand-rolling the finished product."[15] In such clandestine environs, cigarettes, which already represent one of the most efficient ways of destroying human health, often become even more deadly.

> Tests on counterfeit cigarettes at St. Andrews University in the UK found that they had on average five times as much cadmium as genuine cigarettes, and cadmium causes kidney disease and damages your lungs. There's six times as much lead in them too, which will damage your nervous system. And then there's the elevated level of arsenic, which could cause cancer. You don't need to be told that smoking can kill you: but if you just bought 200 cigs, no questions asked, from a man in a bar, it probably just got a lot more dangerous.[16]

As a smuggling strategy, the cigarettes are often exported along with, and within, packets of tea. Because tea and tobacco weigh roughly the same, the contraband is difficult to detect. Moreover, the profit margins are astronomical: "With the typical cost of a container just $120,000, counterfeiters can make millions of dollars of profit on just one shipment."[17]

Snake Oil for the World

> Counterfeit drugs kill people.

—Lembit Rägo, World Health Organization

> Until recently, Marilyn Arons' only experience of counterfeit goods was the fake Louis Vuitton handbag she bought on the street 25 years ago. "It's something you never think about," says the 64-year-old New Jersey resident. When she learned in March that her refill of Lipitor, a popular cholesterol-lowering drug, contained fake pills, she had plenty of angry, anxious thoughts on the matter. "If it wasn't Lipitor I was taking," she worried, "what was it?" ... Arons, who is suing several drug distributors, says she was furious when her

pharmacist told her she would be fine. "Would you be fine,"
she demanded, "if I paid you with counterfeit money?"

—*U.S. News & World Report*[18]

With at least one out of every ten packets of medicine worldwide now fake, drug counterfeiting has become a big business. Just consider this small sample of the twenty-first-century version of the world's medicine cabinet: "cough syrup" laced with antifreeze; "meningitis vaccine" and anemia drugs made from tap water; "birth control pills" that are nothing but compressed wheat flour; "Lipitor" and "Norvasc" without any active ingredients; "Viagra" and "Cialis" with twice the recommended dose; "flea medicine" made of chalk; "malaria" pills without a trace of its critical ingredient, *artusenate.*

As with many other counterfeit goods, China is not the only country that engages in the production of these fake kinds of pharmaceuticals. India, for one, is deep in the game, as are Mexico, Brazil, and Argentina.

China is, however, certainly one of the major players, and it is not just because of a huge production capacity and sophisticated distribution network. It is also because as fast as you can say, "Can you fill this prescription, please," China's highly skilled pirates are able to reproduce the so-called blister packaging, vacuum-formed clamshells, fake holograms, and distinctive pills so artfully and faithfully that drug companies typically can only detect fakes by using complex lab testing. This counterfeiting capability is no small feat, particularly as pharmaceutical companies worldwide continue to boost the complexity of their packaging in an effort to thwart counterfeiting.

Note, however, that this uncanny ability of the Chinese to excel in highly sophisticated piracy is attributable to precisely the same factors that have allowed China to become the world's factory floor. Chief among these factors is the flood of *foreign direct investment* (FDI) that has brought in all the latest sophisticated machinery necessary to knock off whatever drug or product from which money can be made. When the pills and packaging are complete, China's counterfeit "drug dealers" then harness many of the same transportation, distribution, and sales channels established for legitimate purposes by foreign companies in China to distribute the illegitimate products worldwide.

Nor does it necessarily take a huge factory to produce counterfeit drugs. One of the simplest ways to create a phony batch of Viagra is to start with some of the authentic pills. Grind these up, add a little bulking agency, and remold the pills. Presto; you now have Chinese-style "Viagra Lite."[19]

The World Wide Counterfeit Web

Fake Chinese medicines can find their way into your medicine cabinet in many ways. In some cases, it happens when a big chain such as Rite Aid gets fooled by a supplier. In other cases, it happens when a small local pharmacy tries to keep its costs down by buying odd lots from wholesalers. More often than not, however, it is that increasingly double-edged sword called the World Wide Web that delivers these deadly drugs from the bowels of eastern China to people's doorsteps. Consider these typical profiles of Internet drug consumers, who become easy prey for China's drug pirates:

> A Social Security couple is getting eaten alive by medical expenses and need a drug not covered by insurance or Medicare. So, they try an online "Canadian" pharmacy that offers cheap drugs but that is really operating out of Heilongjiang Province.

> A post-partum depressed housewife wants to keep her Prozac habit a secret from Dad and the kids, a sweet 16-year-old daughter and weight-lifting 17-year-old son, both of whom go in on a post office box and monthly orders of birth control pills and muscle-popping Deca-Durobolin anabolic steroids. Meanwhile, world-traveler business Dad is off on another

*intercontinental trip and is too busy to do anything but order
his Ambien sleeping pills online.*

*Finally, and as the anchor of the Internet boom in counterfeit
drugs, there is the aging Baby Boomer who is not as good as he
once was in the bedroom but wants to be as good once as he ever
was. He is the easiest mark of all for the pirates and the number
one reason why Viagra is the Internet's top-selling counterfeit
drug. (In this regard, in a study conducted at the University of
London, Dr. Nic Wilson used a technique called infrared
microscopy to measure accurately the amount of the active
ingredient in samples of Viagra obtained over the Internet. The
good doctor found that fully half of the pills were phony.[20])*

It is not just fake drugs that are sold over the Internet. The World
Wide Web is also the primary delivery mechanism for a host of contraband digital media, from music and films to software. It has been
estimated that more than half, and as much as two thirds, of all Internet traffic is devoted to the distribution of stolen content!

In what has become the pirate-infested "South Seas" of Internet
space, the vaunted eBay has also become one of the most efficient
facilitators of counterfeiting and piracy in the world. According to
Brian Brokate, an attorney helping to represent Rolex, a high percentage of the auctions on eBay where high quantities of an item are
available in the same auction are counterfeit goods. Laments Brokate:
"You would think there would be some way to hold eBay liable for
trademark or copyright infringement. Well you can't. . . . eBay benefits enormously from the sale of counterfeit goods. Every trademark
owner knows this is a huge problem and it's not stopping."[21]

Piracy Economics 101

*China's failure to police intellectual property, in effect, cre-
ates a massive global subsidy worth hundreds of billions
of dollars to its businesses and people. Seen another way,
China's vast counterfeiting schemes act on the rest of the*

> *world the way colonial armies once did, invading deep into the economies of their victims, expropriating their most valued assets, and in doing so, undermining their victims' ability to counter. As China grows into a great power, the wealth transferred into the country by stealing intellectual property will propel it forward.*

—Ted Fishman, *China, Inc.*[22]

Piracy is a highly profitable venture for a variety of reasons—many rather obvious, some perhaps more subtle. For starters, pirates and counterfeiters do not have to engage in research and development to produce a product or design. They simple steal the intellectual property after it is produced.

Pirates also do not have to spend huge sums of money on advertising and marketing to build and sustain a brand name and open new markets. They just piggyback on the efforts of legitimate companies—while in the process, destroying much of the brand value and goodwill that a company builds up at huge expense.

Nor do Chinese pirates have to abide by various environmental or worker safety regulations or pay their corporate contributions to the government for Social Security or workers' compensation—much less pay corporate income or sales tax.

Chinese counterfeiters also appear to be every bit as sophisticated at achieving both "economies of scale" and "economies of scope" in production as any legitimate organization and supply-chain management executive team. As noted in the *Chinese Business Review*, "[A] smart counterfeiter is likely to produce fakes of several companies' products in a particular product line." Moreover, "this duplication occurs in many product lines, whether software, film, batteries, or auto parts."[23] This ability to use production facilities to churn out multiple but related products at larger volumes is the very definition of economies of scope and scale and allows counterfeiters to produce at substantially lower unit costs.

For all these reasons, counterfeiters have a huge cost advantage over legitimate producers. That's just part of the economic equation, however. From the perspective of legitimate producers, it is not just a loss of profits and market share and the dilution of brand name that corporations suffer. In many industries, there are real legal costs, too.

Consider that most big corporations now have to maintain large intellectual property enforcement armies that constantly roam the planet looking for knock-offs. Nike, for example, "has full-time anti-counterfeiting officers in Beijing, Shanghai, and Guangzhou, and initiates about 300 raids in China a year."[24] Louis Vuitton "employs a network of 250 trademark agents, investigators and lawyers."[25] The cost to the companies maintaining such teams, conducting raids, and paying for litigation and enforcement already runs into the millions and millions of dollars, and such expenses are growing rapidly.

In some cases, corporations have also been sued because of the failure of a critical knock-off part that led to product failure. Most subtly, companies are also bearing the burden of higher warranty costs as products break down because of inferior phony parts that often go undiscovered.

Perhaps the largest, most difficult to quantify, and as yet not fully realized economic cost of counterfeiting and piracy will be its future effect on stifling the rate of global innovation. Consider that the single most important economic reason why intellectual property law and patents exist is to spur innovation. Without the prospect of being able to capture the rewards of innovation, individuals and companies will expend far less time, money, and other resources to produce innovative new products.

The Many Faces of Chinese Piracy and Counterfeiting

Producers in the fake product industry are a diverse bunch, ranging from a large dedicated facility to the individual who concocts an imitation shampoo at home and outsources the packaging and labeling. Large-scale manufacturers can be state-owned firms, township and village enterprises (TVEs), or private, entrepreneurial firms.

Among the participants are legitimate enterprises that resort to bogus production because they have fallen on hard times or because they are pressured to become profitable, which is the case for many in the state sector. Such players, often joint venture partners with a foreign firm, will divert some output without the knowledge of the foreign investor or will run another line using the same designs or equipment. Others are "shadow" enterprises, established for the purpose of fake manufacturing.

. . . All players share cost advantage based on zero investment in technology and reputation building, low-cost raw materials and components, and labor cost that is usually below that of legitimate firms.

—Oded Shenkar, *The Chinese Century*[26]

China's pirate producers and counterfeiters come in many shapes and sizes and under many guises and disguises. Here is one typical "ghost-shift" scenario of how such piracy occurs in what has become a "global supply chain" of piracy and counterfeiting.

A factory in China is hired by a multinational to make 1,000 units of a product per day. However, rather than just run two regular eight-hour shifts to produce the contracted-for amounts, the factory also runs a third "ghost shift" and then ships the extra 500 items out the back door.

Another variation on this theme is to reverse-engineer Western technology. Through reverse engineering, Chinese counterfeiters have been able to get knock-offs of everything from Suzuki motorcycles to Callaway golf clubs on the street just weeks after these new products are introduced to the market.

Still another variation is the "start-up counterfeiter." Consider the case of the Taiwanese folding-bike maker Dahon. Its investigators discovered a competitor called Neobike that was producing bikes almost identical to the existing Dahon models. Three of the five Neobike founders turned out to be former Dahon employees.[27]

According to James Nurton, much of the "counterfeiting takes place in the coastal provinces of southern China, with trading centers based in cities such as Yiwu, Ningbo and Ninghai. Some is transported westwards by land to Urumuchi, where it can be sent onwards via Kazakhstan into Russia and the west. More commonly, goods are shipped out of China's ports, either directly to markets in the west and Africa, or to a free-trade zone such as Jebel Ali in Dubai where shipments can be rearranged into mixed containers, and forwarded by sea or land into Europe."[28] Indeed, whole towns have come to rely on the counterfeit economy:

> So if you are manufacturing in Chaosan, in Guangdong Province, your specialty is likely to be [fake] electronics, cigarettes, pharmaceuticals or CDs. For car parts, it's more likely you'll be in Wenzou City or the Pearl River Delta. In Yuxiao County, the expertise is in manufacturing fake cigarettes; in Jintan City, it's pesticides. Meanwhile the China Small Commodities City in Yiwu, 5 hours drive from Shanghai, is to knockoffs what Wall Street is to stocks and bonds: 200,000 buyers, 30,000 wholesale stalls and 3,500 retailers trade around 100,000 products that are available here; 2,000 tonnes of product are bought and sold every day.[29]

Organized Crime Economics 102

The handbag has a much better mark-up than heroin.

—Andrew Oberfelt, Abacus Security[30]

When the contraband leaves Chinese soil, it can find its way into the world's supply chain or distribution network in a thousand different ways. Many of these conduits are increasingly being controlled by organized crime networks, particularly China's infamous Mafia equivalent, the Triads.

Perhaps most disturbingly, with a sophistication rivaling any MBA-trained top executive corps, these crime networks are now diverting resources out of traditional gang staples such as drugs or prostitution and into counterfeiting on the basis of pure economics: Whereas a drug dealer might double his money on a kilo of heroin, that same dealer "can buy 1,500 pirated copies of Microsoft Office 2000 and pocket a 900 percent profit."[31] Moreover, if a Chinese gang member is caught peddling heroin or speed, its ten years or more in the slammer, depending on the country. But if he is caught peddling something far more deadly—impotent Lipitor or heart-stopping Viagra—it is a small fine and slap on the wrist:

> *Counterfeit trafficking is part of a broader, organized-crime problem. In June, U.S. immigration and customs-enforcement agents busted 17 people for smuggling tens of millions of dollars' worth of bogus Louis Vuitton, Prada, Coach, Chanel, Christian Dior and Fendi merchandise in thirty 40-foot containers to Port Elizabeth, New Jersey. According to the customs officials, 15 of the defendants are Chinese nationals who are part of two separate crime networks that use shell companies to import counterfeit luxury goods from China and distribute them through storefronts on [New York's] Canal Street. Each organization paid undercover agents $50,000 a container to look the other way. . . . Once the goods hit the U.S., there is little deterrent. "In narcotics, they get 20 years to life," says Pat Stella, U.S. customs assistant special agent in charge of New York City. "But a guy caught on Canal Street in the morning is back on the street by the afternoon.[32]*

In some cases, the counterfeits are fobbed off on big multinational corporations by unscrupulous wholesalers and used in brand-new products or equipment. That's what happened, for example, to Kyocera, which "had to recall a million cell-phone batteries that turned out to be counterfeit, costing the company at least $5 million."[33] In other cases, the softest targets for Chinese piracy are struggling small businesses and value-conscious consumers at the bargain-priced end of the retail network—easy prey for a large cadre of unscrupulous middle men.

China's Legal System of Pirate (In)justice

A Chinese law professor has first-hand proof that the country's counterfeiters have turned their attention to more highbrow publications. Zheng Chengsi, a professor at the Chinese Academy of Social Sciences and a member of the National Congress Law Committee, was surprised to find unauthorized digital versions of his own work being offered for sale by a Beijing-based web site. Of the eight books on offer, seven dealt with piracy and copyright law issues and one was enti-tled Knowing the Enemy in Yourself: Winning the Intellectual Property War.

—*Managing Intellectual Property*[34]

Every year, the Chinese government increases the number of raids it conducts, and every year Chinese counterfeiting and piracy grows ever larger. Behind this phony "get tough on pirates" shell game is a system of laws and regulations that, through the fundamental laws of economics, encourages rather than deters the tens of millions of Chinese pirates. In doing so, this system of government-sanctioned piracy blatantly violates the rules of the World Trade Organization and many other treaties and agreements.

One major problem is that the fines the Chinese government imposes on counterfeiters and pirates are absurdly small. In a cynical sleight of government hand, these fines are calculated *not* on the basis of the value of the true product but rather on the pirated good itself, which is far, far less.

A second major problem is that most cases are handled by administrative enforcement bodies rather than by the criminal justice system. The enforcement powers of many of the relevant agencies are limited to confiscating the fakes and imposing monetary fines rather than imposing any jail terms. As *Womens' Wear Daily* notes: "Under current law, only violators with extremely high monetary amounts of counterfeit activity are punished in criminal courts—a difficult case for police and brand owners to prove since records are rarely kept by piraters. To make matters worse, the monetary thresholds are currently calculated on the infringer's prices, almost always much lower than the legitimate product."[35]

A third problem is that in China's relatively young free market economy, there is both a lack of adequate resources and training for criminal enforcement and intellectual-property protection as well as pervasive corruption in the courts. As New Balance president John Larsen has put it: "There really is no established rule of law in China. They have laws, but they don't have enforcement opportunities and practices there. And of course corruption in China, particularly in the courts, is from our experience pervasive."[36]

Beyond these problems, there is this outrage: The export of pirated or counterfeit goods from China is *not* considered illegal. That means that even if an investigative team from Louis Vuitton or Pfizer or Bosch can detect a big shipment of phony goods, the Chinese government will not stop it. When these goods enter the distribution network, they become almost impossible to trace—particularly when organized crime is running the delivery chain.

Equally outrageous, there is the manner in which the Chinese judicial system adjudicates patent and trademark infringements. China is a so-called first-to-file country. Under country rules, a trademark that is well known around the world will not be protected unless it is also well known in China. This interpretation of Chinese law has allowed many local entrepreneurs to register a foreign trademark *before* the legitimate company does—and then exact a hefty "ransom" for its use:

The story of Zhejiang Xiandai serves as a cautionary tale. There were media reports that Beijing Hyundai Motor had to

> *pay Zhejiang Xiandai Group for the exclusive rights to use the xiandai qiche trademark, the widely accepted Chinese translation for South Korea's Hyundai Motors. The Zhejiang company reportedly spent Rmb100,000 ($12,000) registering the trademark "xiandai" in 43 classes of goods and services and it is estimated that the Zhejiang company gained Rmb40 million ($4.8 million) when it sold the trademark to Beijing Hyundai Motor. This story is a strong reminder to foreign trademark owners that they must take steps to protect their trademarks in China as early as they can.*[37]

In fact, trademark protection in China is often a rigged game in which corrupt judges and administrators have ruled against some of the largest multinational corporations with some of the most well-known trademarks in the world. Intellectual property litigation is on a steep rise in China, and the outcome is always uncertain.

For example, China's *Trademark Review and Adjudication Board* (TRAB) refused to grant Daimler Chrysler a trademark for its signature Mercedes hood ornament, and "Apple Computer has sued TRAB for disallowing the registration of its apple logo on clothing on the grounds that Apple's logo is similar to an apple logo already registered on clothing by Guangdong Apples Industrial Co."[38] In one of the most absurd cases, Toyota lost its lawsuit against the China Geely Group, an automaker in Zhejiang, for the inappropriate use of its logo.[39] The irony in this case is that Toyota did take the time to file its trademark as far back as 1990. Even so, it was unable to defend its misappropriation.

As a final point, it is useful to note that in a pattern repeated constantly with international agreements over everything from air and water pollution to nuclear proliferation, China has refused to sign the Internet-related provisions of the Trade Related Intellectual Property Agreement. Its laws also sanction the free use of copyrighted material, including software, for "learning purposes," and government agencies are similarly exempt from any adherence to copyrights or trademarks.

The bottom line: China will never crack down on its counterfeiting and piracy operations until it becomes in its best interest to do so *or* until the international community puts sufficient pressure on the Chinese government to do so. As Pfizer's VP of Global Security has noted: "Let's be practical here. It won't get much better until China has its own intellectual property to protect."

Inevitably, as China's buccaneer nation continues to grow and prosper at the expense of the rest of the world, conflict between China and its global neighbors will only intensify. However, should the Chinese government crack down successfully on its pirates, that will only contribute to the many budding "wars from within," the subject of Chapter 8, "The Bread and Water Wars—Nary a (Clean) Drop to Drink."

3

KILLING US (AND THEM) SOFTLY WITH THEIR COAL

China's population is so big and its resources so scarce that if we continue to ignore our environmental problems, that will bring disaster for us and the world.

—Pan Yue, Deputy Director
Chinese State Environmental Protection Administration[1]

A larger fraction of the haze we see is Asian, far more than we ever dreamed. We're a small world. We're all breathing each other's effluent.

—Professor Tom Cahill, University of California-Davis[2]

As an example of the severity of China's self-inflicted air pollution crisis, it would hard to top the northeast city of Benxi—one of the 20 largest cities in China.[3] At one point, this heavy industry center, which burns roughly 7 million tons of coal per year and produces more steel per capita than any other city in China,[4] literally disappeared from satellite images because of the dense cloud of haze and soot that enveloped it.

The obvious question for those of us living outside China is this: Why should we care? Indeed, if one were to view the heavily polluted Chinese landscape from a totally free-market perspective, one might arrive at this conclusion: If the Chinese want to pollute their air and water so that they can raise their standard of living while consumers in other countries are thereby able to enjoy lower-priced products, so be it.

One problem with this way of thinking—aside from its obvious disregard for the hundreds of millions of innocent Chinese victims of pollution—is this: As you saw in Chapter 1, "The 'China Price' and Weapons of Mass Production," in our discussion of the "China Price," China's extremely lax environmental regulations and weak enforcement allow Chinese manufacturers to produce at an unfair cost advantage over competitors. China's wanton fouling of its air and water thus represents an important source of competitive economic advantage that is helping to put millions of people out of work and depressing wages in other countries.

There is, however, an arguably even bigger problem with China's pollution that affects literally every one on the planet. China's prodigious pollution is now spewing well beyond its environmentally porous borders.

Some of the fallout is regional—such as increased acid rain in neighboring Japan, Korea, and Taiwan. Some of environmental fallout is global—such as an increase in a particularly virulent brand of Chinese smog known as "chog" reaching as far away as Canada and the United States. Some of the effects of the China Air-Pollution Wars are long range and more speculative such as an increase in coastal flooding and hurricanes that may result from China's ever-growing contributions to global warming.

In the analysis that follows, two things should become readily apparent. The first is that the scope of China's environmental degradation is quite literally breath-taking. The second is that China is not really making a "choice" to be one of the world's worst polluters. Rather, like the dust storms in China's Gobi Desert that send pollutants swirling up into the jet stream and eventually to American shores, the Chinese people are being swept along by a complex set of factors and a model of unsustainable economic development that can only end badly not just for the hundreds of thousands of Chinese dying annually from air-pollution-related diseases, but indeed, for all of us.

The Air-Pollution Wars Scorecard

The Middle Kingdom[China] is hurtling toward environmental catastrophe—and perhaps an ensuing political upheaval. Already, most Chinese cities make Los Angeles look like a Swiss village.

—Joshua Kurlantzick, *The New Republic*[5]

Any discussion of the China Air-Pollution Wars must start with the most salient statistics. Here, then, is China's horrific air-quality scorecard as compiled by respected bodies such as the World Bank and China's own *State Environmental Protection Administration* (SEPA):

- China is home to 16 of the 20 most polluted cities in the world.
- China has almost 100 cities with more than a million people each, and fully two thirds of these large Chinese cities fail to meet World Health Organization air-quality standards.
- China is the world leader in the sulfur-dioxide emissions—a key ingredient of photochemical smog. Smog not only reduces visibility; it also kills by attacking both the heart and lungs.
- Carbon dioxide is a principal ingredient driving global warming. China produces the second highest CO_2 emissions in the

world, and it will surpass the world-leading United States over the next several decades.

- China releases 600 tons of mercury into the air annually, nearly a fourth of the world's non-natural emissions.[6] Mercury is particularly harmful to the nervous system, and "children exposed to mercury may be born with symptoms resembling cerebral palsy, spasticity . . . convulsions, visual problems, and abnormal reflexes."[7]

- China is the world leader in the generation of substances that deplete the world's ozone layer—a phenomenon that increases cancer risks, harms plant and marine life, and is leading to the melting of the polar ice caps and attendant rising sea levels and coastal flooding.

- Acid rain, which severely damages forests, fisheries, and crops, affects one fourth of China's land and one third of its agricultural land. As much as 50% of the acid rain in Japan and Korea is of Chinese origin.

- Dust storms associated with Chinese desertification regularly dump tens of thousands of tons of debris on cities from Beijing and Seoul to Tokyo, and their effects have spread as far as North America. These blizzard-like storms can "cause destruction on the scale of a serious earthquake. They can kill people and livestock, destroy crops, and force whole communities to abandon their homes."[8]

According to the Chinese Academy on Environmental Planning, more than 400,000 Chinese die prematurely from air-pollution-related diseases, primarily from lung and heart disease.[9] That number is expected to reach more than 500,000 within a decade.

The World Bank estimates that pollution is annually costing China between 8% and 12% of its more than $1 trillion GDP[10] in terms of such problems as increased medical bills, lost work due to illness, damage to fish and crops, and money spent on disaster relief.

Killing Themselves (and Us) Softly with Their Coal

On a recent hazy morning in eastern China, the Wuhu Shaoda power company revved up its production of electricity, burning a ton and a half of coal per minute to satisfy more than half the demand of Wuhu, an industrial city of two million people.

—*The Wall Street Journal*[11]

When an American hockey player suffered symptoms from mercury contamination, he never expected that he might have power plants half way across the world in China to blame. With its growing appetite for energy, China is finding its many coal-burning power plants hard at work generating the much needed electricity power—as well as huge amounts of air pollutants like sulfur dioxide and mercury. The earth's climate system, however, does not recognize national borders, and that is how increased quantities of Chinese pollutants have joined . . . a global "conveyor belt of bad air." This conveyor belt circles around the world, sending airborne polluting chemicals and particulates from one country to another, posing global health threats. Some scientists have estimated that 30% or more of the mercury settling into America's ecosystems comes from abroad—China, in particular.

—Yale Global Online[12]

At the root of many of China's air-quality problems is its heavy dependence on relatively high-sulfur, low-quality coal for everything from electricity generation and industrial production to cooking and space heating in the home. China relies on coal for almost 75% of its energy needs.

The large amount of coal in China's "energy mix" is quite different from virtually all the other major economies of the world, which depend much more on oil. The result of this heavy coal dependence, coupled with a woeful lack of pollution-control technologies, is that China's air-quality problem is a different one from that of developed countries such as the United States and Germany in at least three ways.

First, unlike in the United States, Germany, or Japan, where sophisticated pollution-control technologies are deployed, much of what Chinese power plants and factories spew in the air is not just sulfur dioxide but also a high percentage of fine particulate matter, the most damaging airborne pollutant.

Second, small cities in China are no better off than large cities in terms of ambient air quality because small cities are as likely as large cities to depend on coal in both their residential and commercial sectors. That means that China's pollution woes are spread over the entire country in cities small and large rather than concentrated in a few large industrial hubs.

Third, unlike the developed world where the automobile is the single largest source of air pollution, China's current problem is primarily a "stationary source" one. These stationary sources range from large coal-fired power plants in huge factory towns to small coal-fired stoves and heaters in peasant homes.

The nightmare here is that even if China is able to get better control of pollution from factories and power plants and even if it is able to convert some of its population to natural gas cooking, it is likely to be overwhelmed in the next several decades by an explosion in the market for cars and trucks. Hundreds of millions of new cars and trucks are projected to crowd China's rapidly expanding highway system over the next several decades—in large part because of people like Jason Yu and a booming economy:

Growing up in Beijing, Jason Yu rode his bicycle to school each morning. Last year, the 38-year-old accountant put away his bike, borrowed $33,000 and bought a black Volkswagen Passat. With cream-leather seats, a sunroof and a CD player, Mr. Yu's new car helps explain one of the main drivers *of the oil crunch: China's voracious appetite for energy. Professionals such as Mr. Yu, who makes more than $20,000 a year, have stormed into the car market, helping turn China into the world's second-largest petroleum consumer after America.*[13]

China's Long Reach of Acid Rain

Acid rain . . . now falls over two-thirds of China's land mass. Of 340 major Chinese cities surveyed last year, 60% had serious air pollution problems.

—Pan Yue, Deputy Director
China State Environmental Protection Administration

Just what exactly is acid rain? By definition, it is rain with a pH reading of less than 5.6 (where 7 is neutral). It occurs when the sulfur-dioxide and nitrogen-dioxide emissions from power plants burning fossil fuels react in the atmosphere with water, oxygen, and various chemicals to form sulfuric and nitric acids.

Although the general public appears split over whether acid rain is a serious problem, numerous scientific studies have found abundant evidence that acid rain is, in fact, an efficient killer. It kills fish when it falls into lakes, rivers, and streams. It directly kills crops and damages soil and thereby substantially reduces harvests. It indirectly kills forests by weakening trees and making them more susceptible to diseases. Acid rain also reduces visibility and eats away at building materials and on house and car paint—with the damages running into the billions of dollars.

As noted by China's State Environmental Protection Administration, roughly a third of China's territory and half of its cities suffer from acid rain,[14] and the problem continues to worsen despite efforts to boost controls. Moreover, a third of Chinese cities currently have acid rain strong enough to damage aquatic life and vegetation. Acid rain is an environmental problem that knows no boundaries—as Canada has painfully learned from the contributions of the United States to its acid rain.

Japan and South Korea are hardly model citizens when it comes to controlling the pollutants that cause acid rain. That said, it is also true that roughly half of Japan's acid rain and a smaller but significant fraction of Korea's acid rain carries the "made in China" label. With no small irony, Japan has sought to subsidize the use of pollution-control technologies in China to protect itself, but it has also helped to finance the construction of new coal-burning power plants, so the net environmental effect on Japan has been negative.

A Mongolian Grapes of Wrath

The once green pastures of eastern Inner Mongolia lately resemble a scene from the American Dust Bowl of the 1930s. Sand storms emanating from these desertified grasslands have become an increasingly common irritant in Northern Chinese cities, and their effects have recently been felt as far away as Colorado.

—American Embassy in China[15]

If ever there is a place to grasp the climatic and environmental changes in China, it is not out on the vast plains, where herds-men and farmers battle over dwindling water resources and tillable land. Instead, it is along an odd stretch of towering sand dunes just 70 km northwest of the capital [of Beijing]. In olden times, this area was a favorite hunting ground of the imperial family, with forests and lakes for picnics.

Now the woods are gone. Nearby sits the junction town of Huailai—except that no one calls it that anymore. Even on the road signs it is Shacheng—Sand City.

—*Asia Week*[16]

Say the word *desert* and the first word that is likely to pop into your head might be *Sahara* or *Mojave*—certainly not *China*. In truth, China is one of the most desert-plagued nations on Earth. Fully one fourth of its land mass, primarily in the northwestern part of the country, is desiccated dust. Within another 20 years, some experts predict that almost 40 percent of China will have been ground into sand.

Turning China into desert is hardly new. The Chinese philosopher *Mencius* noted the problem as far back as 300 B.C., and even pinpointed human causes of the problem such as overcultivation and overgrazing.[17]

What is both new and alarming is the accelerating speed with which this process is now taking place. As related by Wang Tao of the Chinese Academy of Forestry,[18] between the 1950s and 1970s, China lost about 600 square miles (about 1,500 square kilometers) to desert. Today, as the desert has approached within 150 miles of Beijing, roughly 1,500 square miles (4,000 square kilometers) of Chinese real estate are being lost to desertification annually and that number continues to rise despite massive efforts of the central government to contain it.

It is not just that the speed of desertification has been accelerating. According to the China Meteorological Administration, the frequency of the sand and dust storms that represent the environmental fallout from it is also increasing. This claim has been corroborated by the United Nations Environmental Program, which notes a five-fold increase in dust storms in Asia over the past half century.[19] Prior to the 1990s, these storms were relatively rare. Now, however, China is likely to experience more than 20 episodes a year, with at least half of China being affected. These dust and sand storms, which travel on winds of 60 miles (100 kilometers) per hour or more, are serious business to the Chinese, as evidenced by this passage:

> *Two severe dust storms struck North China March 15–20, dumping 56,000 tons of wind-eroded topsoil on Beijing. The March 19–20 storm was the strongest since China began*

*monitoring the phenomenon in 1995. Practically every area
north of the Yangtze River was affected to some degree. At the
peak of the second storm in Beijing between 10 a.m. and noon
March 20, many capital residents fled for cover indoors.
Shopkeepers reported a sharp drop in business, save for a few
enterprising kiosk operators who enjoyed heavy sales of
scarves and facemasks. . . . Various sources reported the con-
centration of suspended particles in the air reached an amaz-
ing 100 times the city's already dangerously high average.
Visibility fell to 100–200 meters, despite low humidity.*[20]

It's not just Beijing and much of northern China that are now being
regularly pummeled by China's dust storms. These storms have now
become a global phenomenon. As *New Scientist* has grimly observed:
"[I]n Korea and Japan, dust blown from China has closed airports,
turned the rain brown and choked rivers and lakes with algal blooms. It
has even found its way across the Pacific to hang as an orange haze over
Colorado. China's dustbowl is becoming a global problem."[21]

Just why are China's dust storms accelerating and intensifying?
Certainly Mother Nature has played some role. However, most
experts believe that the majority of this accelerating and intensifying
problem is purely man-made. The major causes are well worth high-
lighting and include the aforementioned overcultivation and overgrazing first noted by Mencius centuries ago. Other causes include
rampant deforestation, the mismanagement of water resources, and,
more indirectly, global warming. These causes are all intimately tied
to China's rapid economic growth and imperative to feed its people.

Overcultivation: From Grasslands to Granary to Dust Bowl

*. . . to cultivate grassland in the first year, to get a little grain
in the second year, and to turn them into sand in the third or
fourth year.*

—Global Alarm: Dust and Sandstorms from the World's
Drylands[22]

The overcultivation problem began in earnest back in the late 1950s with Mao's Great Leap Forward. Ethnic Han Chinese were dispatched by Beijing to the hinterlands—hitherto occupied mostly by non-Han Mongolian and other ethnic tribes. These cadres of Han farmers began in earnest to plow up the grasslands and cultivate grain as part of the more general effort to bootstrap the economy. The typical result was not to turn these grasslands into granaries but rather into more sand and dust.

Since that time, there have been repeated and equally futile efforts to turn pastureland into farmland. The perverse result has been that even more sand and dust has been freed to be swept up into the atmosphere with the spring winds that whip across the abandoned farms, often with gale force.

Overgrazing: A Chinese-Style "Tragedy of the Commons"

The United States has 8 million sheep and goats; China has a staggering 290 million. The sheep and goats that range across the land are simply denuding western and northern China, a vast grazing commons. In China . . . there is no administrative mechanism for limiting livestock populations to the sustainable yield of rangelands.

—Lester Brown, *The Earth Policy Reader* [23]

The overgrazing problem illustrates how well-intentioned economic policies can have far-ranging environmental effects. A key triggering event in this case was Deng Xiaoping's 1979 economic reforms.

When Deng initiated the "responsibility system" for agriculture in 1979, meat production was decoupled from the central planning process, so that cow, sheep, and goat ranchers were free to multiply their herds and stock as they saw fit. One perverse result has been an explosion of grazing animals in Inner Mongolia, where millions of sheep and goats now denude and destroy these grasslands. This is a "tragedy of the commons" of historic proportions. All efforts by the central government to control the population of grazing animals have thus far been a dismal failure.

Deforestation: China's Chain Saw Massacre

Population growth in traditional forest regions and rising demand for various forest products and services due to increased national income have and will continue to put tremendous pressure on remaining forest resources, especially natural forest resources in China. The existing legal system and institutional framework have failed to protect the forest ecosystems, especially those in the ecologically fragile regions, from being misused and depleted. Despite the strong political will from the national leadership to restore forest ecological functions in the most critical areas, current trend will not alter unless more economically viable means can be adopted and the economic efficiency of the proposed actions can be improved.

—Pelii Shi, Chinese Academy of Sciences
Jintao Xu, Chinese Academy of Agricultural Sciences[24]

Rampant deforestation is a third major contributor to desertification. Forests not only help anchor the topsoil; they also act as a buffer and "wall" to the winds and can prevent a storm from gaining critical mass. More broadly, deforestation results in everything from a loss of biodiversity and flooding to a reduction in rainfall.

Rampant deforestation is driven by China's economic needs. As it has risen to become the largest furniture manufacturer in the world and biggest consumer of raw lumber, both legal and illegal logging has exploded.

Deforestation is not the only problem. By overpopulating the hinterlands region with farmers and ranchers in a bid to increase agricultural and meat production, the Chinese have created a large army of firewood foragers that further decimate the trees and shrubs that grow on the dry and infertile steppes of western China.

In addition, as discussed in the next chapter on China's Water Wars, China is also draining dry its lakes, streams, rivers, and groundwater aquifers. To the extent that this has created water shortages in the desert areas, even more topsoil has shriveled into dust.

Chinese "Chog" Rides the Gobi Express

The Asian Brown Cloud puts millions of people at risk not only for various respiratory diseases but also for severe natural disasters as weather patterns are radically altered and become more extreme and unpredictable. The haze, 80 percent man-made, is composed of a grimy cocktail of toxic ash, black carbon, sulfate, nitrates, acids, and aerosols—tiny solid or liquid particles suspended in the atmosphere. . . . Aerosols in the Asian Brown Cloud also present numerous health hazards. Most often these are respiratory diseases such as asthma, but the composition of the haze also exposes people to carcinogens including arsenic, lead, chromium, and selenium.

—*Global Environmental Issues*[25]

The net result of overcultivation, overgrazing, deforestation, and inefficient water use has been a dramatic increase in both the intensity and frequency of China's dust storms. If that were the end of China's story, the rest of the world might not really care much about the issue. The problem, however, is that China's "chog"—a particularly virulent brand of smog—is now a highly contentious global issue.

Consider this ever-more typical scenario: It is spring and the latest windstorm whips across the steppes of Inner Mongolia. These gale-force winds send vortices of dust clouds high up into the air for a ride upon the jet stream. As this giant swirl moves eastward first toward Beijing and then across the Chinese industrial heartland, it attracts a host of other pollutants, from the fine particulates spewed from coal plants to toxic mercury from industrial smokestacks.

After dumping tons of this toxic stew along a string of Chinese cities and towns, the swirl first makes a "stopover" in Japan and Korea. There, according to South Korea's Rural Development Agency, "a single storm can dump more than 8,000 tons of sand."[26] The worst storms close airports, roads, shops, and schools. More broadly, according to the United Nations Environmental Program, the cost of these dust storms to the region's economy is now tops $6 billion a year.[27]

The swirling cloud—now jam packed full both of fine particulate matter and toxic pollutants—then continues at speeds of upward of 1,500 miles per day, to complete its 7,000-mile journey to North America. Upon arrival, it indiscriminately pollutes the skies of cities ranging from the already smog-filled Los Angeles to the typically pristine skies of the ski resort of Aspen.

China's Ever-Expanding Role in Global Warming

Global warming causes the level of the ocean to rise in two ways: by unlocking vast amounts of water from melting glaciers around the world, and because warmer waters expand. Records of sea level drawn from around the world show that the sea has risen by between 4 and 10 inches in the last century, according to the IPCC [Intergovernmental Panel on Climate Change], and "it is likely that much of the rise in sea level has been related to the concurrent rise in global temperature."

—Global Warming is Here: The Scientific Evidence[28]

Then there is the long-term issue of global warming and rising sea levels. Within 80 years, 30 million people in China are going to be under sea. We know it is going to happen so we must look at ways of how to protect the area.

—Dr. Peter Walker, International Federation of Red Cross and Red Crescent Societies[29]

For tens of millions of years, greenhouse gases and a collateral "greenhouse effect" have been Earth's best friend. Soon, however, these gases may become Earth's worst enemy.

Greenhouse gases consist primarily of carbon dioxide but also include methane, nitrous oxide, ozone, and water vapor. They have been our friend because they act like a "thermal blanket" to keep Earth at a livable temperature. When the sun's radiant energy beats down on the planet, Earth, in turn, wants to radiate this energy back into space. Greenhouse gases help to trap some of that energy and, thereby, keep some of the heat in.

This "greenhouse effect" occurs in much the same way you would observe in an actual greenhouse. Without this natural global warming, Earth's average temperature would be much lower than around 60 degrees Fahrenheit, which is quite hospitable for our species and all the other animal, marine, and plant life that help make up the "food chain" and support the broader ecosystem.

By the way, if, as you are reading this, you react negatively to terms such as *ecosystem* and roll your eyes at the idea of global warming, you are not alone. A lot of people, particularly in the United States, believe that global warming is a left-wing hoax perpetrated by fuzzy-headed environmentalists.

As a purely scientific matter, however, the vast majority of climatologists believe the greenhouse effect and attendant global warming is a real, serious, and largely uncontroversial phenomenon. According to the U.S. Environmental Protection Agency, since the industrial revolution began more than a century ago, "atmospheric concentrations of carbon dioxide have increased nearly 30%, methane concentrations have more than doubled, and nitrous oxide concentrations have risen by about 15%." In the same time frame, average surface temperatures have increased by anywhere from one half to one degree, and the sea level has risen anywhere from 4 to 10 inches in the past century.

Of course, these changes do not sound like much—and as yet, they may not be much. Now, however, the much bigger concern among climatologists is that global warming appears to be increasing at a much more rapid rate.

Consider that the 10 hottest years in the twentieth century all occurred in the past 15 years leading up to 2000. Even more alarming, the area of the Arctic's perennial polar ice cap is now declining at the rate of 9 percent per decade. In addition, both the snow cover in the northern hemisphere and floating ice in the Arctic Ocean have visibly decreased. This relatively modest global warming thus far is already causing considerable damage around the globe.[30] Its effects range from increased wildfires, dust storms, floods, and more intense and frequent hurricanes in the United States to extreme "killer heat waves" in Europe and India that have claimed tens of thousands of lives.[31]

So where does China fit into all of this? Simply that, as noted earlier, China is the second largest producer of carbon dioxide behind the United States.

The Troubles with China's Environmental Destruction Agency

[T]he central government promotes big solutions that gives regulators little power to enforce them. Local officials have few incentives to crack down on polluters because their promotion system is based primarily on economic growth, not public health. It is a game that leaves poor, rural regions clinging to the worst polluters.

—*The New York Times*[32]

Why has China allowed itself to become both the black lungs and biggest dust bowl of the planet? This is an important question within the context of China's Air-Pollution and Water Wars, particularly because, at least on paper, China appears to have a set of environmental regulations almost as tough as those of the United States or Japan.

In practice, however, the laws are almost a total sham. At the root of the problem lies a perverse set of economic incentives that have derailed effectively all attempts by the central government to control pollution.

For starters, China's SEPA is woefully understaffed and under-budgeted. Whereas the United States EPA employs close to 20,000,[33] China's SEPA has only 300, to oversee environmental protection in a country with more than a billion people and with close to 100 cities of a million people or more.

Second, it is not just that there are not enough federal regulators to go around. Also, the local environmental bureaus that are most empowered to enforce the central government's environmental edicts are both highly autonomous and often corrupt. This problem of local autonomy goes far back into China's history and its imperial times and is reflected in the ancient Chinese proverb "the mountains are high and the emperor is far away." The practical effect of a weak central government is that putatively "federal" environmental regulations are not generally enforced at the local level. Instead, "local officials either collude with corrupt local businesses or believe that nothing must be allowed to slow economic growth."[34]

A third, highly interrelated problem is that many of China's worst polluters are state-run enterprises or companies in which the government is a major shareholder. This raises an obvious conflict-of-interest problem because it requires the government to police itself.

Fourth, in a given locality, some of the worst polluters are also some of the largest employers. In many cases, cracking down on such offenders becomes almost impossible because to do so would exacerbate an already serious unemployment problem.

Fifth, there is the large matter of the small fines Chinese regulators impose on polluters. Rather than being an effective deterrent, these fines are seen as a rather small cost of doing business. Moreover, local authorities that collect the fines often recycle the revenues back to the polluters as a tax breaks![35]

Sixth, China's weak legal system makes it difficult to impossible for pollution victims to seek any proper redress. Not only are the laws unclear, but the judiciary is often pro-polluter.

Seventh, and in a related vein, few environmental groups exist to assist pollution victims and mobilize political pressures for compliance. As a by-product of the repressive nature of the regime, would-be environmentalists are subject to fines, jail, or beatings.

In addition, environmental groups face high "barriers to entry" in their formation. Not only are their regulatory reporting requirements formidable; any group has to post a large "bond" with the government to operate. To see how this might discourage environmentalism in China, just imagine if every local chapter of the Sierra Club had to put up a million dollars just for the right to engage in environmental activism.

Eighth, there is China's historical and cultural relationship with the environment. For centuries, the country's rulers have subjugated their surroundings to their needs rather than attempting to live in harmony with them. Most explicitly, Mao once declared that man must "conquer nature and thus attain freedom from nature."

It's not just China's "master-servant" relationship with the environment that is problematic. There is also a blatant disregard for private property and the rule of law, coupled with precious little respect for the more diffuse rights of others to everything from clean air and water to human rights. Many scholars have speculated on why these attitudes are so embedded in the Chinese culture, with some blaming the problem on everything from Confucianism and Communism to atheism.

Regardless of the sources of the attitudes, in China's permissive atmosphere, it is routine for Chinese executives and factory managers to either ignore environmental rules or, in some ways far worse, to engage in elaborate ruses to fool environmental inspectors.

One such ruse, which is practiced by as many as one third of all large Chinese companies, is to switch on the company's pollution-control technologies only during government inspections. This is easy to accomplish because inspections are always scheduled in advance by compliant and complicit regulators rather than conducted in surprise fashion. Because of these kinds of ruses used by business executives to avoid and evade regulation, Joseph Kahn of the *New York Times* has correctly noted that

> *[T]he enormous human and environmental toll of China's rapid development is not just an unintended side effect but also an explicit choice of business executives and officials who tolerate death and degradation as the inevitable price of progress.*[36]

To a Westerner, the obvious question arises: What are these business executives thinking when they do this? I do not really know the answer to that. What I do know is that the problem is endemic and cuts to the heart of the Chinese psyche, at least in the People's Republic.

As a final cause of China's lack of environmental protection and enforcement, one must also note the rise of powerful foreign business groups and lobbyists in the political and economic fabric of China. As noted in Chapter 1, much of the foreign direct investment that is flooding into China comes from countries such as Japan, Korea, Taiwan, and the United States, whose multinational companies are actively seeking to "export" some of their most polluted industries to China.

There is both a danger and an irony here that should not be lost on any student of Chinese history aware of the "foreign humiliation" that China was subjected to in the nineteenth and twentieth centuries. The danger is that these powerful foreign economic interests are overpowering the political will of the central government, thereby rendering it impossible for China to get a handle on its own pollution problems. The irony is that as China's Communist Party seeks to mold the country into a superpower, it is quickly losing control of its own destiny to powerful foreign economic interests.

Add all of this up and you get what you get: one of the most heavily polluted countries on the planet with problems that are not just regional but global in their trans-border implications. Indeed, it is precisely China's dysfunctional system of environmental protection that continues to make China such a magnet for foreign investment.

4

THE "BLOOD FOR OIL" WARS—THE SUM OF ALL CHINESE FEARS

Throughout the summer and into the fall of 1941, Japanese negotiators and the United States were at loggerheads. The U.S.-led embargo would not be suspended until the Japanese stopped their militaristic expansion; indeed, Japan would have to roll back some of its gains. . . . By September 1941, Japanese reserves had dropped to 50 million barrels, and their navy alone was burning 2,900 barrels of oil every hour. The Japanese had reached a crossroads. If they did nothing, they would be out of oil and options in less than 2 years, If they chose war, there was a good chance they could lose a protracted conflict. Given the possibility of success with the second option, versus none with the first option, the Japanese chose war.

—Lieutenant Colonel Patrick H. Donovan, U.S. Air Force[1]

It may come as a surprise to many people—particularly Americans—that it was America in 1941 and not Saudi Arabia and its Arab allies in

1973 that imposed the first oil embargo in modern history. In response to Japan's invasion of China, the United States cut off Japan's imported oil.[2]

This attempt to pressure Japan to withdraw from China constituted a deep humiliation to a country with a premium on "saving face." The oil embargo left the Japanese military with a petroleum reserve that would be quickly exhausted. Some historians cite the American embargo of oil and other strategic war materiel as the major trigger for the Pearl Harbor attack and the start of World War II.

Since the embargo and the ensuing "day of infamy," oil and war have hardly been strange bedfellows. With oil being the lifeblood of every modern economy, considerable blood is being shed in the Middle East and elsewhere to control or protect the vast network that brings this "black gold" from faraway places to the world's factories and transportation systems. What is disturbingly new about today's "blood for oil" wars is how China's rapidly expanding thirst for petroleum is changing the battlefields.

On the economic front, China's rapidly increasing oil demand is creating persistent and significant oil price shocks and increasing volatility in the world's oil markets. These shocks destabilize the global economy.

On the foreign-policy front, China's oil thirst is rapidly accelerating the global arms race and the further spread of weapons of mass destruction—from long-range, intercontinental ballistic missiles to the nuclear warheads that ride atop them. China's self-professed "amoral" approach to its foreign policy and business dealings is also helping to prop up both dictators and rogue nations with a propensity to loot their public treasuries, trample human rights, and, in at least two cases to date, conduct campaigns of genocide and ethnic cleansing.

Finally, on the "hot-war" front, the China Oil Wars may also spill over into a dangerous array of ugly military confrontations. One possible trigger may be the discovery of large oil reserves in the South and East China Seas. China has been engaged in long-term territorial disputes with Japan, Indonesia, the Philippines, Vietnam, and other neighbors in these areas, and has already used military might to seize several islands in dispute and assert its claims.

China's Growing Thirst for Oil

China's growing energy demands, particularly its increasing reliance on oil imports, pose economic, environmental, and geostrategic challenges to the United States.

—The U.S.-China Economic and Security Review Commission[3]

The long-run impact of sustained, significantly increased oil prices . . . will be severe. Virtually certain are increases in inflation and unemployment, declines in the output of goods and services, and a degradation of living standards. Without timely mitigation, the long-run impact on the developed economies will almost certainly be extremely damaging, while many developing nations will likely be even worse off.

—U.S. Department of Energy[4]

Any discussion of China's growing thirst for oil must first acknowledge that the biggest guzzler on the global oil block is the United States. With less than 5% of the world's population, the United States annually consumes about 25% of the world's oil production. In comparison, with about 20% of the world's population, China currently consumes only about 7% of the world's oil. Note, however, that as China's economy continues to grow rapidly, so, too, will its oil consumption and share of the world oil market—even as the U.S. share of that market stabilizes. The most salient facts are these:

- China is the world's second-largest petroleum consumer behind only the United States.

- China is already heavily dependent on oil imports. It currently imports more than 40% of its needs, and oil import dependence is projected to reach 60 percent by 2020.

- As the largest economy without a substantial strategic petroleum reserve, China is highly vulnerable to oil-market disruptions. It has on hand less than 10 days of supply versus about 60 days for the United States and 100 days for Japan.[5]

In large part as a result of China's growing thirst for oil,[6] today's oil market is characterized by both dramatically higher prices and significantly greater price volatility. Because of surging oil demand in emerging countries such as China and India, the International Monetary Fund is now warning of a "permanent oil shock" and possible sustained global recession over the next several decades.[7]

Such a permanent shock portends a difficult economic future. Higher oil prices increase the costs of production of goods and services, lowering capital investment and causing inflation. Oil price shocks also act as a "tax" and reduces the demand for goods other than oil. The typical result is recession, an attendant reduction in tax revenues, an increase in the budget deficit, and upward pressure on interest rates.

It is also well worth noting that whereas the developed nations of the world are highly vulnerable to oil price shocks, developing countries—from Bangladesh and Cambodia to Haiti to Mexico—are hurt even more. This is partly because developing countries "generally use energy less efficiently and because energy-intensive manufacturing accounts for a larger share of their GDP." It is also because developing countries typically have a much more "limited ability to switch to alternative fuels." In addition, increased oil costs "can destabilize trade balances and increase inflation more in developing countries, where financial institutions and monetary authorities are often relatively unsophisticated."[8]

Despite the serious economic impacts of inflation and recession that may result from China's increasing participation in world oil markets, it is the other more geopolitical and foreign-policy-oriented effects—driven by China's highly provocative energy security strategies—that may ultimately prove to be most dangerous to global economic and political stability. To understand these effects, it is first useful to understand China's deepest oil-security fears.

The Sum of All Chinese Energy-Security Fears

At the end of the day, you've got two very large consumers [the U.S. and China] competing over the same sandbox. Sooner or later the Chinese are going to run out of places they can look for oil.

—Gal Luft, Executive Director
Institute for the Analysis of Global Security[9]

The paramount fear of the Chinese is that at some point, the United States might attempt to do what it once did to Japan—disrupt China's oil supplies as a means of exerting pressure on Chinese economic, trade, or foreign policies. This is not an idle fear—particularly from the Chinese perspective.

In the economic arena, many analysts believe that a U.S. "trade war" with China is inevitable as it continues to gobble up world market share and shift jobs from other countries to its own "factory floor." At issue with the United States, as well as Europe and Japan, and as discussed in the previous chapter, will certainly be China's mercantilist and "beggar thy neighbor" exchange rate, trade, and tariff practices and its failure to comply with World Trade Organization requirements. Many members of the U.S. Congress have already begun to "demonize" the Chinese, and tough negotiators are regularly dispatched to Beijing for serious talks.[10]

The most likely U.S. oil-embargo scenario would involve a Chinese invasion of Taiwan. China has made it very clear to the world community that this small island nation "belongs" to the Chinese mainland. Should Taiwan continue to resist China or, far more provocatively, officially declare its independence, a "blitzkrieg"-style invasion of the island is certainly well within the scope of Chinese military plans. That such an attack could quickly escalate into a larger "world war" should be evident in this missile-rattling passage from the *New York Times*:

> *China should use nuclear weapons against the United States if the American military intervenes in any conflict over Taiwan, a senior Chinese military official said Thursday. "If the Americans draw their missiles and position-guided ammunition on to the target zone on China's territory, I think we will have to respond with nuclear weapons," the official, Maj. Gen. Zhu Chenghu, said at an official briefing. . . . General Zhu's threat is not the first of its kind from a senior Chinese military official. In 1995, Xiong Guangkai, who is now the deputy chief of the general staff of the People's Liberation Army, told Chas W. Freeman, a former Pentagon official, that China would consider using nuclear weapons in a Taiwan conflict.*[11]

The U.S. Navy has already confronted the Chinese military several times over Taiwan—once during the Eisenhower administration and once during the Clinton administration. With the United States continuing to promise to protect Taiwan, one response to Chinese aggression might well be for the U.S. Navy to attempt to block the flow of oil to China.

As a practical matter, this would be a relatively simple task because the U.S. Navy currently controls most of the shipping lanes through which oil now flows. This includes the Strait of Hormuz, which is the critical entryway for all tanker-based oil deliveries from the Middle East. It also includes the very narrow Straits of Malacca, the link between the Indian and Pacific Oceans that provide passage for about 80% of China's oil imports and are considered to be the key chokepoint in Asia. That is why, from the Chinese perspective, if a trade war erupts or China invades Taiwan, a military confrontation between the United States and China could well follow.

Chilling to note is that "China is estimated to have about 20 intercontinental ballistic missiles capable of reaching U.S. territory and another 12 submarine-based missiles that can hit U.S. cities from international waters. These missiles have very large nuclear warheads that are the equivalent of three to five million tons of TNT or, by comparison, 240 to 400 times more powerful than the blast that destroyed Hiroshima. Just one of these warheads could completely destroy a large city."[12]

China's Highly Provocative Oil-Security Strategies

China's approach to securing its imported petroleum supplies through bilateral arrangements is an impetus for nonmarket reciprocity deals with Iran, Sudan, and other states of concern, including arms sales and WMD-related technology transfers that pose security challenges to the United States.

—The U.S.-China Economic and Security Review Commission[13]

With its overriding goal of securing oil and gas to fuel China's economic growth, the Chinese government has actively cultivated its relations with the oil-rich Middle East, especially Iran and Saudi Arabia. In their dogged pursuit of this goal, Chinese policymakers have been more than willing not only to undercut U.S. nonproliferation efforts but also to work closely with governments that export Islamism. . . .

—Dan Blumenthal, *The Middle East Quarterly*[14]

How has China sought to address strategically its oil-security fears? At the heart of its strategy is an approach that is radically different from that of the United States. Whereas the U.S. focus has been primarily on ensuring the security of the international oil market, China has adopted a "bilateral contracting approach" in which it seeks to lock down physical supplies of oil with other oil-producing countries.

In essence, this is a strategy designed to obtain *physical* control rather than merely financial control of the oil *before* it ever gets to market. China's approach involving the lockdown of oil reserves is a hard-edged, conflict-generating strategy that is designed to lock out other potential buyers such as the United States or Europe.

Achieving physical control is arguably not the worst feature of China's oil-security strategy, however. That distinction is reserved for China's own self-professed "amoral" approach to its bilateral negotiations. China is quite willing to engage in what the U.S.-China Commission has dryly described as "nonmarket reciprocity" deals with some of the most dangerous rogue nations in the world.

In some cases, Chinese bilateral deals have involved the sale of weapons of mass destruction—including highly sophisticated ballistic missiles in return for oil. In other cases, these deals have involved the exchange of nuclear resources and technology for oil, which creates attendant concerns about nuclear proliferation. In still other cases, these deals have quite literally involved genocidal "blood for oil."

In all of these dealings, everyone from China's business leaders right up to its president and premier openly boasts to dictators and rogue states alike that it will never condition its business dealings on any issues that challenge the sovereignty of its trading partners.[15] As President Hu Jintao has put it, "Just business, with no political conditions."[16]

Even more profane, given the broader humanitarian goals of the United Nations and its peacekeeping mission, China has repeatedly promised that in exchange for oil, other resources, or market access, it will use its U.N. veto as a tool to protect dictators and rogue states from any U.N. sanctions.

The following examples demonstrate some of the more disturbing aspects of China's oil policy—and its far-ranging effects. Note, however, that these examples involving Iran, the Sudan, and Angola are just the tip of an iceberg and are, by no means, an inclusive list of problems.

Accelerating the Global Arms Race

Beijing has sold thousands of tanks, artillery pieces, and armored personnel carriers to Iran, more than 100 combat aircraft, and dozens of small warships. Beijing has also sold Iran an array of missile systems and technology, including air-to-air missiles, surface-to-air missiles, and antishipping cruise missiles. Most worrisome have been China's transfer of ballistic missile technology and its assistance with Iran's [nuclear] programs. . . . China has sent entire factories to Iran for producing chemicals that, although they have legitimate purposes, can also be used to make poison gas, and tons of industrial chemicals that could be used in making nerve agents.

—The Rand Corporation[17]

Chinese foreign minister Li Zhaoxing flew to Tehran to conclude an oil and gas deal between China's state-owned Sinopec and the Iranian oil ministry worth approximately $100 billion (U.S.) over thirty years. The purpose of Li's visit was clearly to exploit tensions between Washington and Tehran over Iran's nuclear program. His trip came against the backdrop of delicate European Union-led negotiations with Iran over its nuclear program and U.S. threats to refer the Iranian nuclear matter to the United Nations Security Council.

After the oil deal was signed, Li announced that China would refuse to refer the issue of Iran's nuclear program to the Security Council. Li's announcement signified that decades of Sino-Iranian cooperation was bearing fruit for both parties: China would get the oil and gas its economy desperately needs while Iran would finally win the political support of a

*reliable and weighty friend. Beijing bet that an open chal-
lenge to U.S. policy would not result in any negative repercussions—and it won. The fact that the Chinese establishment
considers its actions a victory should worry the Bush administration. If Beijing continues to view access to Middle Eastern oil as a zero-sum game and the Middle East as a playing
field for great power competition, more direct confrontation
between China and the United States will be not the exception
but the rule.*

—Dan Blumenthal, *The Middle East Quarterly*[18]

As a "charter member" of President Bush's "axis of evil," Iran possesses the world's second-largest natural gas reserves after Russia and
controls fully 10% of the world's oil reserves. Perhaps not surprisingly,
oil export revenues account for 80% to 90% of the country's total
export earnings. More important, they fund roughly half of Iran's government budget.[19]

According to the U.S. State Department, Iran's radical fundamentalist Islamic regime has consistently been the "most active" state
sponsor of terrorism.[20] This regime also plays a key role in the desta-
bilization of Iraq—at the real cost of American military lives. It has
done so by exerting its considerable influence on the majority Shiite
population in Iraq and by acting as a haven for terrorists and a launch-
ing point for insurgent activity into Iraq.

In addition, Iran has aggressively sought to acquire nuclear
weapons. A major concern is that such weapons might be used in a
preemptive strike against Israel. A second concern is that Iran's quest
for a nuclear capability is already triggering a nuclear arms race
among other nations such as Saudi Arabia and Egypt.[21]

Perhaps not surprisingly, the United States has tried to counter
Iran's rogue behavior in a number of ways, the most important of
which has been the application of economic sanctions against the
regime. Unfortunately, China's willingness to trade diplomatic favors

for oil rights makes it far more difficult for the United States to deploy an effective sanctions strategy.

In this regard, while the United States attempts to dissuade other nations in Europe and Asia from doing business with Iran, China exploits this "sanctions vacuum" to strengthen its Iranian ties and seal a number of mega-deals to develop Iranian petroleum reserves. These deals include the massive Yadavaran field that geologists believe contains up to 3 billion barrels of recoverable reserves and a total production capacity of as much as 300,000 barrels a day.[22]

China's unwavering support for Iran has three unfortunate effects. First, it has helped prop up a regime that is so highly unpopular among much of the populace *that might otherwise have even collapsed by now.* Second, China's willingness to ignore the U.S. campaign has resulted in Japan and many European nations essentially "throwing in the sanctions towel" and seeking to make their own business deals with Iran. Their clear argument: We cannot stand by as China locks down all the best undeveloped petroleum reserves.

The third effect is the most unsettling. In exchange for petroleum access, China has supplied Iran with highly sophisticated weaponry such as ballistic missiles and a chemical weapons capability. China has already supplied Iran with most of the advanced nuclear technology that is enabling its development of nuclear weapons. To say that this is highly destabilizing to a region that is already a perennial powder keg would be to vastly understate this effect.

China's U.N. Shame and Propping Up Dictatorial Regimes

Unlike their increasingly publicity-sensitive western rivals, the Chinese have no qualms about making deals with oil-rich dictators, however corrupt or nasty.

—*The Economist*[23]

As the previous discussion of Iranian oil deals mentioned, one of the most potent weapons in the China Wars is China's ability to veto any U.N. Security Council resolution.[24] China's top business and political leaders regularly "shop" China's U.N. veto to countries with which they seek to strengthen ties. A closer look at two of these countries—Angola and the Sudan—illustrates two different and very ugly faces of this "dances with dictators" problem.

Genocide and Terrorism in the Sudan

All summer, the UN Security Council debated whether to condemn the Sudanese government for supporting the murderous Janjaweed militias in Darfur. . . . Quietly but steadfastly, China's ambassador to the United States, Wang Guangya, has helped defang U.S.-sponsored drafts against Sudan, transforming language threatening to "take further action" against Khartoum into the more benign "consider taking additional measures." . . . Beijing's goal? Probably to protect its investments in the Sudanese oil industry, including a 40% stake in a refinery pumping more than 300,000 barrels a day and a 1500-kilometer pipeline from Sudan to the Red Sea.

—*The New Republic*[25]

Not only the largest country in Africa, with borders touching countries ranging from Chad, Egypt, Eritrea, Ethiopia, and Libya to the Central African Republic and Congo and Kenya and Uganda, but also Sudan is strategically located along the Nile River and Red Sea. Historically, this has made the Sudan a "target of revolving-door superpower intervention and massive arms transfers."[26] China is just the latest superpower to enter into the Sudanese sweepstakes.

China's activities in the Sudan provide a chilling example of the kind of crass Chinese commercialism that is being shopped under the U.N. banner of peace and humanitarianism. The Sudan is one of six countries in the world that the United States has designated as "state sponsors of terrorism."[27] It earned this distinction by refusing to extradite three suspects in the 1995 assassination attempt of the Egyptian president and by allowing its soil to be used for the sanctuary and training of terrorist groups.

To isolate the Sudan—and attempt to change its behavior—the United States has banned all imports, exports, and investment into that country. In addition, the United States has tried to enlist European countries, Japan, and other countries in this boycott. The net result has simply been to make the Sudan and its oil reserves that much easier pickings for China.

China has given the Sudan a complete package of economic and diplomatic incentives in exchange for access to its oil reserves. A key part of that incentives package has been China's brazen willingness to use its diplomatic power and permanent veto in the United Nations to protect the Sudan from U.N. sanctions. During Sudan's campaign of genocide in its Darfur region, China repeatedly thwarted U.N. attempts to stop the ongoing rape, massacre, and systematic starvation of non-Arab Sudanese at the hands of Arab Janjaweed militia forces armed and controlled by the Sudanese government. According to estimates by the World Health Organization and the United Nations, this "ethnic cleansing" has led to the deaths of several hundred thousand people and the displacement of almost two million refugees.

It is not just diplomatic incentives that have kept China very much in the Sudanese oil game. China has also become one of Sudan's main weapons suppliers—from small arms and mortars to helicopters, jet fighters, and even SCUD missiles. This steady stream of weapons has, in turn, helped accelerate an arms race throughout sub-Saharan Africa and the Middle East. The result to date has been several billion dollars of investment in Sudan's oil industry from which China currently gets close to 5% of its oil imports.[28]

Corruption and Looting in Angola

China originally broke off relations with newly independent Angola, regarding it as too close to the Soviet Union. Thirty

*years later it has rectified this mistake. The former Por-
tuguese colony has become China's second-largest commercial partner in Africa and exports 25% of its oil production to
China.*

—*Le Monde diplomatique*[29]

*Angola presents a horrifying case of squandered possibilities.
Rich in oil and diamonds, this country on the southwestern
coast of Africa is desperately poor. In the first few years of
this decade, corruption was so extreme that each year, more
than U.S.$1 billion of Angola's oil revenues reportedly were
disappearing.*

—Professor John McMillan[30]

*[O]ne in four of Angola's children die before the age of five
and one million internally-displaced people remain dependent on international food aid.*

—Global Witness[31]

Angola is indeed a country "rich in oil and diamonds" but with a population that is desperately poor. The primary problem is one well
known in economics and referred to as the paradox of the "resources
curse." Although one might think that those countries with the greatest endowments of natural resources would also be those with the
highest per capita income, the seemingly paradoxical result is often
exactly the opposite.

The underlying economic reason is one of "perverse incentives":
The greater a country's natural resources, the more likely it is that the
country's corrupt rulers will try to capture this wealth for their own
Swiss bank accounts rather than use those natural resources riches on
behalf of the people. Nowhere is this more true than in Angola,
where, as the U.S. State Department has reported, the country's
wealth is "concentrated in the hands of a small elite whose members"
use "government positions for massive personal enrichment."[32]

In a concerted diplomatic effort, the United States, the International Monetary Fund, the World Bank, national export credit agencies, and various nongovernmental organizations such as Global Witness have all called for "greater transparency" in the tracking of Angola's oil revenues. However, the biggest obstacle to reform has been China and its willingness to deal secretly with Angola's corrupt leadership.

In exchange for drilling rights in Angola, China regularly shells out huge upfront payments to Angolan officials that are impossible to track. China also provides lavish "soft loans" to the Angolan government, much of which quickly bypass the public treasury for offshore accounts or are funneled into the campaign coffers of the ruling party to help keep it in power.

As a result of these Angolan-Chinese connections, Angola is now China's top energy supplier. Angola is the second-largest producer of oil in sub-Saharan Africa behind only Nigeria. Angola's oil revenues account for almost 50% its total annual economic output, 90% of total exports, and 80% of government revenues. It has been estimated that as much as one third of Angola's annual revenues "go missing" each year while the Chinese happily facilitate this theft with its nontransparent contracts.

A Coming "Hot War" in the South China Seas?

The Spratlys and the Paracels are island chains hardly worthy of the name. Consisting of a few dozen rock outcroppings each, many of which are under water at high tide, they lack a source of fresh water and have never been inhabited. What they lack in land area, however, they more than make up in sweep. The Paracels, located equidistant from China, Vietnam, and the Philippines, are hundreds of miles in extent. The Spratly Islands, another five hundred miles further south, stretch across additional hundreds of miles of open ocean between Vietnam, Malaysia, and the Philippines.

China is aggressively moving to take control of the two archi-
pelagos, ignoring the competing claims of a half-dozen other
nations. In a December 15, 1998, report to House Republican
leaders, Congressman Dana Rohrabacher reported that "the
pattern of Chinese naval bases in the Spratlys shows an encir-
cling strategy of the energy-rich islands and an intimidating
military presence along the vital sea route that connects the
strategic Strait of Malacca with the Taiwan Strait." Some
eleven Chinese bases have been detected to date.

China's claims are usually interpreted in economic terms.
Indeed, China's already voracious appetite for energy is
straining domestic sources, and the continental shelf of the
South China Sea is suspected to possess vast oil and natural
gas fields. Yet Beijing's efforts to transform the South China
Sea into a Chinese lake has strategic reasons as well. The
Strait of Malacca is a maritime chokepoint connecting the
Pacific and Indian oceans; through this a vital sea lane passes
70% of the crude oil used to fire the economies of Japan,
Taiwan, and South Korea. Free passage through the Strait of
Malacca is critical to any effective U.S. response to crises in
Asia and the Middle East.

From the bases that it is building on Mischief Reef and else-
where in the Spratlys, Chinese air, naval and Marine forces
could strike not only at shipping, but at all the countries that
surround the South China Sea, including such U.S. allies as
the Philippines, Brunei, and Thailand.

—Steven Mosher, *Hegemon*[33]

The previous passage from Steven Mosher's controversial book is
worth quoting for several reasons. The first is that it provides an accu-
rate description of a looming hot spot in the China Oil Wars.

According to the U.S. Energy Information Agency, the South
China Sea has proven oil reserves of around 7 billion barrels, and the
U.S. Geological Survey has estimated there may be another 20 billion
barrels to be discovered; China optimistically claims the undiscovered reserves could top 200 billion barrels. This latter amount would

be enough to provide China with one to two million barrels of oil a day, or roughly 15% to 30% of its current consumption. Should substantial oil reserves be discovered in the contested areas of the South China Seas defined by the Spratlys and Paracels, this could well lead to a military conflict between China and one or more of its neighbors.

More broadly, this Hegemon excerpt is interesting because it illustrates how the Chinese military is moving in a strategic manner to ensure China's energy security. Throughout modern history, China has never been a naval power. However, over the past decade, China has embarked upon an ambitious program to build a "blue-water navy." A clear goal is to develop the capability to challenge those U.S. fleets that currently control key oil-shipping "chokepoints" as near to China as the Straits of Malacca and as far away as the Strait of Hormuz.

The strategy also underscores the point that in any given arena, Chinese strategy is likely to operate at multiple levels—not just focusing on oil security but on other and broader foreign-policy goals. For example, as a Rand study has pointed out, sometimes Beijing will sell weapons to a country such as Pakistan as a way of forcing "India to devote more resources to its border with Pakistan and less to its border with China."[34] In a similar fashion, China has sold arms to Myanmar as a way of gaining access to Myanmar's Indian Ocean naval bases, including a radar installation on the Coco Islands that is close to India's naval base in the Andaman Islands.[35]

The broader point is that China will use any and all economic, political, and military weapons at its disposal to achieve any one of a number of goals. Perhaps none of those goals is as important in both the short- and long-term as energy security.

Fear and Loathing in the "Sea of Conflict"

The [Japanese] Center for Safety and Security Research (CSSR), a research institute under the Education, Science and Technology Ministry, has released a report on two crisis scenarios concerning China that predict China's actions regarding energy and their impact on Japan.

The first scenario is a battle over energy sources. It assumes that if China reinforces its procurement of energy without taking cost efficiency into consideration, the world will be plunged into a situation in which each country competes for oil by ignoring international market mechanisms. As a result, political tension between the two countries over resources in the East China Sea will mount. *[emphasis added]*

—Asia Times Online[36]

Japanese enterprises' act of trial extraction of oil and gas resources in China's exclusive economic zone . . . will not only make the East China Sea the most dangerous area for possible eruption of conflicts between the two countries, but will also worsen China-Japan relations.

—The People's Daily Online[37]

China's budding blue-water navy strong-arming Brunei or Vietnam out of oil in places such as Mischief Reef and the South China Seas is one thing. It is quite another for China to confront an economic superpower such as Japan over oil resources in the Sea of Japan and East China Sea. That's why the consequences of an escalating Oil War between China and Japan are even more dangerous and far-reaching than the war already brewing in the South China Seas. Such a war would pit China not against a small collection of lesser states with far less ability to fight back but rather against an economic superpower that is already a de facto member of the nuclear weapons "club" and which has the resources necessary to remilitarize quickly.

The simmering to a boil China-Japan Oil War revolves primarily around a fierce dispute over oil and gas reserves located deep below the waters of the East China Seas. Although there is a theoretical middle or "median line" proposed by Japan that equally separates Chinese and Japanese claims to the mineral rights below these seas, there are two major problems with using this line to settle this long-simmering territorial dispute. The first is that China rejects such a territorial demarcation. Instead, as in the South China Sea, the Chinese prefer a much more expansive "Chinese lake" definition that would drive the Japanese back toward their shores. Rather than counting from land's edge, China wants to count its boundaries from the edge of its *underwater* continental shelf. As described in the *Economist*:

> *Under the UN's Convention on the Law of the Sea, an EEZ [Exclusive Economic Zone] can extend up to 200 nautical miles from a country's shoreline. But the East China Sea between China and Japan is only about 360 nautical miles at its very widest. Japan says the boundary should be the median line between the two countries. China says its EEZ [and right to drill oil] should extend to the edge of its continental shelf, which would put the line almost up against Japan's shores.*[38]

The second and far greater problem is that even if China accepted the middle line proposed by Japan, the highly fluid oil and gas fields underlying this middle line know no such boundaries. As geological survey studies have shown, "China's Chunxiao and Duanqiao gas fields are linked to Japan's gas fields."[39] This means that whoever drills first and pumps the fastest will get the petroleum no matter whose side of the line the resource falls on—and the same may apply to any additional reserves found in the area.

Since 2003, the Chinese have been drilling first. Predictably, Japan protested China's move and, perhaps equally predictably, their protests led to negotiations that dragged on for years. When the negotiations went nowhere, a frustrated Japan responded with their own efforts to test drill on their side of the median line. China's sharp reaction to this Japanese "provocation" is highly instructive because it illustrates both the high stakes involved and the ease with which conflicts can quickly escalate or spiral out of control.

For starters, the Chinese government's press strongly condemned the action by Japan. As part of its attack to whip up public indignation, the Chinese press also waved the perennial "bloody shirt" of Japan's brutal occupation of China from 1937 to 1945 by specifically pointing out how Japanese history textbooks have treated this episode.

The irony of the Chinese accusing anyone of "revisionist history" would not be lost on any true China watcher. Nowhere in Chinese history texts can be found an account of the scope of human suffering and deaths inflicted by Mao's Great Leap Forward or the Cultural Revolution.

The bigger point in assessing the probability of war between China and Japan—either economic or military—is that there is certainly no love lost between the two nations. The Japanese occupation of China—including the infamous "Rape of Nanking"—was certainly one of the most brutal episodes of imperialism in recorded history and it is unlikely to ever be forgotten by the Chinese.

More broadly, the clash over oil and gas in the East China Sea has not simply been a childish war of words. In reaction to the Japanese attempts to test drill, China quickly dispatched two warships into the area to harass the Japanese team. These were not just any warships. They were two high-tech Sovremenny-class missile destroyers— some of the best in the class. Purchased from Russia as part of China's bid to build its deep-water navy, both warships are heavily armed with cruise missiles.

Episodes such as this are having a troubling effect on both Japanese public opinion and government policy. As concerns mount that China will eclipse Japan as an economic power and attempt to muscle Japan out of the way in its quest for both markets and energy resources, there is a growing view that Japan will have no other choice but to do what it has resisted for more than 50 years since the end of World War II. That would be both to remilitarize and to "go nuclear" officially.

Japan is technically under the U.S. nuclear umbrella, and therefore arguably has no need for its own nuclear arsenal. Japan can, however, "go nuclear" quickly in its own right because it has one of the more extensive nuclear energy programs in the world, relying on nuclear power for more than 30% of its electricity needs.[40] Because of Japan's nuclear power program, it also has a veritable mountain of reprocessed plutonium that could be devoted to building hundreds of nuclear warheads.

To date, the deep scars on the Japanese psyche from the bombs falling on Hiroshima and Nagasaki have played a key role in keeping Japan out of the nuclear weapons "family" of nations. The growing Chinese threat on so many fronts could finally tip what has become a delicate balance leading to development of nuclear weapons and the remilitarization of Japan.

5

THE "NEW IMPERIALIST" WARS AND WEAPONS OF MASS CONSTRUCTION

People say China is a sleeping giant, but it's wide awake. It's the elephant creeping up behind us. Only, it's so big we can scarcely see it moving.

—Zainab Bangura, Sierra Leone Political Activist

In 1916, Vladimir Lenin, a forefather of Chinese Communism, described imperialism as the "highest form of capitalism."[1] In its modern form, the imperialist nation uses its superior financial resources and managerial expertise to gain economic control over the minerals, raw materials, agricultural products, and other natural resources of the colonized country. Such economic control is often achieved by lavishly bribing the corrupt rulers and bureaucrats of the developing nation who facilitate the influx of capital, skilled labor, and managerial talent from the imperialist country. This first wave of capital and labor—the imperialist's "weapons of mass construction"— build the transportation and communications networks and the extraction infrastructures needed for the subsequent natural resource "rape."

When the imperialist nation gains control of the resources, it ships them back to the home country to feed its industrial machine. While the exploited country is stripped of its wealth and sees its environment degraded, the imperialist country produces high valued-added, finished goods that it exports to world markets. It thereby earns, in Lenin's terms, "super profits" on the backs of the poor.

In the Marxist-Leninist view, this is arguably what the imperialistic British Empire did in its colonial heyday in its relations with East African colonies such as Kenya and Uganda. France also did it in West African colonies such as the Ivory Coast, Guinea, Mali, and Senegal. Before African independence, even lesser nations such as Belgium and Portugal got into the imperialist act in places such as the Congo, Angola, and Mozambique. Viewed from this Marxist-Leninist perspective, the real winners from World War II were not France and Great Britain and the allied forces but rather all the former colonies that would achieve independence.

Today, however, in a supreme historical irony, there is a new imperialist on the block preying on many of those former colonies. It is none other than one of the loudest critics and worst former victims of British and Japanese imperialism—the putatively Marxist-Leninist People's Republic of China. Throughout Africa, Latin America, and Asia, China is using the Trojan horse of a "South-South" message that allies China in a workers' coalition with other developing countries against "northern hemisphere" imperialists such as the United States, France, Russia, and Great Britain. Under the cover of this South-South diplomacy, China is deploying a potent mix of state-subsidized capital, managerial expertise, skilled labor, and rapidly gaining economic control of a lion's share of the world's metals, minerals, raw materials, and agricultural resources.

The unwitting developing countries now ensnared in China's South-South imperialistic web are starting to have an increasingly rude and painful awakening. At the root of China's new imperialism is an economic appetite for resources and raw materials that is voracious.

The China Wars for Minerals and Raw Materials

Chinese geologists estimate that the demand for minerals over the next 30 years may exceed product by as much as a factor of five. The projections are staggering: 5.3–6.8 million tons of copper by 2023, and 13 million tons of aluminum by 2028.

—*Asia Pacific Bulletin*[2]

In choosing to be the "factory floor" of the world, China has hitched its star to a heavy manufacturing model that, in less than three short decades, has transformed the country from a quiet agricultural backwater into one of the world's largest consumers of metals, minerals, lumber, and other raw materials. China's strategy is different from that other emerging behemoth, India, which is focusing much less on heavy manufacturing and much more on software, other information technology niches, and global service industries.

Pursuing its heavy manufacturing model, China has already overtaken the United States and Japan as the world's largest steel consumer. It is the largest buyer of copper, the second-largest buyer of iron ore, and the third-largest buyer of alumina, which is used in smelters to produce aluminum.

China is also one of the top consumers of Thai rubber, Burmese teak, Chilean and Philippine copper, cobalt from the Congo, and Indonesian pulp and paper. Other minerals high on China's list but low in the consciousness of the general public range from "industrial minerals" such as limestone, dolomite, phosphate rock, and sulfur to "process minerals" such as titanium slag, and phosphoric acid.

China's strategy for securing supplies of all these various production inputs is similar to that for oil, as discussed in Chapter 4, "The 'Blood for Oil' Wars—The Sum of All Chinese Fears." It seeks to gain as tight *physical* control of these resources as possible. The way China gains ownership control is by first ingratiating itself to foreign governments and then encircling the country's economy with virtually every strategy described by Lenin in the "imperialist playbook."

In the first stage of China's relationship with a developing country, China dangles lavish, low-interest loans as bait and uses its huge army of engineers and laborers to help the country build up its infrastructure—from roads and dams to hotels and stadiums, from parliament buildings and palaces to satellite capabilities and telecommunications networks. In this regard, over the past few decades, more than a thousand Chinese firms, private and state-owned, have been deployed to the overseas construction market along with an estimated three million construction workers.[3] Backed by heavily subsidized, low-interest loans from the government—the financial capital described by Lenin—both state-owned and private Chinese construction firms are able to penetrate these overseas markets. The Chinese government then "uses the funding to gain political and economic leverage in developing countries, as well as to encourage the purchase of Chinese equipment and labor."[4]

In some cases, China also sells weaponry to the country as a means of ensuring continued political control by the ruling elites it courts. As discussed in the previous chapter, in the worst cases, China offers political favors ranging from the use of its veto at the United Nations to threatening retaliation if the United States, Europe, or Japan engages in any type of economic embargoes aimed at curbing human-rights abuses or violations of democratic freedoms.

The Chinese diplomatic approach has great appeal to many Africans, who for decades felt the colonial/imperialist yoke of European nations. As Zhou Wenzhong, the assistant deputy foreign minister in China, has succinctly described this seductive message in the case of

Sudan, where rampant human-rights violations and genocide are part of a cruel and ruthless feature of Sudanese daily life: "I think the internal situation in the Sudan is an internal affair, and we are not in a position to impose upon them. You have tried to impose a market economy in multiparty democracy on these countries, which are not ready for it. We are also against embargoes, which you have tried to use against us."[5]

These various economic and diplomatic gambits by China not only build "goodwill" between the two countries; they also provide ample opportunity for China to enrich the developing country's ruling elites through favors and bribes and thereby directly win their favor. In many cases, China is also able to encumber the loans directly with a promise of repayment through claims on the actual raw materials.

Of course, investments in highway systems and communications quite literally and digitally pave the way for precisely the kind of "high-low" trade that China is seeking. When completed, the next stage of the relationship kicks in. This is when China directs its financial capital and human resources to the development of the extraction and harvesting activities and transport of the natural resources back home for the production of higher value-added goods. One of the useful by-products of this relationship is to provide considerable employment opportunities for Chinese workers. In this way, China's weapons of mass construction and global economic strategy also act as a political safety valve.

In effect, then, China is using foreign aid and the promise of capital investment to leverage one-sided "joint ventures" for massive resource extraction operations. In the process, it systematically strips nations of their raw materials and natural resources while recovering the costs of these resources and materials by dumping cheap finished goods into these same countries—often driving out local indigenous labor and driving up the local unemployment rate. This scenario is playing out with chilling effectiveness, particularly in Africa and Latin America.

Heart of Darkness—China's Parasitic African Safari

We should unite and drive U.S. imperialism from Asia, Africa and Latin America back to where it came from.

—Mao Tse-tung, 1959[6]

While western governments may fret about China's growing influence in the region [Africa], some Chinese analysts see a measure of irony in the country's new role. Back in the 1960s and 1970s, China was more interested in world-wide revolution, third-world solidarity and the backing of African liberation movements. Now, according to one scholar at the Chinese Academy of Social Sciences, China's behavior has more in common with that of the colonizers. "Since we are mainly there to make money and get hold of their resources," he says, "it's hard to see the difference."

—*The Economist*, 2006[7]

China and Africa formally started their economic relationship in 1414 in the most spectacular of fashions. With great fanfare, the emperor of the Ming Dynasty dispatched a fleet of more than 60 galleons with a crew of more than 30,000 to the "Dark Continent" on a mission of trade and exploration. This initial round of China-African trade also started in the most fair, equal, and promising of ways—with a pair of magical giraffes gifted to Chinese explorers by African leaders and the opening of trade routes that saw African tortoiseshell, elephant ivory, and rhinoceros-horn medicine exchanged for Chinese gold, silk, and spices.

The relationship was short-lived. When the emperor died, China quickly withdrew into an isolationist foreign policy.[8] Five *centuries* passed before the Chinese government would again take an active interest in Africa.

The new China-Africa relationship began during the 1960s shortly after Mao formally broke with the Soviet Union. In seeking to provide a strategic counterweight to both the United States and the Soviet Union, Mao threw the full weight of China's resources behind the various revolutionary and independence movements in Africa.

In many countries, the Chinese helped arm and train rebels. They sent doctors and nurses. They also helped educate thousands of African students in both Chinese universities and local schools using imported Chinese teachers.

Perhaps most important in currying African favor and cultivating goodwill was China's first deployment in Africa of its "weapons of mass construction." Thousands of Chinese contractors and engineers helped build strategic infrastructure such as the "TanZam" railway linking Tanzania to Zambia as a way of isolating then-apartheid South Africa.[9] Chinese contractors also built stadiums for soccer and political rallies and other "prestige projects."[10]

The goal during the Cold War era was to build solidarity with the new, anticolonial regimes and spread Communism, and these ideologically motivated efforts bore a sweet economic fruit for China beginning in the 1990s. That's when, after a significant withdrawal from Africa in the 1980s to tend to its own struggling economy, China returned in force.[11] This time, however, China's business in Africa was to be just that, purely business. Its strategic goal was nothing less than gaining full economic control of the metals, minerals, raw materials, and agricultural riches of a continent that is as wealthy in these resources as it is lacking in political and social structures to defend itself from the imperialistic Chinese assault.

Many of the same rebels who China had supported were now waiting with trusting, and unsuspecting, open arms for this new wave of Chinese emissaries and entrepreneurs. A select but important few had wound up in high positions in governments across the continent. Many of the now-middle-aged rebels had also exchanged their military uniforms and camouflage for three-piece business suits. Former rebels were standing side by side with thousands of former students who had joined the elite economic classes using the currency of their Chinese-subsidized education.

Today, as U.S. former Assistant Secretary of State for African Affairs, Walter Kansteiner, put it, "China has simply exploded into Africa,"[12] and it has with a significant presence in all 54 African nations.

China's Parasitic African Adventure

Chinese contractors have stitched together a road network that reaches Ethiopia's northern border with Sudan to the eastern seaport of Djibouti to the southern border area with Kenya. [The company] China Road secured most of its contracts through public tenders. Yet Mr. Deng says he is instructed to slice projected profit margins so thin—about 3%—that losses are inevitable, given perennial cost overruns in Africa.

Western businesses, by contrast, typically pad bids with projected profits of 15% and more. Even so, Mr. Deng has his eye on a range of new projects, including water reservoirs, airport facilities and a railway project. "We're a government company and the Chinese government wants us here building things," he says.

—The Wall Street Journal[13]

Just as it was in the 1960s and 1970s, one of China's most powerful weapons of influence in Africa continues to be its heavily government-subsidized weapons of mass construction. The difference now is the close and obvious ties of this aid to resource exploitation.

In the copper-rich Congo and oil- and timber-rich Equatorial Guinea, China is laying down the roads needed to move the resources to port cities for shipment to China. In Algeria, which has the fifth-largest natural gas reserves in the world, China is building everything from airport terminals and five-star hotels to nuclear reactors.

Rwanda, which is rich in gold, tin, and tungsten, has been on the receiving end of everything from roads and railways to convention centers and government buildings. In diamond- and gold-rich Sierra Leone, China has built a new parliament building, stadium, and government office buildings, along with tractor and sugar plants and the country's biggest hotel, while helping strategically located Ethiopia build Africa's largest dam.[14]

China's Zambia gambit is particularly instructive. This country supplies 20% of the world's cobalt and is the world's seventh-largest copper producer. China is not only erecting dams and hydropower stations, but also has poured more than 100 million investment dollars into Zambian copper mines. Illustrating China's penchant for owning resources, a Chinese company is now the proud owner of the Chambezi copper mine, one of the biggest Chinese mining operations on the continent.

Meanwhile, even in the tiny African Kingdom of Lesotho, "Chinese businessmen own and operate nearly half of all the supermarkets and a handful of textile companies."[15] Chinese businesses also run major timber operations across the continent. Africa's largest timber producer, Gabon, is China's major African supplier, and China has emerged as the largest consumer of African timber.[16]

What's wrong with all of this? Isn't China simply helping Africa bootstrap itself into the twenty-first century?

It is important to reiterate that one major kind of construction that China does in Africa is not aimed at developing the broader African economy. Instead, China's aim is to build extraction and transportation infrastructures that facilitate the export of African raw materials and resources to China—rather than into African factories to manufacture their own finished goods. This is a model of development for Africa that is unsustainable, and one that will lead not to prosperity but

simply to environmental degradation and impoverishment—just as
Lenin warned.

A second major kind of construction focuses on erecting lavish
government buildings for the ruling elites who are already looting the
public treasuries. In the process, these African nations go deeper into
Chinese debt—all the more so if China is also selling large amounts
of weaponry to protect African despots.

China's military and economic support for Africa's ruling elites is
closely related to a third problem previously discussed in Chapter 4.
This is that China is also using its amoral foreign policy and diplomatic powers at the United Nations to protect African dictators and
strongmen from all manner of international pressures and sanctions—thereby facilitating its penetration of Africa.

The first excerpt below from the *Wall Street Journal* offers a
broad overview of the strategy. The second excerpt from the *New
Republic* offers chilling specifics.

> *Unlike the U.S., which bars U.S. companies from doing busi-
> ness with some outlaw regimes, Beijing expresses no qualms
> about dealing with the continent's most brutal and corrupt
> leaders. Instead, Chinese leaders prefer to view their relation-
> ship through a North-South prism, emphasizing the need for
> developing nations to band together against the industrialized
> West. "China is ready to coordinate its positions with African
> countries . . . with a view to safeguarding the legitimate rights
> and interests of developing countries," said Chinese Premier
> Wen Jiabao during a 2003 speech in Ethiopia.[17]*

> *Unencumbered by principles, Chinese companies are free to
> go where many Western firms cannot. Beijing moved closer to
> Nigeria in the mid-'90s, when, after the execution of writer-
> activist Ken Saro-Wiwa, the U.S. Congress considered block-
> ing new investments by U.S. oil companies. Chinese companies
> positioned themselves in Libya well before the U.N. sanctions
> against Tripoli were lifted last year. Consider also Beijing's
> tactics in the CAR [Central African Republic]. When the*

*European Union and international lenders refused last year
to bail out the new authoritarian government until it restored
constitutional order, Beijing stepped in, bankrolling the entire
civil service. The move was savvy: Being in the CAR government's good graces won't hurt when, as energy experts predict, access to Chad's oil fields opens up on the CAR side of
the Chad border.*[18]

The diplomatic danger from China on the human-rights front
should be obvious: As Africa watcher Lindsay Hilsum noted: "It is
easy to moralize at regimes which you have no reason to cultivate. But
such regimes will not cow to this new moralizing if China is offering
practical support without conditions."[19]

On the ground in Africa, China's amoral foreign policy is in sharp
contrast to that of the United States. As noted by Mustafa Bello, head of
the Nigerian Investment Promotion Commission, "The U.S. will talk to
you about governance, about efficiency, about security, about the environment. The Chinese just ask: 'How do we procure this license?'"[20]

At this point, it is critical to name China's other African agenda—
one far more strategic than economic. Both Africa and Latin America
are playing an ever-increasingly important role in Beijing's strategy of
the "diplomatic encirclement" of Taiwan.

For example, in 2005, after Beijing announced cancellation of
almost $20 million worth of debt and offered close to $4 million for
the construction of critically needed roads, hospitals, and other infrastructure, Senegal broke off relations with Taiwan. A few years
earlier, Liberia had abandoned Taiwan after Beijing ponied up
$25 million in reconstruction funds and a $5 million interest-free
loan.[21] Beijing is sometimes not subtle with its bribes.

How Tight the Panda's Hug

*Over the past year, South African clothing manufacturers
have lost one-third of their market share, shedding some
17,000 jobs in the process. Thousand more jobs are on the line*

*as Chinese imports of clothing, textiles and footwear flood
into the South African market. In just two years, the value of
Chinese imports has more than doubled.... According to
Ebrahim Patel, general secretary of the South African Clothing and Textile Workers' Union, the undervalued renminbi
gives China a currency advantage of at least 40%. Even if
clothing industry workers were paid nothing the industry
would still not be competitive.*

—*Business Africa*[22]

The dangers that many African nations now face from getting into
China's imperial bed is aptly illustrated by the parasitic relationship
that has developed between China and arguably the richest of the
African nations, South Africa. South Africa's mineral wealth is
absolutely staggering. Besides being home to more than half of the
world's gold reserves, it also possesses more than three fourths of the
world's manganese and almost three fourths of the world's chromium.
Both are essential in the alloying process for steel and other metals.
South Africa is also home to more than half the world's platinum
group metals, which are critical in auto production, and almost half of
its vanadium—essential in the production of aerospace titanium
alloys.

One would think that, with such an embarrassment of mineral
riches, South Africa would run substantial trade surpluses with virtually all of its trading partners. Not so with China.

In fact, South Africa's exports to China have more than doubled in
five years, but the trade has been largely in raw materials rather than
manufactured goods. Never missing a strategic beat, however, China is
at least providing South Africa some jobs by using factories there (and
elsewhere) as staging areas for garments that are then shipped duty
free to the United States.[23] More broadly, the punishing effects of the
China Price are now reaching deep into the poorest pockets of poverty
as garment workers from Mozambique and Swaziland to Uganda are
being pushed onto the unemployment line.

Moeletsi Mbeki, the deputy chairman of the South African Institute of International Affairs, has commented on the current neocolonial relationship: "We sell them raw materials, and they sell us manufactured goods with a predictable result—an unfavorable trade balance against South Africa." Indeed, South Africa's trade deficit with China has soared from a mere $24 million in 1992 to more than half a billion dollars today.

It is not just minerals, metals, and raw materials that China is gaining control of in Africa. In the boldest case yet of Chinese agro-imperialism, there is Zimbabwe. In the past, Zimbabwe sold its tobacco at international auction for top dollar. However, "now the auction houses in Harare are silent—tobacco goes directly to China's 300 million smokers, as payment in kind for loans and investment from Chinese banks to Zimbabwe's bankrupt state-run companies. As Zimbabwe's agricultural sector collapses, the Chinese are taking over land the Zimbabwean government confiscated from white farmers, and cultivating the crops they need."[24]

The Chinese relationship with Zimbabwe provides glaring testimony to the inability of African nations to protect their resources, particularly when the top leadership is corrupt. As the Greek proverb says, "A fish rots from the head down."

Zimbabwe's "Look East" Strategy

Zimbabwe doesn't have oil, but it is the world's second-largest exporter of platinum, a key import for China's auto industry. Chinese radio-jamming devices block Zimbabwe's dissident broadcasts, and Chinese workers built [President Robert] Mugabe's new $9 million home, featuring a blue-tiled roof donated by the Chinese government. While Western politicians railed against Mugabe last year for flattening entire shantytowns, China was supplying him with fighter jets and troop carriers worth about $240 million in exchange for imports of gold and tobacco.

—Fortune[25]

We are looking to the east where the sun rises, and have turned our backs on the west where the sun sets.

—President Robert Mugabe, Zimbabwe

Zimbabwe is a country ruled with an iron fist by President Robert Mugabe and, like Angola, which was discussed in Chapter 4, it is a country whose vast mineral riches are being systematically looted by its ruling elites. The looting would not be possible without the active economic and military assistance of the Chinese.

The problems in Zimbabwe are just the tip of a much larger iceberg that is rapidly sinking the African continent into a deeper abyss of chronic poverty among the masses and unimaginable corruption among the elites. No one has described this problem better than South Africa's Mbeki:

> *The political elite uses its control of the state to extract savings from the rural poor who, if they could, would have invested those savings either in improving their skills or in other productive economic activities. The elite diverts these savings towards its own consumption, and to strengthen the state's repressive instruments. Much of what Africa's elite consumes is imported. So state consumption does not create a significant market for African producers. Instead, it is a major drain on national savings that might have gone into productive investment. This explains Africa's growing impoverishment. The more the political elite consolidates its power, the stronger its hold over the state, and therefore the more rural societies sink into poverty and the more African economies regress.*[26]

Ultimately, it is because of these dynamics that China's African strategy is a threat that will colonize and economically enslave the vast majority of the continent's population that lives outside the elite circles. It is an imperialist marriage manufactured in China and made in hell.

China's Latin American Tangos

China is a world power. She doesn't come here with imperialist airs; she comes here like a sister. God bless China.[27]

—President Hugo Chávez, Venezuela[28]

In the 1960s, the Soviet Union defied America's Monroe Doctrine by supporting Fidel Castro's military buildup in Cuba. Later, it supported insurgencies in Central America. This triggered a competition among existing right-wing dictatorships, Marxist authoritarianism, and the U.S. democratic model. In the end, democracy and open markets won. Promoted by the United States, these principles have generally made Latin American states more viable politically, economically, and commercially.

Today, another communist state—the People's Republic of China (PRC)—is seeking trade, diplomatic, and military ties in Latin America and the Caribbean. The region is rich in natural resources and developing markets for manufactured goods and even arms.

—Stephen Johnson, The Heritage Foundation[29]

Just as China is on the prowl for metals, minerals, raw materials, and agricultural resources in Africa, so, too, does it seek to lock down a wide variety of nature's wealth in Latin America. This is hardly an idle adventure.

The world's largest copper reserves are in Chile. Bolivia has the second-largest natural gas reserves in South America and is rich in cassiterite, the chief source of tin. Both Argentina and Brazil play host to large iron ore reserves. Even Cuba, most known for its sugar, is an important player in the mining market, with the world's fourth-largest nickel reserves and the sixth-largest cobalt reserves. On the wings of Chinese demand and financial capital, Paraguay, Brazil, and Argentina have become the world's major areas for new soybean cultivation.

China's Latin America offensive began in 2001 with a loud blast from Mao's old Marxist trumpet. A 12-day trip by Chinese President Jiang Zemin played primarily to left-wing favorites such as Cuba and Venezuela but also to populists in Argentina and Brazil. This was a trip that seemed overtly political, with Zemin attacking Washington's "unipolar" scheme.[30] However, it was merely a prelude to the real economic offensive begun in earnest in November 2004. That's when Zemin's successor, Chinese President Hu Jintao, began his own whirlwind Latin American tour with a pledge to invest $100 billion in the region over the next decade. The imperialistic roots of this new voyage were hard to miss:

> *The day before Hu landed in Argentina, Shanghai's A Grade Trading scooped up the rights to rebuild and reactivate the defunct Hiparsa iron ore mine and processing complex there—a U.S.$25-million deal. In neighboring Brazil, China's steel giant Baosteel continued negotiations with Companhia Vale do Rio Doce for the construction of an iron-ore production plant potentially worth U.S.$2 billion. In Cuba, Hu pledged a U.S.$500-million investment in the nickel industry [while] China will build a new mine in the island's northeastern Moa Bay area.[31]*

The recent dealings with Fidel Castro have been particularly troublesome for the United States, which continues to try to isolate Cuba economically. China, however, has never had any such qualms about allying with dictators, particularly those who ascribe to Marxist principles. Now, China has an ever-growing appetite not just for ideological bedfellows but also for Cuba's mineral reserves, which have been languishing through decades of America trade sanctions.[32]

More broadly, China is employing many of the same tricks it has used successfully in Africa to bore its way into Latin American hearts. In any given country, the China connection invariably starts with small commercial agreements and loans. It then moves to joint venturing and perhaps even military ties. Free-trade agreements are always a prize.

China is also quick to exploit any vacuums that might arise when Western interests get cold feet for either political or economic reasons. For example, when Argentina's financial collapse rippled through South America's southern cone, China quickly seized the chance to increase its stake in Argentina and Brazil, while U.S. investment declined by nearly half.[33]

Just as it does so lavishly in Africa, China spreads its goodwill by building infrastructure and through promises of large investments and debt forgiveness. Of course, many of the agreements that China is entering into with Latin American nations "are loans for the expansion of the infrastructure such as ports and railroads" and such investments are squarely "focused on getting resources out of the region."[34]

A case in point is that of Brazil. "China is partnering with Brazil to improve that country's railways and establish a rail link to the Pacific to cut transportation costs of iron ore and soybeans." Similarly, Chile's congested port at Antofagasta may get a facelift thanks to the PRC,[35] and China already loads almost $3 billion of copper a year into its ships at ports along the Chilean coast[36]—more than half of Chile's copper exports.[37]

In exchange for its copper connection, in 2005, China coaxed Chile into signing what threatens to be the bane for so many African and Latin American nations, a free-trade agreement and China's first-ever free-trade agreement with a Latin American country. As the *Economist* notes about this self-serving strategy:

> *The problem with supplying China with resources is that countries in the Americas are missing out on the manufacturing or processing work that could keep more wealth in the local economies. This has already tarnished relationships with Mexico and many Central American countries, which have lost employment in textiles and electronics to lower-cost China.*

*Moreover, the financing projects, which involve tied loans,
mean that Latin America will pay for much of the infrastructure expansion that will allow China to purchase and export
these natural resources—and the project themselves could go
to Chinese companies.*[38]

Perhaps no country in Latin America has suffered more than
Mexico from China's emergence as the world's factory floor. As Tom
Buerkle from Institutional Investor notes:

*China's export industries compete head-on with manufactur-
ers in Mexico's maquiladora sector and have been grabbing
market share aggressively. China surpassed Mexico as the
biggest exporter of textiles to the U.S. in 2002, and the expira-
tion in December of the Multifiber Agreement, an international accord that regulated the international textile trade, will
heighten the competition by removing protective quotas.*[39]

*China also has moved steadily upmarket in recent years to
become the leading supplier of computer components, consumer electronics and motor parts to the U.S. market. "In the
past three years, Mexico lost market share in the United
States in product lines that had the greatest sales," says
José de la Cruz, an economics professor at the Instituto Tec-
nológico de Estudios Superiores de Monterrey. "We are losing
the opportunity to do business in products that generate more
wealth."*[40]

The contrast is startling: "Chinese goods are made by laborers
who work for one-third of the wages of their Latin American counter-
parts and who tolerate worse working conditions."[41] Not surprisingly,
"for every dollar that Mexico makes from exports to China, the PRC
makes $31 from exports to Mexico."[42]

Unlike many African and Latin American nations, Mexico is fighting back. It has imposed "compensatory quotas on more than 1,000
Chinese products."[43] Brazil is already growing increasingly uncomfort-
able with the Panda's bear hug. As Roberto Giannetti da Fonseca of

Brazil's Federation and the Center for the industries of the State of Sao Paulo, has remarked: "China is 'not a strategic partner.' It merely wants to buy raw materials with no value added and to export consumer goods."[44] Statistics back up this claim as "nearly 60% of Brazil's exports to China are primary goods, largely soya and iron ore. Imports from China are more high-tech and varied, with electronics, machines and chemicals in the lead. Now China is making inroads into such labor-intensive sectors as textiles, shoes and toys, too."[45]

There is a clear and present danger for Latin America from China's imperialism. As analyst Stephen Johnson has noted:

> [T]he commodities-based trade model used by China will undermine the progress that Latin America has made toward industrialization. [Countries] with powerful presidents or ruling oligarchies may be tempted to fall back on plantation economics. Income gaps between the rich and poor may widen as a result. Moreover, such narrowly focused economies are vulnerable to downturns in commodity prices. Some 44 percent of Latin Americans already live below the poverty line. If these countries fail to adopt reforms, social inequality and political instability could depress U.S. exports to the region and increase migration problems.[46]

Imperialism with a Taiwanese Twist—and Spies R Us

In Latin America, as in Africa, China is pursuing its imperialistic agenda with a Taiwanese twist. Almost half of the remaining 25 countries that now diplomatically recognize Taiwan are in Latin America, and China is aiming to pick off each of them with promises of lavish aid.

One of the first defectors since the onslaught of China's Latin America offensive was the tiny island of Grenada. It offers a stark lesson in not only Beijing's "dollar diplomacy" but also the personal and sometimes quite penny ante politics of corruption.

The triggering event for Grenada cutting Taiwan loose was the donation by China of $50,000 to a hurricane relief fund. This money promptly found its way not into Red Cross coffers where it was supposed to go but rather into the "pockets of Grenadian Prime Minister Keith Mitchell's government."[47] Of course, it did not hurt the cause of severing Taiwanese ties that Beijing had already pledged $100 million in aid over a 10-year period.[48] "The tiny Caribbean island of Dominica made a similar switch in March 2004 after China promised it $100 million in aid over five years, more than $1,400 for each of the island's 70,000 people."[49]

There is a final and important observation on China's imperial strategy that must be noted. Although this book is primarily focused on the coming *economic* wars with China, China often intertwines its longer-range military objectives with its imperialistic economic goals. This chapter ends, therefore, with the rather stern warning from journalists Jane Bussey and Glenn Garvin to the United States, which has been distracted by the war on terrorism so much so that it is ignoring its own backyard:

> *"The strategic equation in our own hemisphere is changing like a cancer that you can't feel," says Al Santoli, senior foreign policy advisor for Rep. Dana Rohrabacher, a California Republican. Across the region, China is making its mark:*
>
> *At tracking stations in Brazil, Chinese technicians familiarize themselves with new digital reconnaissance equipment that might someday enable them to stalk and destroy U.S. intelligence satellites.*
>
> *In computerized listening posts in Cuba, Chinese experts in electronic espionage scoop up signals from U.S. military satellites and sift through the contents of millions of American telephone conversations for intelligence.*
>
> *At airfields in Venezuela, Chinese military officers instruct pilots in the fine points of new transport planes that the government of President Hugo Chávez has purchased from Beijing. From this toehold, China hopes to expand military*

sales—eventually including jet fighters—throughout South America.

. . .

Because China's initiative in the Western Hemisphere has involved tiny nibbles rather than a single bold thrust, it has attracted little public attention. But that doesn't make it any less real. . . .[50]

6

THE 21ST CENTURY OPIUM WARS—THE WORLD'S EMPEROR OF "PRECURSOR CHEMICALS"

China's large landmass, close proximity to the Golden Triangle [countries of Burma, Laos, and Thailand], and numerous coastal cities with large and modern port facilities make it an attractive transit center to drug traffickers. China's status in drug trafficking has changed significantly since the 1980s, when the country for the first time opened its borders to trade and tourism after 40 years of relative isolation. As trade with Southeast Asian countries and the West has increased, so has the flow of illicit drugs and precursor chemicals from, into, and through China.

—U.S. Drug Enforcement Administration[1]

Jimmy [a European drug dealer] might not know it but these days he is effectively a salesman for the Triads, the Chinese gangs which have all but cornered the market in the production of the raw materials needed to make Ecstasy and cleverly exploited China's burgeoning trade relationships with other countries to distribute the chemicals around the world.

—*The London Observer*[2]

Cocaine, heroin, methamphetamine, and Ecstasy. These are the four major "hard drugs" of the illicit global drug trade. Each has its own special way of frying brain cells and destroying lives. Together, the annual sales of these hard drugs generate hundreds of billions of dollars. The costs to the victims of drug-related crime and the toll in human misery for the world's 200 million-plus drug users is inestimable.

Although China has conquered many an export market—from bicycles and microwave ovens to toys, cameras, and DVDs—the same cannot be said for hard drugs. At least in this particular "China War," the Middle Kingdom has lots of bad company.

Consider Afghanistan. It is located in the poppy-rich "Golden Crescent"[3] at the crossroads of Central, South, and West Asia. Post 9/11, this newly "democratic" country has emerged as the biggest gangster on the junkie block. It produces more than 4,000 tons of opium a year and provides about 75% of the opium needed for the world's heroin supply. Every ten tons of opium yields a ton of pure heroin with a "street value" of more than a billion dollars a ton.[4]

Then there is North Korea. Its rogue activity is hardly limited to the counterfeiting of U.S. currency and trafficking in missiles to terrorists. Kim Jong-il's factories also churn out tens of millions of methamphetamine tablets renowned for their purity—particularly in the dope dens of Japan.

Such illicit activity is hardly limited to poorer developing countries. As competently as Merck and Pfizer, clandestine "designer drug" labs in Belgium and the Netherlands synthesize more than half the world's Ecstasy tablets—replete with branding logos. Meanwhile, as an example of a highly effective division of labor that would make Adam Smith turn over in his grave, Israeli and Russian mafias operate much of the global supply chain and distribution channels for all four of the world's major hard drugs.

Despite the overabundance of bad company China has in the global drug trade, there remains this hard and troubling fact: *No single country plays more of a key role than China in the global production, transportation, and distribution of all four illegal hard drugs and their "precursor chemicals."* Consider the following:

- China annually produces more than 100,000 metric tons of acetic anhydride, with much of this precursor chemical diverted to transform the poppies of the Golden Triangle and Golden Crescent into pure "China white" and the more pedestrian "Afghan heroin."

- China is the world's second-largest producer of potassium permanganate, the key precursor chemical used in the oxidation and separation process to turn the coca leaves of South America into cocaine.

- China and India are the world's largest producers of bulk and synthetic ephedrine. Smuggled over land, air, and sea, this key precursor is used in methamphetamine "superlabs" from Bangkok and Pyongyang to the Mexican heartland and Australia bush.

- China is the world's leading producer of sassafras oil and safrole, which are used to make "PMK," the key precursor chemical for Ecstasy.

- China has retained its historical role as a major transit area for the heroin from the Golden Triangle countries of Burma, Laos, and Thailand and expanded that role into the Golden Crescent and Central Asia.

- China is emerging as a highly efficient production center in its own right for "finished goods"—including most prominently, heroin, Ecstasy, and speed.

- Awash in illicit cash, China's banking system is becoming an important hub for global money laundering.

China's rapidly emerging role as the world's "factory floor" for precursor chemicals, and, increasingly, as a hard-drug producer in its own right has come despite apparently sincere and severe attempts by the central government to control the trade. China's failure, however, to curb its drug trade portends great conflict with other nations.

The Sad, Sordid Economics and Politics of the Heroin Trade

Britain's East India Company would wage three wars on the people of China in order to secure the right to sell opium there. . . . They were the world's first drug wars. Their sole purpose was to secure the importation of an addictive substance that provided a bountiful flow of profits.

—Kristianna Tho'Mas[5]

Mark 1874 in blood red ink on your history calendar as the date of one of the world's first major milestones in the global drug trade. This was the year English chemist C. R. Wright "unwittingly synthesized heroin (diacetylmorphine)" by boiling "morphine and a common chemical, acetic anhydride, over a stove for several hours."[6]

Today, one of the most important roles that China plays in the global heroin trade is to provide criminal syndicates with the vast quantities of the precursor chemicals needed to turn opium paste into heroin. These chemicals range from chloroform and ethyl ether to hydrochloric acid. However, no precursor chemical is more important to the heroin trade than the acetic anhydride first used by C. R. Wright.

How China came to be a major player in the global heroin trade is a sad and sordid story in which some of the most sophisticated principles of economics collide with the *"realpolitik"*[7] foreign-policy goals of some of the most powerful nations in history.

The China Drug Wars story necessarily begins with the world's first major drug cartel—the British government of the 1800s. It was the British government working with and through its trading arm, the British East India Company, that first began to move opium along a truly global supply chain. The mighty mercantilist Britannia did this as a means of both promoting economic growth and controlling inflation throughout its colonial empire.

The initial problem Britain faced in its trade with China was this: As British traders bought more and more of China's teas and silks and rice, Britain's trade deficit with China ballooned. This severe trade imbalance created strong downward pressures on the British pound and strong upward inflationary pressures throughout Britain's colonial empire.

Britain responded to this growing trade imbalance with all the ruthlessness and cynicism of any modern drug cartel. It began exporting opium from its colony of India into China. Given China's reputation as the Emperor of Opium, you may be surprised to know that it had little indigenous poppy cultivation of its own at the time.

Britain's mercantilist trade strategy worked with stunning speed and appalling consequences. As millions of Chinese became quickly addicted to "the pipe," the trade balance equally quickly shifted back in favor of Britain. The East India Company's profits soared as this explosive drug trade wreaked havoc on the Chinese economy and population.

When the Chinese government attempted to interdict this opium trade and restore order, it was British (and later French) warships that protected the drug dealers. They used their vastly superior firepower, cannonry, and training to blow Chinese junk warships out of the water. It was during these "opium wars" that China suffered its "foreign humiliation." As part of the Treaty of Nanking signed in 1842, China was forced to cede control of Hong Kong to Britain and forced to open five ports to foreign trade: Canton (Guangzhou), Shanghai, Ningbo, Fuzhou, and Xiamen.

That's hardly the end of the story. The most important legacy of these opium wars was China's response to what quickly became its own burgeoning trade deficits with Britain. China began growing its own opium, thereby not only institutionalizing drug addiction in China but also poppy cultivation as a lucrative livelihood.

When Mao Zedong rose to power in 1949, one of his first acts was to eliminate both opium production and opium addiction in China. Within just three years, both were almost entirely suppressed—at least one happy by-product of a brutal and repressive regime. Mao's crackdown, however, had an unintended consequence every bit as pernicious as Britain's eighteenth-century opium gambit, which was to drive the opium trade deep into the "Golden Triangle" of Burma, Laos, and Thailand.

The CIA's Shame—The Golden Triangle and Golden Crescent

Southeast Asia's Golden Triangle has long been a major [heroin] supplier for North American markets and in this trade there has been a significant Chinese role . . . mainly in the transportation portion of the drugs through Panama, that in many ways has become a Chinese protectorate in all but name. In aid of this trade, there is the international agreement that allows sealed containerized shipments from Southeast Asia to be exempt from inspection in intermediary stops. This allows for untouchable illicit shipments from the Golden Triangle to arrive in Columbia (via Panama) for distribution in the United States.

—Tom Marzullo[8]

In the beginning, the Golden Triangle heroin trade was overseen, in large part, by the remnants of the defeated Kuomintang army of Chiang Kai-Shek that had fled to Burma in 1949 with Mao's Red Army hot on its heels. With the help of the American *Central Intelligence Agency* (CIA), these Nationalist Chinese forces sought to use their drug dealing revenues to finance a counterrevolutionary campaign to "take back China" as part of a broader official U.S. foreign policy to "contain China."[9] Eventually, however, as Mao consolidated power, the Kuomintang used its growing drug trade merely to pay their living expenses and, eventually, this military organization morphed into an equally well-organized gang network. Today, in conjunction with an eclectic group of Burmese, Laotian, and Thai hill tribes and ethnic groups, these gangsters run the China drug trade.

Of course, the American CIA's role in expanding the China drug trade was hardly limited to helping the Kuomintang. During the 1960s, in the early stages of the Vietnam War and as part of its "containment policy," the CIA also used the drug trade and its infamous "Air America" operation to fund anti-Communist guerrilla warfare by Hmong tribes in Laos. This further boosted drug production in the Golden Triangle, and, paradoxically, helped accelerate drug use in the United States by increasing the supply, lowering the price, and improving heroin quality.

During the 1980s, the CIA similarly assisted a drug-financed Islamic mujahideen resistance against the Soviets in Afghanistan. After the mujahideen Taliban came to power in the wake of the Soviet retreat in 1989, poppy cultivation flourished. However, in July 2000, Mullah Omar of the Taliban ordered a ban on poppy cultivation, and production fell dramatically.

In the short run, the only effect was to stimulate worldwide poppy cultivation in the Golden Triangle and other countries such as North Korea. Even more unfortunate, after the U.S. military toppled the Taliban following the 9/11 terrorist attacks and established a "democratic regime" in Kabul, poppy farmers were again allowed to run free as a means of courting the support of the countryside against the Taliban and quelling rebellion.

Today, Afghanistan is again producing opium at record levels and is to the world heroin trade what the Saudis are to oil. As American military advisors and personnel chase the Taliban, hunt for Bin Laden in caves, and extol the virtues of the new democracy, Afghan opium, often processed with Chinese precursor chemicals and shipped through Chinese gang networks, winds up as heroin in the dark alleyways and big city streets of nations around the world. As Interpol has noted: "An increasingly large portion of Afghanistan's opium is processed into morphine base and heroin by drug laboratories in the country, significantly reducing its bulk and facilitating the movement of the drug to markets in Europe, Asia and the Middle East."[10]

One final episode in this sad and sordid hard drug history is worth noting: The political vacuum that ensued in Central Asia after the fall of the Soviet Union has created yet another drug monster on China's border. This monster consists of the Central Asian states of Kazakhstan, Uzbekistan, Turkmenistan, Tajikistan, and Kyrgyzstan.

The "independent" governments established in the early 1990s in the wake of the fall of the Soviet Union quickly succumbed to the powerful influence of the drug cartels. Today, "50% of the world population in Central Asia now grows drugs on their land,"[11] and these republics serve as major transit points for drugs both into and out of China.

A Methamphetamine Primer

All the superlab equipment has been taken out of the barn and laid out, to be dusted for fingerprints prior to being hauled off as toxic waste. Here are the empty cases of off-brand ephedrine tablets. And here are the boxes that held the Martha Stewart bedsheets—favored for straining meth because of their high thread count, but also . . . because the

Mexican national trafficking organizations simply like her cachet. "Who doesn't like her?" my colleague Serena muses, looking down at the boxes. "We all love Martha."

—Mitchell Koss, *LA Weekly*[12]

"Speed" has a long and interesting history, including high-profile addicts ranging from Adolph Hitler and JFK to Johnny Cash. Its history begins with the synthesis of amphetamine in Germany in 1887 followed by that of methamphetamine in Japan in 1919.

In the United States, the first "speed freaks" were victims of the common cold who bought Benzedrine inhalers and then kept using them as a stimulant long after the cold was gone. However, the biggest spur to speed came during World War II when the Nazis first used amphetamines during their blitzkriegs across Europe. In the Pacific theater, both Japanese and U.S. soldiers were similarly issued "bennies" in their field kits, and "some soldiers attributed the long, unrelenting battles on the Pacific Islands to the drugs issued the soldiers on both sides."[13]

During the 1960s, speed hit the mainstream as outlaw biker gangs learned to produce a low-grade and highly toxic form of speed called DL-methamphetamine. The key producers were gangs such as the Hell's Angels, and the major consumers were initially long-haul truck drivers and later budget-conscious addicts who could not afford the more up-scale cocaine.

The 1980s gave us Ronald Reagan and the fall of the Berlin Wall. It also gave rise to what is now the most potent, addictive, and frequently abused form of meth.[14] D-methamphetamine, short for dextrose-methamphetamine, is produced using ephedrine and pseudoephedrine reduction methods. It is this type of meth that is cranked out in the "superlabs" with much of the precursor chemicals for production—and at least some of the final product—coming from China.

Even the Devil Doesn't Like to Bargain Over Speed

I don't have a bedtime
I don't need to cum
For I have become
An amphetamine bum.

—The Fugs[15]

Whether it comes in powdered form, tablets, as a liquid injectable, or as shards of "ice" (known in China as *shabu*), speed truly does kill. This stimulant is an artificially synthesized version of adrenaline, one of the human body's most important hormones. It is a drug that "releases high levels of the neurotransmitter dopamine, which stimulates brain cells and enhances mood and body movement."[16]

The dangerous allure of speed is that "in the short term, it makes you, not high, strictly speaking, but more: more capable, more powerful, more attractive, more clever, more sexy, more smart, more efficient, more happy. It boosts you into the euphoria of superlatives. And initially, it can be tough to see what's wrong with that."[17]

What's wrong is plenty. Psychologically, by overstimulating the brain's pleasure nodes, the initial rush of speed inevitably leads to a longer-term depression. According to many psychologists:

> *The biggest problem for recovering meth addicts is then it can take anywhere from two to five years to heal the damage of pleasure receptors in the brain. During that time of recovery, life seems like terminal boredom. "So addicts keep taking meth, not because they're physically addicted, as heroin addicts are, but because, without meth, it's impossible to enjoy anything."*[18]

Physiologically, the neurotoxicity of meth results in damage to brain cells, and over time, meth reduces dopamine levels that "can result in symptoms like those of Parkinson's disease, a severe movement disorder." Meth can also "cause irreversible damage to blood vessels in the brain, producing strokes" and frequently leads to respiratory problems, an irregular heartbeat, or extreme anorexia.[19]

Speed not only kills directly but also indirectly. Unlike heroin, methamphetamine guns the sex drive but with a perverted twist—it is difficult for a man to achieve an orgasm. Moreover, speed dries up the mucus membranes, including the rectal mucosa. The result for many gay men has been both rectal injury and a rise in HIV infections "because of the long periods of sexual activity due to delayed orgasms."[20]

After long-term use, many meth addicts become paranoid, delusional, and often violent. In one of the more spectacular cases of such "amphetamine psychosis," a San Diego speed freak stole an army tank and then went on a 30-minute rampage, crushing cars and everything else in his path.

The truly evil part of meth addiction may well be that speed freaks do not even enjoy a "Devil's bargain" where they exchange a "good" for a "bad." Instead, after the first, ever-fleeting, ephemeral honeymoon rush, "the paradox of meth is that it seems to take away whatever you want from it. You take it for sex, you can't have an orgasm. You take it to work, you become more and more inefficient."[21]

Today, methamphetamines and related amphetamine stimulants "are abused by more people than cocaine and heroin combined."[22] Meth labs—from small "Beavus and Butthead" operations for personal consumption to the sophisticated cartel superlabs—wreak environmental havoc, too. "Each pound of manufactured methamphetamine produces about 5 to 6 pounds of hazardous waste" and "clandestine drug lab operators commonly dump this waste into the ground, sewers, or streams and rivers."[23]

The World's Methamphetamine "Tap Root"

China is a source country for significant amounts of the ephedrine and pseudoephedrine exported to Mexico and subsequently used to manufacture methamphetamine destined for the United States.

—U.S. Drug Enforcement Administration[24]

As with the heroin trade, Chinese criminal syndicates facilitate the production, transportation, and distribution of various forms of methamphetamine across Europe, Asia, and the Americas—from tablets and powdered form to the high-purity "ice" crystals known in China as *shabu*. Although scattered across the country, most of China's numerous methamphetamine laboratories are concentrated in the provinces of the eastern and southeastern coastal areas, and crime syndicates running mobile meth labs "are particularly active in Guangdong and Fujian."[25]

"Several ports in southern China serve as transit points for crystal methamphetamine transported by containerized cargo to international drug markets."[26] The irony here is that the birth and subsequent rapid growth of the China meth trade were largely a response to events in the early 1980s when "Chinese drug lords began synthesizing methamphetamine as a way to diversify their drug business away from its dependence on heroin, which was facing harsh government crackdowns."[27]

While China is playing an ever-more-important role in world meth production and distribution, its far more important role in the international "speed" trade is to serve as the world's leading supplier of bulk ephedrine. Ephedrine is the principal precursor chemical used to mass produce meth all over the world in so-called superlabs—highly sophisticated clandestine factories that can generate up to 100 pounds of speed "per cook"—and explode in a fiery ball with the slightest misstep.

China is not the only country to produce bulk ephedrine for meth production. India, Germany, and the Czech Republic are also major players, but "China is the only country that still mass produces ephedrine from [ephedra] grass . . . and gets a better-quality product that is 60% cheaper to make."[28]

With its combination of a strong expertise in basic chemical manufacturing and its lax environmental laws, China is also one of only three countries that can cost-effectively mass produce chemically synthesized ephedrine and has the capacity to produce roughly 100 tons annually.[29]

Favorable economics and market positioning have made China the de facto "factory floor" for meth precursors. Big customers such as the Mexican drug cartels are not the only customers that are serviced by the Chinese. China also clandestinely exports precursor ephedrine to Russia for the "domestic production of methamphetamine in kitchen labs in quantities for personal use."[30]

Potentially a significant generator of political conflict is this startling fact: Although ephedra grass grows wildly in northern China, it is produced by the tons on China's own state-run farms. Despite the presumed strict controls on its distribution, much of this government-produced ephedra winds up in the hands of criminal syndicates, often with the help of corrupt government officials.[31]

The Chinese Ecstasy Connection

Federal authorities have seized a record $25 million haul of the amphetamine-type stimulant, MDMA, also known as Ecstasy. . . . The seizure occurred on 28 March after Customs officers in Sydney targeted a shipping container for inspection and allegedly found concealed within a consignment of pineapple tins, approximately 500,000 tablets (125.25kgs) of MDMA as well as 15 kilograms of heroin. The drugs have a combined estimated potential street value of $34 million. . . .

*The container, which was shipped from China, held 5,908
sealed tins of pineapple packed into 985 cartons.*

—Australian Ministry for Justice and Customs[32]

The chemical name for Ecstasy is 3,4-methylenedioxymethampheta-
mine, or MDMA for short. It is a white, bitter-tasting crystalline solid
typically taken as a tablet or capsule and quickly absorbed into the
bloodstream. Within 20 to 60 minutes, users begin "coming up." During its four- to six-hour high, this "love drug" induces strong feelings
of "closeness and connectedness," it "triggers intense emotional
release," and it dramatically enhances the senses, particularly the
sense of touch.[33] At a biochemical level, what MDMA is actually
doing is flooding the brain with both serotonin and dopamine, two of
the brain's principal chemical messengers of pleasure, mood eleva-
tion, and satisfaction.

The German pharmaceutical company Merck first synthesized
and patented MDMA in the early 1900s, but it remained on Merck's
back shelves until the American CIA dusted it off in the 1950s. Along
with other drugs such as LSD and scopolamine, MDMA was tested
as a possible brainwashing and mind-control agent. That experiment
went nowhere. MDMA was tested only on animals, and the drug
remained off the public's radar screen.

That all changed in the late 1970s and early 1980s when the "love
doctor" Alexander Shulgin, a Ph.D. biochemist from Berkeley, almost
single-handedly popularized the drug. While working on the development of a number of highly profitable insecticide patents for Dow
Chemical, Shulgin also experimented with MDMA. As the first
human known to take MDMA, his own personal experience, as
recorded in his lab notes, was remarkable:

*I feel absolutely clean inside, and there is nothing but pure
euphoria. I have never felt so great or believed this to be*

possible. The cleanliness, clarity, and marvelous feeling of solid inner strength continued throughout the rest of the day and evening. I am overcome by the profundity of the experience. . . .[34]

The experience and his experiments soon turned him into a proselytizer for the drug's therapeutic virtues, and MDMA quickly caught on. By 1981, in a stroke of drug-culture marketing genius, MDMA was dubbed "Ecstasy" by a Los Angeles distributor who chose the name because he thought "it would sell better than calling it 'Empathy.'"[35] By the mid-1980s, Ecstasy was being profiled in newspapers such as the *San Francisco Chronicle* and magazines such as *Newsweek* and *Harpers Bazaar* referred to the drug as "the Yuppie psychedelic" and "the hottest thing in the continuing search for happiness through chemistry."[36]

Perhaps surprisingly, MDMA's American cradle was not in hip and liberal California but rather conservative, cowboy bar Texas. In the 1980s, when it was still legal, Ecstasy was "distributed openly in bars and nightclubs in Dallas and Fort Worth. It could be purchased via toll-free 800-numbers by credit card. The drug was even marketed through pyramid-style selling-schemes."[37]

At this point, an alarmed U.S. Drug Enforcement Agency successfully lobbied to turn MDMA into a "schedule one" illegal drug just like heroin, cocaine, and speed. As both U.S. producers and users were forced underground, the followers of the Indian guru Bhagwan Shree Rajneesh began introducing MDMA on the European continent—slipping it into people's drinks primarily as a way to woo potential contributors to the cult.[38]

By the early 1990s, MDMA drug production had set down deep European roots. Today, sophisticated labs in Belgium and the Netherlands produce as much as 80% to 90% of the world's MDMA. The bulk of the precursor chemicals needed for production comes from China.

The Agony of Ecstasy[39]

MDMA is a stimulant whose psychedelic effects can last between 4 and 6 hours and it is usually taken orally in pill form. The psychological effects of MDMA include confusion, depression, anxiety, sleeplessness, drug craving, and paranoia. Adverse physical effects include muscle tension, involuntary teeth clenching, nausea, blurred vision, feeling faint, tremors, rapid eye movement, and sweating or chills. Because of MDMA's ability to increase heart rate and blood pressure, an extra risk is involved with MDMA ingestion for people with circulatory problems or heart disease.[40]

—Office of National Drug Policy Control, The White House

MDMA advocates insist that the only reason that Ecstasy is considered a dangerous drug is because it has been driven underground by legal systems around the world that mistakenly equate this "highly spiritual drug" with heroin, cocaine, and speed. There is at least some merit to this argument. One of the major health risks associated with "Ecstasy" today occurs because it does not contain MDMA at all. Instead, unscrupulous dealers pawn off adulterants ranging from mescaline and meth to codeine, dextromethorphan, and the synthetic hallucinogen paramethoxyamphetamine.

Many users who seek to "rave" wildly at all-night dance parties rather than have the kind of religious experience originally proselytized by Dr. Shulgin, now combine MDMA with drugs such as speed, the dissociative psychedelic ketamine, and other psychedelics such as LSD and psilocybin.

Even if MDMA is taken in its pure form under ideal conditions, heavy users will suffer a variety of psychological and physiological effects. An unlucky few also die. Consider this poignant story from *Counselor* magazine:

The languid high came on smoothly as [18-year-old Alexa Stevens] breathed in the fresh air off the Charles River. Thinking she had received a weak dose of Ecstasy, Alexa popped two more pastel-colored pills with the word "sex" engraved on them. Within minutes her heart began to race, terrified and confused she rushed down the stairwell, hair drenched in sweat, and dropped to her knees and convulsed. Twenty-four-hours later, after being admitted to a large University hospital, her condition deteriorated rapidly and doctors had to intubate. Forty-eight-hours later, discovering her liver was about to fail, they found a donor and grafted part of the donated organ. The liver graft failed, she slipped into a seizure, and her brain hemorrhaged. At that point, her family requested she be taken off life support.[41]

It's Not Your Father's Root Beer Anymore

Today a handful of Chinese chemical companies are practically the only firms to produce PMK, ostensibly for use in the perfume industry. These firms benefit from the fact that China is the world's biggest producer of sassafras oil, way ahead of its nearest rivals, Brazil and Vietnam, whose supplies are thought to be diminishing. But apart from perfume, PMK has few legal uses: these days almost all of it is used to produce Ecstasy and other synthetic drugs.

—*The London Observer*[42]

Ecstasy is big business. According to the United Nations, clandestine labs now churn out more than 125 tons a year for close to 10 million users. Together with the meth market, organized crime rings up the cash registers to the tune of about $65 billion a year.[43]

As with the synthesis of heroin and the production of speed, the lowest common denominator for MDMA criminal activity is China because, although there are many different ways to manufacture MDMA, the primary method for its mass production typically involves several essential precursors supplied in large part by China. The first ingredient is the same sassafras that has been used to make root beer for more than a century. Oil from the sassafras tree is used to produce "safrole" and then, from safrole, piperonyl methyl ketone or "PMK" is made.

PMK is a versatile chemical, used in everything from perfumes and insecticides to soap. Today, however, the primary use for PMK is to produce Ecstasy. More than 100 tons of PMK alone are smuggled into European MDMA labs each year, which is enough to make more than 100 million tablets, and it comes principally from China.[44]

China has become the ideal source for PMK for two reasons. It is the world's leading producer by a large margin. China is also one of the world's leading chemical and insecticide manufacturers. This means that China has the raw materials, expertise, and capacity to produce large amounts of PMK. It also has the distribution channels to legally export PMK and illegally hide PMK in shipments of other chemicals. As noted by the *London Observer*:

> *US Drug Enforcement officials have become so alarmed at PMK shipments that they have practically banned the chemical from being imported into the country. Such was their concern that two years ago they signed a resolution with the European Union to crack down and monitor PMK shipments. Yet this has had little if any effect. [China's] Triad gangs have created a series of front companies to buy the chemical and ship it on to Ecstasy factories around the world, giving them profit rates of up to 3,000 per cent. Numerous internet sites market the chemicals to eager importers in places as diverse as Mexico, Indonesia and Europe.*[45]

More broadly, Chinese gang syndicates use a variety of methods to smuggle illegally both precursor chemicals and finished product to world markets. These methods include "mislabeling the [shipping] containers, forging documents, establishing front companies, using circuitous routing, hijacking shipments, [and] bribing officials."[46]

Although China's economy and its manufacturing facilities are first class, much of its banking system is still very much Third World, which[47] has made China easy prey for drug syndicates seeking to launder money through the rickety Chinese banking system. As a result of the drug trade, China is now emerging not just as the "factory floor" for the world's hard-drug production but also as a major money-laundering center.

7

THE DAMNABLE DAM
WARS AND DRUMS
ALONG THE MEKONG

Before the Chinese Communist Party came to power in 1949, China had only 23 large and medium-scale dams and reservoirs. Fifty-five years later, China has 22,000 of the world's 45,000 large dams (those more than 15 meters [about 50 feet] in height). Excluding small farm-scale irrigation dams and mini and micro hydropower units, China has about 85,000 dams and reservoirs. And China continues to proudly be the most active large-dam builder in the world, despite the growing scientific evidence that large dams are not economical and sustainable in the long run. [Essayist] Dai Qing calls this trend "a blind faith that engineers and technical fixes can solve all problems," a "conscious failure by China's leaders to . . . respect and follow ancient [Chinese Daoist] wisdom [of self-restraint]."[1]

—Tashi Tsering, Tibet Justice Center

Dam happy. That's the only way to describe China's water-management policy. At more than 85,000 dams and counting, Chinese leaders boast of having the tallest dams, the largest by reservoir capacity, the dam with the highest ship lift, and the most powerful electricity producer. From arch dams, earthen dams, and gravity dams to cascade and concrete-faced rockfill dams, China has it all.

China should not be boasting about dams. Instead, China's top leadership may well want to reconsider the perilous path it has chosen to take. For if ever there were a double-edged sword, a large dam strategy would be it. On the beneficial edge of that sword, large dams generate significant amounts of cheap electricity. They store water when there is a surplus for use in irrigation during times of scarcity. They protect arable land from flood and soil erosion. They can help promote aquaculture and fisheries development as well as tourism, recreation, and inland navigation. They can even change the local climate (for better *or* worse) by increasing humidity and precipitation.[2]

On the other far more costly and dangerous edge of the sword, large dams are quite capable over time of destroying the very waters they harness as well as the agricultural lands they are trying to improve. Because dams tend to slow down river flows, they decrease the ability of rivers to rejuvenate and cleanse themselves of pollutants naturally. They interfere with, and often destroy, natural habitats and fish reproduction. The reservoirs created by large dams displace significant population segments when they inundate villages and towns. Archaeological sites are literally drowned.

Perhaps the worst aspect of large dams is their relatively short useful shelf life. As silt builds up behind a dam and the reservoir becomes shallower and shallower, less electricity is generated, less water for irrigation is stored, and flood control becomes increasingly more difficult. Last, but hardly least, is the possibly of a catastrophic accident should a dam be breached and collapse and send a roaring wave of water downriver on a devastating path of destruction.

For all of the reasons mentioned previously, and based on significant historical experience, most environmentalists now believe that large dams often represent an unacceptable risk, particularly over the long term. Increasingly, many scientists have come to share this bleak view of dams, too. As the World Commission on Dams has noted:

> *Large dams generally have a range of extensive impacts on rivers, watersheds, and aquatic ecosystems—these impacts are more negative than positive and, in many cases, have led to irreversible loss of species and ecosystems.*[3]

China's leadership emphatically does not share the view of the World Commission on Dams. This leadership is hip deep in the construction of an ever-larger and larger set of dam projects. These projects will be built on one of the most highly polluted and, not coincidentally, heavily dammed set of river basins in the world. The result of this damnable dam strategy is a set of great risks not just for the Chinese people but for all of China's downstream neighbors.

Of Dying and Dried Up Rivers—China's New Sorrow

> *She gave birth to one of the world's most glorious ancient civilizations. For more than 4000 years, she has nurtured millions of fields and farmers spread alongside her. Millions still rely on her bounty today. But like so many working mothers, the Yellow River is exhausted, her resources dwindling, her energy flagging. The 3600-mile-long waterway known throughout history as "China's sorrow" because of a penchant for spilling over is now causing despair for precisely the opposite reason: It is drying up.*

—*The Los Angeles Times*[4]

China has seven major rivers, the two largest and most well-known of which are the Huang and Chang—known in the West as the Yellow and Yangtze. Other major rivers, which cross China from north to south, include the Shonghua, Liao, Hai, Huai, and Pearl.

The Yellow River is considered by many historians to be the "cradle" of Chinese civilization. It is China's second-longest river and, along with the Huai River, plays a critical role in both irrigation and soil replenishment as it runs through China's fertile Northern Plains or "breadbasket."

The Yellow River derives its name from the large amounts of silt that give it a distinctive color. Fifty years ago, China's "Mother River" ran bountifully to the sea. Today, however, as stark testimony to China's growing water-scarcity problems (discussed in the next chapter), the Yellow River can run dry for more than 200 days a year. For much of the year, the easternmost portions of the river turn into a highway, with cars and trucks traversing the dusty riverbed.

The Yangtze River has no such problem, at least as yet. The world's third-largest river behind only the Nile and the Amazon, its flow for now is abundant. The Yangtze, however, carries its own heavy burdens—flooding and rampant pollution.

A commercial workhorse, the Yangtze is both a key transportation route and convenient dump site for much of China's heavy-industry heartland, particularly in its lower reaches, which link the industrial city of Chongqing to Shanghai through Wuhan. Along this route beats the pulse of Chinese heavy industry, which releases all manner of organic and toxic effluents into the river. Chongqing alone, with its population of more than 30 million, produces more than a billion tons of industrial waste water and more than 300 million tons of sewage a year.[5]

The Pearl River Delta is a magnet for foreign direct investment in the southern province of Guangdong near Hong Kong. As discussed in the next chapter, like most of China's rivers, the Pearl is severely polluted; it has become a major dumping site for China's leading light-industry sectors.

In managing its seven major river systems and complex web of more than a thousand other rivers, lakes, and streams, China historically has faced three major enemies. The two most well known are chronic drought and flooding. However, China has also suffered from severe "water-logging," which refers to the accumulation of rainwater in fields. Water-logging can greatly increase the salinity of arable land, starve plant roots of needed oxygen, drastically reduce crop yields, and create prime breeding grounds for mosquitoes. China has a long and often tragic history associated with these problems, and it is understandable why the country has been so attracted to dam building as part of its broader water-resource management program.

It is useful to know that only "about 8% of the land located in the mid- and downstream parts of the seven major rivers of the country are prone to floods." However, it is also true that about 50% of the total population of the country lives in these areas, which "contribute two thirds of total agricultural and industrial product value," and "according to historical records, large flood events occur once in every two years."[6]

The Great Leap Upriver

Dam construction in China has a long history. Tracing back to ancient Chinese history, one can find that the most ancient reservoir, Shaopi, was built in Eastern Zhou Dynasty (598–591 B.C.) in Anhui Province. It is an earth dam, 10m [about 30 feet] high, and has been in regular operation up to now. The later Zhibo irrigation canal in Shanxi Province (453 B.C.) and Dujiangyan irrigation project in Sichuan Province (219 B.C.) are very famous engineering works, especially the invented masonry spillway dam, 3.8m [about 12 feet] high, on the navigation canal in Guangxi Autonomous Region which was constructed in 219 B.C. and is still operating now.

—Chinese National Committee on Large Dams[7]

Despite a rich and ancient history, dam construction did not really begin on a widespread scale until the Communist revolution. Only 22 large dams existed prior to 1949.[8]

All that changed beginning with the Great Leap Forward (1958–1960). Although this period is best known for the calamities it wrought in trying to jump-start China's steel and manufacturing industries, the period also marked the beginning of China's thoroughly myopic quest to be the dam capitol of the world. Within 40 years, as part of a broader campaign to conquer nature, Mao's cadres had dammed every major river in China, building more than 80,000 dams of various sizes in the process.

Today, the poster child for China's dam-happy proclivities is the Three Gorges Dam, an undeniable engineering feat. Three Gorges is 181 meters tall, or almost 600 feet tall. It stretches 2.3 kilometers (almost a mile and a half) across the Yangtze. With a volume of 26 million cubic meters or more than 30 million cubic yards, it will stretch more than 350 miles upstream and inundate an area the size of Switzerland.

The dam has a ship lift with a carrying capacity of 11,500 tons that is more than twice the height of any existing ship lift. Three Gorges also sports the largest hydroelectric station in the world, with an installed capacity equal to about 15 large nuclear power plants—18,200 megawatts.

At present, the Three Gorges Dam is basking in the glow of its apparent success. Mind-boggling in its size and audacity, and often likened to China's modern-day version of the "Great Wall," it is providing desperately needed electricity as the country faces widespread electricity shortages. It has even become a premier tourist attraction.

Now here's the other side of the Three Gorges coin: If ever there were a disaster waiting to happen, it is this very same dam. For starters, the dam is located close to a major earthquake fault line, which is even more a concern because the dam has experienced numerous cracks. At one point, China's Premier Zhu Rongji warned that, because of rampant corruption and shoddy construction management, much of the dam's infrastructure was made not of solid, reliable concrete but rather of "tofu."[9]

There is also the matter of cost. Originally budgeted at about $20 billion, current estimates of completion range as high as $70 billion, which wreaks havoc with any original cost-benefit analysis that might have been done to justify the project. Perhaps most threatening to the longevity of the dam, is the fact that the Yangtze is one of the most silt-heavy rivers in the world, which makes the Three Gorges Dam particularly susceptible to the problem of massive silt buildup. Scientists have warned that silt buildup may eventually reach back as far as Chongqing, clog this critical river port, and dramatically lessen its ability to generate electricity and prevent flooding.

Longer term, there will be the issue of the receding headwaters that fuel the Yangtze River. As a result of global warming, glaciers in Tibet that now feed the Yangtze are melting ever faster. At least one Chinese scientist has predicted that the Yangtze will eventually begin to have dry periods like the Yellow River and eventually stop its flow from reaching the sea near Shanghai.[10]

Finally, there is the matter of the intense political and social unrest among farmers and villagers caused by the dam's huge footprint. The reservoir created by the dam, which will be full by 2009, will eventually destroy more than 17,000 acres of forest and arable land. Far more contentious, it is forcing the eviction and relocation of close to two *million* people. This forced relocation involves "13 cities, 140 towns, 4500 villages and 1600 industries"[11] as well as the deepwater burial of more than 1,000 archeological sites.

Three Gorges as a Distraction and the Broader Problem

The sheer pointlessness of the vast investment in dam building was brought home by the 1998 floods, which killed 4,000 people and cost the economy $36 billion. The dams have done

*nothing to stop the floods, which have been increasing in
frequency and severity. Even the Three Gorges Dam, big
though it is, will make no practical difference.*

—*Asia Times*[12]

In many ways, the debate over the Three Gorges Dam has distracted
analysts from the much broader issue of China's dam-happy strategy.
As a simple matter of fact, as the world remains mesmerized by Three
Gorges, China is in the process of cementing its reputation as the
dam capitol of the world by building more and ever-larger dams.

The dam-building strategy is both economically and environmentally unsound. As Elizabeth Economy has persuasively argued, China
would be much better off if it abandoned its focus on large dams and
huge diversion projects and focused instead on "ensuring that the
existing water supply is used more efficiently." In her view, "demand
management is more effective, if less dramatic, and could enable
China to live within its means."[13]

In fact, many dams are also deathtraps waiting to be sprung.
According to a report by China's Water Resource Department,
30,000 of China's dams are in "critical condition," and they "threaten
over 400 cities" and almost 150 million people.[14,15] That same report
indicated that "3,484 dams collapsed from the year 1954 to year
2003"—an average of 71 collapses annually.[16]

One of the reasons for the mishaps is sheer neglect. As China
pours billions and billions of dollars more down the dam chute for
ever-larger and shinier new projects, it continues to underfund even
the most-basic maintenance and repair needs of many of its older
dams—many of which were built with faulty engineering and cheap
materials during the Mao years. As the section chief of the Shangrao
City Water Resource Department Section JianXin points out: "The
fundamental maintenance of the dams has been paralyzed."[17]

There is also the larger problem of corruption that plagues everything from enforcing environmental and workplace safety laws to the

cracking down on piracy and counterfeiting. As Tashi Tsering has ruefully noted:

> By the time project money reaches [dam] project builders, corrupt officials at the state, provincial and county levels would have typically embezzled more than half the project budget. This results in use of cheap, poor-quality raw materials for construction such as cement. Since construction on most dam projects typically begins before completing all studies required by law, issues of structural safety of the dams—will they withstand earthquakes or landslides?—are of concern to millions of innocent people downstream.[18]

Corruption and neglect are all the more surprising given China's numerous tragic experiences with dam failures. The collapse of the Banqiao and Shimantan Dams during the 1970s offers a textbook case of what can go wrong when large dams collapse.

The Tragedy of the Banqiao

The Banqiao Dam was originally built in the early 1950s. When cracks were found in the dam and its sluices, they were dutifully repaired and reinforced by Soviet engineers. The Banqiao Dam was then dubbed the "iron dam." Like the Titanic, it was supposed to be indestructible. Then, in 1975, Typhoon Nina hit.

In the span of just a few short days, Nina rained down a mind-boggling 63-inch deluge. At times, it rained 6 inches per *hour*. Under this onslaught, the smaller, upriver Shimantan Dam broke first and sent a wall of water crashing down toward the "indestructible" Banqiao. Half an hour later, the Banqiao was crested and collapsed. Waves of water more than 20 feet high rushed downstream at speeds of up to 50 kilometers (about 30 miles) per hour, wiping out 60 more dams along the way. As many as 200,000 people died, about a third from the initial flooding and the rest from famine and disease as the breach effectively isolated millions of people from basic communications and transportation networks.[19]

Drums along the Mekong

From its origin in the high plateau of Tibet, the Mekong River is 4500 km [about 2,800 miles] long and the 12th longest river in the world, flowing through six countries that include China, Burma, Thailand, Laos, Cambodia and Vietnam. True to its name (Mekong means Mother River in Laotian), the Mekong River is the lifeline to more than 60 million inhabitants in downstream countries such as Laos, Thailand, Cambodia and Vietnam. Most of them are poor fishermen living off the river fish catch or poor farmers using the river water and rich silt to grow rice. They also use the river as their principal means of transportation. . . . The biggest threat to their livelihood is the hydroelectric dams built or planned by the Chinese in Yunnan Province. Moreover, the Chinese are clearing and enlarging the river as a navigation channel for large commercial boats. These development projects by China will cause serious economic and environmental consequences in countries within the river basin, especially Cambodia and Vietnam. In going ahead with these projects, China has not considered the interests of these countries. This may be the cause for conflict, political crisis and even war in the near future. Even the survival of the river may be in serious doubt in the next few decades.

—Trần Tiến Khanh[20]

China's dam projects are not just threatening Chinese citizens. A particularly ambitious set of projects targeted for the Mekong River is already generating considerable conflict between China and its downstream neighbors.

China's upstream positioning on the Mekong relative to its neighbors, coupled with its overwhelming size and military might, put it in a position to dam the river with impunity. This is power, at least to date, China seems fully intent on wielding.

Unlike its downstream neighbors, China and the other upstream country, Myanmar, have refused to join the Mekong River Commission, whose goal is the cooperative and environmentally sound development of the river's resources. In a pattern typical of its U.N. behavior, China was one of just three countries that voted against the 1997 U.N. convention that established basic guidelines and principles for the use of international rivers.[21]

Positioned as it is to control the Mekong's development, the Chinese have embarked on a far-ranging plan to construct as many as 15 large dams. The first two of these dams are already in place. The Manwan and Dachaoshan were completed in 1993 and 2002, respectively. Together, they generate close to 3,000 megawatts of electricity—equivalent in output to about three large nuclear reactors.

It is the third dam now under construction that most alarms China's neighbors. When the Xiaowan Dam is completed in 2013, *it will be as tall as a 100-story building, rank as the tallest dam in the world,* and generate more than 4,000 megawatts of power.

The problems that China's damming of the Mekong are likely to create are vast and far-ranging. Already, the two dams in place have begun to affect the seasonal flow of the river. From the Chinese perspective, this is a good thing because it allows them to run large ships along the Mekong year round while at the same time preventing seasonal flooding. However, the downstream perspective differs decidedly.

To understand the high stakes involved, consider the possible impact of China's dams on the legendary Lake Tonle Sap in Cambodia. This lake is one of the world's most fascinating ecological treasures. For much of the year, it is relatively small—only a yard or meter deep with a footprint of only a bit more than 1,000 square miles. During the rainy season, however, flow from the Mekong River helps deepen the lake to roughly 30 feet and increases the area of the lake more than five-fold. The result is to turn Lake Tonle Sap into one of the best breeding grounds for fish in the world. This eloquent passage from London's *Independent* explains why this is so:

> The waters carry fertile sediment, fish larvae and fingerlings into the forest, which turns into a vast fecund nursery ground for fish—the source of one of the world's biggest inland fisheries.
>
> Here you will find the last of the Mekong catfish, the largest freshwater fish, which grows to three metres [ten feet] long and can weigh more than a cow. There's also the striped snakehead, which lives among tree roots and in lakes and swamps, and is known for its ability to slither overland between pools. Of greater value to millions of Cambodians is the fact that the flooded forest is also the breeding ground for the trey riel (Henicorhynchus siamensis), a sardine-like fish found in almost every net on the river.
>
> As the forest slowly drains each autumn, the fattened fish migrate throughout the Mekong River system, where local fishermen, many living in floating villages, know almost to the hour when the fish will pass by. The peak moment of the annual flood on the Tonle Sap is precisely 10 days before the January full moon.
>
> The intensity of fishing on the Tonle Sap in particular is extraordinary. Nets stretch for miles around the edge of the flooded forest. And near Phnom Penh, small wicker "bags" lowered into the river can catch half a ton of fish in 20 minutes.
>
> About 50 million people in the river's lower basin—in Cambodia, Vietnam, Thailand and Laos—depend on it for food and income. Cambodians alone catch about two million tons of fish a year and are more dependent on wild protein than almost any nation on earth.
>
> . . . According to Matti Kummu of the Helsinki University of Technology, who is modelling the river's hydrology, as much as half of the river's natural annual sediment load comes from

China, and an increasing amount is being captured behind the new dams [in China]. He believes that the sediment, which is carried mostly in the monsoon floods, is critical to the fertility of the Mekong's fisheries, and especially to those in the Tonle Sap.[22]

The obvious problem with China's dam program for the Tonle Sap is that the dams will even out the flow of water and thereby prevent the world's most fertile natural fishery from realizing its full depth and breadth in the critical fish breeding season. Already, fish catches have declined dramatically. In addition, the Mekong is now much more prone to rapid rises and falls as an upstream China regulates its own rivers, seemingly oblivious to the natural habitat and concerns of its downstream neighbors. As noted in *The New York Times*:

Water levels and temperatures have fluctuated widely, threatening the river environment and disrupting the livelihoods of the fishermen and others who depend on the $2 billion annual catch of migratory fish.

For the fishermen, their revered [Mekong] river, once nearly untouched and steady in its moods, has turned into a fickle sea. "In the past the river was up and down like nature— every three or four days up and down," said Tan Inkew, 72, a fisherman who lives in Meung Kan village. "Now the river is like the sea—up and down, up and down very quickly."[23]

The nation most at risk from China's Mekong River dams is Vietnam, the "last stop" of the Mekong on its way to the South China Sea. If anyone thinks that the mighty Mekong cannot go dry during certain periods of the year as it approaches Vietnam, one would do well to remember that the once-mighty Yellow River in northern China, which just 50 years ago flowed year round, now runs dry more than 200 days a year. Already, for the Mekong, the death knell has begun to sound. Government officials recently reported that the

Mekong River had recorded its lowest level ever and that it was "flowing 'close to rock bottom'" near the end of its journey in Vietnam.[24]

It may be useful to close here with the observation that Vietnam continues to maintain one of the largest armies in the world, in large part because of its historical enmity with China. Few people may remember that "other Vietnam war." This exceedingly bloody 1979 war occurred when China invaded Vietnam with tanks and about 90,000 troops in retaliation for Vietnam's pro-Soviet actions in Cambodia. In the space of *fewer than ten days* of fighting, anywhere from 40,000 to more than 100,000 Chinese and Vietnamese troops were killed or wounded, depending on the estimates. These figures rival the entire number of American soldiers killed in battle during its more than *ten-year* war in Vietnam (about 52,000). Although the relationship between China and Vietnam is much better today, if the Mekong were truly to dry up because of China's dam strategy, conflict between the two countries would become inevitable.

8

THE BREAD AND WATER WARS—NARY A (CLEAN) DROP TO DRINK

Of the 2000-plus villagers in Huang Meng Ying, nine are deaf, 14 mentally disabled, three blind and nine physically handicapped. The villagers also point to the surge in birth defects, lesions and gall bladder infections in recent years—a sure indication, they feel, that the water is contaminated. . . . A glimpse of the river, which once irrigated what was one of the most fertile regions of the country, reveals why the villagers have arrived at this conclusion. The once-clear waters are today a floating mass of garbage and chemical effluents, unfit for irrigation, let alone drinking.

—*Asian Chemical News*[1]

Water, water everywhere and,
Nary a drop to drink.

—Samuel Taylor Coleridge, "Rime of the Ancient Mariner"

The "Rime of the Ancient Mariner" paradoxically laments the inability of becalmed sailors to slake their growing thirst with the ocean's nonpotable saltwater. In China, the problem is more perverse. Much of China's *fresh* water in its rivers, lakes, streams, and wells is simply too polluted to use in irrigation, much less for drinking, and this pollution contributes greatly to a rapidly growing water scarcity problem. The statistics are startling:

- 70% of China's seven major rivers are severely polluted.

- 80% of China's rivers fail to meet standards for fishing.[2]

- 90% of China's cities and 75% of its lakes suffer from some degree of water pollution,[3] and 700 million Chinese "have access to drinking water of a quality below World Health Organization standards."[4]

- Almost half of China's total population is exposed to "water supplies that are contaminated by animal and human waste,"[5] and one in three countryside dwellers lack access to safe drinking water.[6]

- Liver and stomach cancers related to water pollution are among the leading causes of death in the countryside; for example, "in Shangba, located in northern Guangdong, pollution in the local water supply is so bad that the small towns in the region are known as 'cancer villages' by locals."[7]

- 21 cities along the Yellow River are characterized by the highest measurable levels of pollution, which "has resulted in mercury contamination of rice, increased incidence of intestinal cancer, and rivers devoid of aquatic life."[8]

- All of China's coastal waters are moderately to highly polluted, and the reddish discolorations of these coastal waters (known as "red tides") are dramatically increasing in both frequency and intensity.[9]

The pollution is caused not just by massive industrial dumping and indiscriminate industrial burning of toxic wastes. An avalanche of excess fertilizer and pesticide runoff and a mountain of animal and human waste stand equally tall as culprits.

Industrial Burning and Dumping

China's government rushed Thursday to shield the country's southern business center, Guangzhou, from a toxic spill flowing toward the city of 7 million—the second manmade disaster to hit a Chinese river in six weeks. As a slick of toxic benzene from the first accident in the north arrived in Russia, where worried residents flooded a telephone hot line, authorities in southern China were dumping water from reservoirs into the Bei River to dilute a cadmium spill from a smelter. The twin disasters highlight the precarious state of China's water supplies for industry and homes.

—Associated Press[10]

The Communist Party secretary of the village of Tangan, Zhao Hezeng, surveys the yellowing stocks in the paddy fields and the tar-black water in the gully alongside. The stream that feeds the gully is brown and foamy. It too would be black were it not for a recent fall of rain. Waste from factories upstream has turned the water the village depends on for irrigation into a foul-smelling toxic soup. Farmers get itchy rashes on their arms from working in the fields. No one dares drink from wells closest to the stream.

—*The Economist*[11]

We should have the power to shut down a plant like that immediately, but we don't. We can only fine them, and such a small amount at that. They basically decide it's a cost that doesn't matter.

—Pan Yue, Deputy Director
State Environmental Protection Administration[12]

China's manufacturing industries are not only flooding the world with low-cost products, but also are flooding China's waterways with toxic ash and effluents. The worst-polluting industries include paper and pulp, food, chemicals, textiles, tanning, and mining.

In some cases, small- to medium-size factories without adequate pollution-control technology wantonly dump a toxic stew of wastes and chemicals into rivers and streams. In other cases, large factories equipped with the latest and most sophisticated pollution-control technologies simply do not use the technologies for fear of driving up production costs—and without any fear of sanctions by lax regulators and often complicit local officials.

The most common toxic pollutants being unleashed by the indiscriminate burning of industrial waste and wanton industrial dumping include dioxins, solvents, and PCBs; various metals such as mercury, lead, and copper; and highly persistent pesticides ranging from chlordane and mirex to DDT.[13] Rampant pollution is causing a dramatic increase in liver, stomach, and other types of cancers, as well as everything from anemia to skin rashes. Invariably, the most vulnerable victims are the poor. As discussed in more detail in the next chapter, the high incidence of pollution-related cancers and illnesses in rural China coupled with the continued diversion of water from agricultural to industrial and urban uses is already contributing to significant social unrest.

Although Chinese government officials and regulators are giving lip service to the problem, the flood of toxic industrial pollution is only likely to get worse. One big reason is that many of the polluting factories are small scale and locally owned. Even when such enterprises are highly unprofitable, they represent important job generators in rural areas plagued by high unemployment, making it difficult for a local environmental protection bureau to close down the polluters, fine them, or otherwise force them to comply with the pollution control standards.

Even though China has some strict environmental laws on the books, the fines that are levied to enforce the regulations are often so insignificant they are considered to be merely a cost of doing business rather than a true deterrent. As Wang Yongchen, the founder of China's Green Earth Volunteers has put it, "China doesn't lack laws and regulations. The problem is enforcement."[14] Huo Daisahn of the environmental group Huaihe Guards has similarly noted:

> [E]ven through some factories have been fined and ordered to install effluent-treatment plants, they do not operate them regularly as costs are high. It would cost them 10 times more to operate the treatment plants than to pay the fine for failing to conform to emissions standards.[15]

Massive Fertilizer and Pesticide Runoff

> With increasing affluence, China's per capita consumption of meat, milk and eggs increased fourfold, fourfold, and eight-fold, respectively, between 1978 and 2002; its egg consumption now equals that of rich nations. This means more agricultural wastes, animal droppings . . . , fish droppings, fish food and fertilizer for aquaculture, tending to increase terrestrial and aquatic pollution.

—Professors Jianguo Liu and Jared Diamond[16]

Chinese industry is not the only major contributor to water pollution. China's agricultural sector is also to blame.

For starters, China is the second-largest consumer and producer of pesticides in the world. Chinese pesticide production rose from 1,000 tons in 1950 to more than half a *billion* tons today.[17] A high proportion of the pesticides and insecticides it produces is characterized by both high toxicity and high residue. Its factories also illegally churn out some of the world's deadliest pesticides—many of which have been banned both in China and the rest of the world.

Numerous scientific studies indicate that the problem of excessive pesticide residues in Chinese food crops is both serious and widespread, as are the effects on biodiversity among both plant and animal species. More broadly, toxic pesticides cause an array of negative health effects, from allergies, cancer, and damage to the nervous system to reproductive disorders, birth defects, and a weakening of the immune system.

Besides the *toxic* pollution from pesticides, there is the problem of *organic* pollution from fertilizer runoff. What's the difference between the two? Organic pollution occurs when an excess of organic materials—anything from human sewage to piggery wastes—are dumped into rivers or oceans. As bacteria grow and multiply to "decompose" this matter, they not only consume the oxygen in the water; they also release carbon dioxide. In this oxygen-deficient and CO_2-rich environment, both plants and fish begin to die and become a source of new organic material for decomposition. Add fertilizer runoff to this "soup," and it is like throwing gasoline on a flame.

China is the world's largest fertilizer user, consuming more than 50 million metric tons annually. Astonishingly, China accounts for fully 90% of global fertilizer increase since 1981.[18] The problem with this fertilizer use is widespread misuse. In many cases, poorly educated farmers and peasants misapply the fertilizer. This reduces fertilizer efficiency and therefore requires even larger applications to achieve a given yield. The result has been a new kind of "flooding" problem in China, that of excess fertilizer runoff flooding into China's rivers and streams.

Fertilizer nutrients such as nitrogen and phosphates, in turn, stimulate an overgrowth of plants and so-called algal blooms as part of a process known as "eutrophication." These algal blooms cover the surface of the water and block out light to the plant life below, preventing photosynthesis. The net result is not just dead fish and plant life, but also an increase in the turbidity of the water and an increase in a fine mud substrate that can block the gills of many organisms. As anaerobic organisms (which do not require oxygen) then attack the organic wastes, they release gases such as methane and hydrogen sulfide, and the result is an extremely foul-smelling body of water.

A Mountain of Sewage and a Dangerous Viral Soup

Dongxing is just one example of how Guangdong's 80 million people live close to the animals, poultry and fish they eat. At another piggery close to Mrs. Yang's, a farmer keeps young chickens next to his pigs. All the piggeries empty their waste into the ponds where shrimp and grass-carp are raised for the table.

In other places, battery chickens are kept above the pig pens, feeding their waste into the pigs' food troughs. The close proximity and cross pollution adds to the risk of animal viruses infecting humans, either directly or via pigs

"It's a complete soup of chemicals and viruses," says Christine Loh, a former legislator and head of the Hong Kong think-tank Civic Exchange, who is one of the city's leading analysts of environmental questions.

—The Sydney Morning Herald[19]

On the animal waste front, the United States is the world's red meat "beef king," and China has become the world's "emperor of pork." China's hog farmers produces 70% of all meat produced in China and 50% of all the pork produced in the world. The result is a mountain of piggery and other livestock wastes, much of which regularly is dumped, or seeps, into China's waterways. These wastes provide a rich source of fuel for the organic pollution process.

On the human waste front, China has the largest urban population in the world—and its cities generate more than a *trillion* tons of sewage each year.[20] However, about 90% of these municipal wastes either go untreated or fail to receive proper "secondary treatment."[21] Adding significantly to the problem is the fact that the construction of sewer lines is failing to keep pace with rapid urban growth and many sewage treatment plants are run inefficiently.

Most perversely, the central government will often provide the funds for construction of the plants. However, that same central government leaves financially strapped local and provincial governments with the fiscal burden of operating them (or not operating them, as is often the case).

A very different and even more deadly kind of pollution results from the overflow of animal and human wastes in China—one with the very broadest international reach. China has become *the world's prime breeding ground for new and exotic strains of influenza and other viruses, including both the deadly SARS virus and avian flu.* The primary reason, as the preceding excerpt indicates, is that so many different farm animals live in such close proximity to humans and other species. The resultant "cross-pollution" creates a "soup of chemicals and viruses" that now threaten the world with new and exotic influenza and other viruses and the possibility of a pandemic in which tens of millions of people may die.

The Red (Tide) Menace

A toxic red tide has blanketed the equivalent of more than 1.3 million soccer fields of sea off eastern China, threatening marine and human life, state media says. The tide is caused by plankton reproducing itself in large quantities due to nutrients provided in part by sewage and industrial waste.

—Reuters[22]

Not just China's lakes, rivers, and streams are being choked by a flood of pollutants. China's oceans are also suffering mightily from a growing epidemic of "red tides."

Although some red tides occur naturally, the particularly virulent brand of Chinese red tides is simply an ocean-going version of the eutrophication process described earlier. The tides are ignited by the wholesale dumping of sewage and agricultural and industrial pollution into ocean waters. The problem is particularly acute in the relatively shallow Bo Sea off northern China, which is characterized by minimal tidal exchange.

Perhaps most disturbing about these red tides for both China and its neighbors, besides the large economic costs in terms of the destruction of fish stocks and devastation of marine life, is the rapidly increasing frequency and intensity of the episodes.[23] China has seen an astonishing forty-fold increase in the incidence of red tides in just the past few years.[24]

The Equally Breathtaking Scope of China's Water-Scarcity Problem

China supports 21 percent of the world's population with just 7 percent of its water supplies and its per-capita water consumption is 1/4th of the world average. . . . More than 300 of China's 660 cities are facing water shortages while more than 100 of these cities are facing extreme water shortages.

—Qui Baoxing, Deputy Minister of Construction[25]

The [Chinese] government has forecast an annual water shortfall of 53 trillion gallons by 2030—more than China now consumes in a year.

—*The New York Times*[26]

By reducing the amount of potable water and water available for irrigation, China's severe water-pollution problems dramatically worsen China's water-scarcity issues. But, just how severe is it?

The most common scarcity metric is "total available water resources per capita."[27] If that number is more than 1,700 cubic meters (m^3) per capita, a country has sufficient water. However, when the number is between 1,000 and 1,700 m^3, a country is said to be "water scarce," and countries below 500 m^3 face absolute water scarcity.

Based on this yardstick, China at first glance does not appear to have a severe water problem. Its per-capita water availability is a little more than 2,000 cubic meters. This is only about 30% of the world average of roughly 7,000 cubic meters, but it is still well above the 1,700 m^3 threshold that signals water scarcity. The problem with this rather dry statistical observation is that it obscures one important fact: China suffers from huge *regional* disparities in the allocation of its water resources. The problem is two-fold.

First, in an ironic luck of the draw, China's best agricultural land is in the north, but most of its water resources, including the mighty Yangtze, are in the south. With less than 4% of the water resources of the country, the North China Plain—China's "breadbasket"—possesses a little more than 20% of the country's total cultivated land. It is precisely in and around this "breadbasket" where water scarcity is most dire.

Second, it is not just Chinese farmers who are suffering from an extreme lack of water. Water is also the scarcest in some of China's most heavily populated and industrialized cities, including China's capital of Beijing and its most cosmopolitan city Shanghai.

In addition to the cities of Beijing and Shanghai, water-scarce areas include the key industrial provinces of Hebei, Shanxi, Shandong, Henan, and Ningxia. They also include Jiangsu and Tianjin, where per-capita water availability is *below 200 m^3 a year!* Together, these provinces provide a lion's share of China's GDP. In this regard, reduced flows on many of China's rivers are already significantly reducing the amount of hydroelectric power necessary to keep China's smelters, paper mills, petrochemical plants, and other factories humming.[28]

The Political Economy of Water Scarcity

Farmers now push for higher and higher yields, which demand more and more water, especially with the widespread use of inefficient irrigation systems. Heavy industries present another major drain. Affluent urban lifestyles also strain the water supply, as residents snap up Western-style toilets and washing machines, and consume more meat and alcohol, which requires more grain—and therefore more water—to feed livestock and to produce liquor. . . . In rural areas, the cost of water can be less than half a cent. The low prices induce apathy about waste among much of the population. In public buildings, broken taps spewing water 24 hours a day are not uncommon, with no one around who cares enough to repair them.

—*Los Angeles Times*[29]

China offers a textbook case of how a complex array of economic forces are rapidly propelling the country down the river to water scarcity ruin. The already intense pressures on China's limited water resources are rapidly increasing with the forces of both economic and population growth and attendant urbanization and industrialization.

It is not just more and more people and factories and more-intensive farming driving China's water demands. It is also a rapidly urbanizing and increasing "affluent" population with rising incomes embracing a "lifestyle" that is dramatically increasing the consumption of "more meat and alcohol"—both of which are water intensive to produce. In addition, water demand is set to rise significantly as China rapidly urbanizes for the simple reason that urbanites with showers and flush toilets generally use much more water than their country cousins.

Misguided government policies must also shoulder much of the blame. One major problem is the abject failure of the Chinese government to price its water resources correctly. Chinese water prices are among the lowest in the world, with much of China's water sold at less than half of its true cost.[30] This not only encourages overconsumption and inefficient use, but also provides inadequate incentives for investments in many water-saving technologies and other demand-side conservation measures. As a result, China uses up to 50 tons or more of water to produce a ton of steel, compared to 6 tons of water in Japan, Germany, and the United States.[31] According to China's own Ministry of Water Resources, China uses four times as much water to produce a unit of GDP than the world average—this in a country facing an almost desperate water shortage.[32] The political constraint here is that no one in China wants to pay more for their water.

A second major problem is a lack of adequate infrastructure to manage water resources. Rampant rickety and aged plumbing and rusty pipelines result in prodigious leakages across the vastness of the country. There is also a general lack of any comprehensive water recycling facilities. Rather than directing substantial resources to more efficient water use, the Chinese government is rolling the dice on a high-risk gamble originally envisioned by Mao Zedong known as the South-to-North Diversion Project. This "mega-project is the largest of its kind ever planned." Its three canals "will stretch across the eastern, middle and western parts of China" and eventually link four of the country's seven major rivers—the Yangtze River, Yellow River, Huaihe River, and the Haihe River.[33]

The eastern route has been designed to make use of the existing reservoirs and canals of China's ancient Beijing-Hanzhou Grand Canal. This is the same route once used to move tea and silk in ancient Imperial China and the longest artificial river in the world. The goal is to draw water from the mouth of the Yangtze and then divert it to Tianjin.

The middle route is expressly designed to bring more water to a chronically thirsty Beijing. It is this route that will cause most of the displacement of the population, with the expansion of the Danjiangkou Reservoir on the Han River alone requiring the forced relocation of as many as 400,000 people. Together, the eastern and middle routes are scheduled for completion by 2010 at an estimated cost exceeding $20 billion.

The western route is both the most speculative with its daunting engineering challenges and the most expensive with a price tag approaching $40 billion. Its goal is to "channel waters flowing off the Tibetan Plateau into the upper stretches of the Yellow River, now so overused it often runs dry before reaching the sea,"[34] but it likely will not be completed before 2050.

Although seemingly offering a "magic bullet" for many of China's water woes, these projects and their intricate pumping systems will consume significant amounts of scarce electricity, cut a wide swath of environmental damage by radically altering water levels, put enormous strains on public coffers, and sow considerable social unrest by uprooting close to a half a million people. Even more problematic is the fact that the most technically simple eastern route "cuts across many of the world's most soiled river basins," which raises the practical question as to whether the water, once successfully diverted, will be "safe enough for industry, let alone drinking."[35]

The South-to-North Diversion Project is not China's only major policy solution to its water-scarcity problems. One highly risky short-term strategy involves a massive extraction of groundwater from deep-water aquifers. A second major strategy, which is fueling intense cross-border conflicts, is the construction of the most massive web of dams ever attempted in any country, as discussed earlier.

China's Dangerous Game of Groundwater Extraction

[T]he massive extraction of groundwater in the North China Plain has led to a rapid decline in the groundwater table. In agriculture, one of the consequences of groundwater depletion has been exhaustion and thus desertion of wells.

—Hong Yang and Alexander Zehnder
Swiss Federal Institute for Environmental Science and Technology[36]

To slake its ever-growing thirst, China is aggressively "mining" many of its deep-water aquifers. Of the 52 million hectares of irrigated land in the country (a little more than 125 million acres), about one fourth are watered by ground aquifers. The capital city of Beijing, which alone sucks out more than 200 million tons of subterranean water a year, has sunk almost 30 inches in the past 40 years and continues to sink about an inch a year. Road sections have collapsed, and there is attendant damage to buildings and other infrastructure.[37] Meanwhile, in Shanghai, the land in the city center has sunk by almost 6 feet in the past 40 years.[38]

This groundwater mining is a dangerous game for at least three reasons: First, the reliance is unsustainable. Unlike shallower aquifers, which can be replenished by annual rainfall, the deepest aquifers are nonrenewable resources, which means that any reliance on these aquifers for ordinary needs is taking place on borrowed time.

Second, as these groundwater aquifers are tapped, groundwater tables decline. The water tables beneath much of northern China are shrinking by about five feet per year, which is forcing farmers to drill deeper and deeper wells leading many lakes and streams to dry up.

Third, and most subtly, China's deep-water mining is inducing the salinization of its water supplies. As groundwater is sucked out of coastal aquifers, sea water seeps in and poisons wells and water supplies. The problem is particularly acute in the coastal areas of Dalian and Yantai. Here, more than 5,000 wells have been destroyed, production on 300,000 acres of irrigated farmland has been cut in half, and almost a million people and a quarter of million livestock do not have enough water.[39]

The next chapter looks at how all of these mounting problems of water scarcity and water pollution—together with broader problems associated with rampant corruption, rising income disparities, and forced dislocations of the peasantry—are contributing to China's many "wars from within."

9

CHINA'S WARS FROM WITHIN—THE DRAGON COMES APART AT THE SEAMS

China is at the crossroads. It can either smoothly evolve into a medium-level developed country or it can spiral into stagnation and chaos.

—Lu Xueyi, Director of Sociology
Chinese Academy of Social Sciences[1]

A single spark can start a prairie fire.

—Mao Zedong

The single spark of Mao's day is now replaced by a cascade of fireballs. Economic reforms and industry privatization in China have created a "reserve army of the unemployed" numbering more than 100 million. The Chinese countryside has become both a slave-labor camp and a dumping ground for every imaginable air and water pollutant, while the rural peasantry is being sucked dry by government tax collectors. This is hardly the end of the story. In the largest set of

157

evictions in world history, China's aggressive dam projects have displaced more than two million rural peasants. The onslaught of industrial development has forcibly evicted hundreds of thousands more.

As part of the long march of "progress," corrupt local government officials seize land on behalf of developers, pocket the monies that are supposed to compensate villagers, and then enlist local gangsters to quell protests. In the big cities, wages that go callously unpaid to poor migrant workers number in the staggering billions of dollars. Unpaid construction workers leap to their deaths in protest (*tio lou xiu*). Meanwhile, on China's western prairies, ethnic separatist tensions continue to smolder over the ongoing "Hanification" of the ethnic minority, mostly Muslim, western frontier.

For all these reasons, none of the Coming China Wars outside China's borders are likely to be as sudden, wrenching, and violent as the wars from within. Hundreds of thousands of skirmishes have already been fought. Over the past decade, the number of protests and riots has risen almost exponentially to nearly 100,000 annually, with both their scope and scale increasing.[2] What is perhaps most alarming to the Chinese government about these protests, riots, and strikes is the diversity of causes and their broad geographic sweep. Consider this sampling of major confrontations over the past several years:

- In Xianyang City, in central China's Shaanxi Province, more than 6,000 workers strike after a textile factory is privatized and the new owner seeks to fire and then rehire them as "inexperienced workers" at much lower wages and "without accrued retirement or medical benefits."[3]

- In metropolitan Shenzen, factory workers producing audio speaker parts take two of their Hong Kong bosses hostage out of fear that the bankrupt company will not pay them back wages. In a separate incident, hundreds of workers clash with security guards and police during a protest against layoffs at an electronics company.[4]

- In the city of Chizhou, just 250 miles southwest of Shanghai, a student on a bicycle collides with the Toyota sedan of a wealthy businessman whose bodyguards callously kick and beat the student. Fueled by cell phones and instant messaging, this mushrooms into a "rich versus poor" conflict involving more than 10,000 people, the smashing of the Toyota and a police car, and the looting of a supermarket owned by another wealthy businessman.[5]

- A similar incident occurs in Wanzou City, a town near the Chongqing municipal area crammed with thousands of unemployed workers and a quarter of a million peasants dislocated by the Three Gorges Dam project. After a wealthy local government official assaults a lowly street porter, more than 10,000 people go on a rampage, looting government buildings and torching a police car.[6]

- In a protest against excessive taxes, a woman from the town of Xianqio in Guangdong Province on China's affluent southern coast refuses to pay a bridge toll. After she is badly beaten, villagers surround the toll station and torch it. They are soon joined by a crowd numbering close to 30,000. A thousand police officers use teargas to dispel the rioters, a man is crushed to death by a fire truck, 7 firefighters are injured, and 17 people are arrested.[7]

- In Sichuan, a province as large as France and bordered by the Tibetan Plateau, tens of thousands of farmers in Hanyuan county clash with the People's Armed Police when their land is seized for a hydroelectric plant and they are given what even a local official acknowledges is "compensation too low to accept."[8]

- In China's "Wild West" autonomous region of Xinjiang Province, Chinese troops are called to the frontier town of Yining to quell fierce clashes between Muslim Uighurs and ethnic Han Chinese amid accusations that the Taliban "are training guerrillas to mount attacks in Xinjiang Province."[9]

- More than a thousand miles away in Henan Province in China's rustbelt heartland, a seething ethnic clash between Muslim Hui and Chinese Han peasants leave more than 100 dead after a bloody fight with farm tools.[10]

The New Marxian Struggle and Worker's Revolt

What lies behind the growing protests is the impact of the vast economic restructuring and the huge influx of foreign capital that has taken place over the past two decades. Social inequality has grown enormously as millions of workers in state-owned enterprises have been thrown out of work; farmers compelled to compete on the capitalist market and pay rising levels of tax; and tens of millions of rural immigrants forced to labor in harsh conditions in sweatshops in coastal China.

—*The Wall Street Journal*[11]

To anyone new to the China watching game, one of the most baffling paradoxes of the Chinese "economic miracle" is this: Despite rapid economic growth, the unemployment rate remains stubbornly high. Some estimates peg it at upward of 25%. Moreover, it is likely to rise rather than fall over the next several decades. The obvious question is why, and the answer lies in these two simple but powerful words: *privatization* and *urbanization*.

As discussed in Chapter 1, "The 'China Price' and Weapons of Mass Production," the privatizing of many of China's *state-run enterprises* (SOEs) has smashed the "iron rice bowl" system that all Chinese workers were entitled to during the pre-reform era. This iron rice bowl provided a cradle-to-grave social welfare safety net that included a secure job, a livable wage, free housing and health care, and a pension.

Closing many SOEs and smashing the iron rice bowl has unleashed a wave of entrepreneurial activity and eliminated many inefficiencies in China's manufacturing sector, but it has also cast adrift millions of workers. Today, Chinese workers constitute one of the largest "reserve armies of the unemployed" ever assembled—well over a 100 million people.

China's pool of surplus labor is not likely to shrink anytime in the near—or even distant—future because China's drive to urbanize its citizenry in an effort to reduce rural poverty over the next several decades is likely only to add to its reserve army. Over the next several decades, the goal of the central government is to move the equivalent of the entire population of the United States off the farm and into the industrial work force—300 million or more peasants.

This surplus of labor severely depresses wages. It also results in stark, Dickensian working conditions in venues ranging from small metalworking shops to large coal mines that are the most dangerous in the world. China's coal mines are "death traps for thousands of miners," many of whom are "transient workers from the poorest parts of China, who have no other means of livelihood than working on the deadliest jobs in the country."[12] These peasants are routinely forced to sign what are derisively referred to as "life-and-death contracts" (*sheng si zhuang*) that revoke all legal claims and grant them a small lump-sum payment in the event of death or injury.[13]

Beyond the bodily carnage, there are diseases such as pneumoconiosis (from dusty working conditions), chemical poisoning, and leukemia that rank as the leading causes of early "retirement" in China. These problems are particularly acute in industries ranging from coal production and metallurgy to building materials, nonferrous metals, machinery, and chemicals.[14]

Typically, the smaller private enterprises are located in towns and villages that are the most deadly. As noted in testimony by policy analyst Wing-yue Trini Leung before the U.S. Congressional-Executive Commission on China:

> *They are typically set up and owned or run by one or a small handful of local entrepreneurs, often under the auspices of*

*local authorities. Such factories form the backbone of the
export-processing industries; many serve as subcontractors
and suppliers to the major MNCs [multinational corpora-
tions] around the world. . . . Workers commonly suffer from
long working hours, forced overtime, deprivation of rest days
and sick leave, low wages (nearly always on piece-rate), arbi-
trary penalties and dismissals, and denial of collective bargaining rights. H&S [health and safety] features very low in
the investment and management priorities of these enterprises, if at all. The local law enforcement officials are usually
willing to turn a blind eye to the situation, either because they
are bought off or because they see it in their interests to keep
the entrepreneurs and investors happy.*[15]

It is not just that wages are depressed and working conditions can
be horrific. In many cases, the wages that workers do earn are not
even paid. This most typically happens to migrant laborers in China's
cities who are ruthlessly exploited because of their second-class
status. The amount of monies withheld by unscrupulous employers is
staggering, running into the *billions* of dollars each year.[16]

The problem is most acute in China's frenetic construction industry, where it is common practice to feed and house the migrant workers but withhold their wages.[17] Zhou Xiaozheng, a sociologist at the
People's University of China in Beijing, has likened the situation to
slave labor: "China has 10 million slaves. The definition of a slave is
someone who is given work and food but no wages. That's what these
people are."[18] The tragedy here is that this industry is second only to
mining in terms of the health and safety risks. As in the coal mines,
most construction workers are poor migrants, and their injuries and
casualties typically go unreported.

This is hardly the only slave labor in China. In an economic
arrangement that harks back to the days of the Maoist communes,
many enterprises house their workers in dormitories where they are,
for all practical purposes, either slaves or indentured servants. In
some cases, bars on the windows prevent their escape. In other cases,

the "bars" are purely economic, because many workers are forced to sign labor contracts that effectively indenture their services to a company for a long period. If a worker breaks this contract, the worker will owe the company such a large sum of money that it would be impossible to pay it.

Of course, all the problems are compounded by the outlawing of labor unions by the government, the lack of any meaningful worker-protection laws, and the lack of enforcement of the few laws on the books. Is it any wonder that a seething rage in the Chinese workplace is increasingly spilling over into violent protests and strikes?

Peasants with Pitchforks

In a very short time, several hundred million peasants will rise like a mighty storm, like a hurricane. They will sweep all the imperialists, warlords, corrupt officials, local tyrants and evil gentry into their graves.

—Mao Zedong, 1927[19]

[A]s peasants abandon the land in search of work in the towns and cities, rural communities are sinking into destitution. Village councils, faced with the loss of tax-payers, respond by increasing taxes on those who remain and going into debt in order to finance the operation of schools and other basic services.

Peasants in the area are now paying up to $U.S.365 in taxes per year, more than the average rural income in China, for land, education, holding livestock and owning a home. About 80 percent of peasants in his township were losing money and 85 percent were already in debt. The average village debt is already $U.S.75,000 and is rising at the rate of 20 percent per year.

A vicious circle is in motion, replicated across rural China. As taxes increase and living standards collapse, more peasants

leave. In Li's township of Qipan, 25,000 people out of a total
population of 40,000 had left. Li's letter declared: "The farm-
ers are leaving, hoping only for luck or with the idea that 'If I
die, I'm going to die in the city. In the next life, I don't want to
be a farmer.'"

—Li Changping, Local Communist Party Secretary in a rural
township of Hubei Province, 2002[20]

To the central government in Beijing, there is no specter more
chilling than a peasant-led rebellion. After all, it was just such a
"prairie fire" that propelled Mao and his Communist cadres into
power. Despite this fear, the Communist Party leadership has done
little to quell rising peasant tensions and much to fuel them through
policies of forced evictions, a crushing tax burden, rampant and fla-
grant corruption, and an utter disregard for the environment in which
farmers and fisherman must eke out a meager living.

The problem has been further compounded in many areas by a
sharp rise in "rural gangsterism." This refers to the practice in which
village officials sometimes employ thugs to collect taxes from the peasants and, in cases where peasants actually protest or revolt, they swoop
in to smash the dissent. This situation is so bad that gangsters are
sometimes even appointed as village leaders by higher-level officials.[21]

The Discontent of the Dispossessed

Attempting suicide by burning oneself in public is a particu-
larly powerful form of protest in China, to which even the
most desperate rarely resort. Yet in the past seven weeks, at
least three people have tried to kill themselves in this way.
Their grievances have been the same: forced relocation from
their homes to make way for commercial developments.

—*The Economist*[22]

To make way for capitalist development and growth and the jobs they bring, the Communist Chinese bureaucracy serves as the primary phalanx for land seizures. The problem in many cases is not the evictions per se but rather the accompanying corruption and greed. In far too many cases, local government officials are blatant double dippers. They accept bribes from the developers for executing the land seizure and then siphon off the money that would otherwise be paid as compensation to those forced off their land. Add to this dynamic the fact that the government rarely adequately provides for the relocation of these individuals and there is a powder keg in the making.

In some cases, government evictions are triggered to make way for large-scale public-works projects. The poster child for this activity is the controversial Three Gorges Dam, which spans the Yangtze River just below Chongqing in Hubei Province and is the largest dam in the world. Its construction, begun in 1994, has led to the displacement of more than two million people. Meanwhile, in preparation for the 2010 World's Fair, Shanghai has been evicting and relocating people at a rate of 80,000 a year since 2000, and plans to move another 400,000 by 2007.[23]

The high-profile displacements are, however, just the tip of the eviction iceberg. In city after city, town after town, and village after village, local officials are selling land-use rights without consulting the occupants to make way for everything from freeways and power plants to new upscale housing and shopping centers.

It is bad enough that the peasantry is being uprooted for all manner of public works and industrial projects. It is worse that in so many cases, corrupt government officials drain off most or all the compensation originally intended for the dispossessed. The ability of corrupt government officials to fill local coffers and enrich themselves at the expense of the peasantry has dramatically increased the willingness of these officials to grant entrepreneurs the right to seize lands from the peasants for private, corporate purposes, too.

A Very Taxing Situation

We farmers do not have enough to eat while even a junior township official will be able to own at least a car and a house. We are feeling very bad about this. We have been forced to fight.

—World Wide Socialist Web[24]

Almost 60% of the Chinese population is involved in agriculture, the average farmer's income is a mere $400 and stagnant, and the vast majority of peasant families have only very small plots on which to eke out a living.[25] Under the best of circumstances, subsistence farming could provide Chinese peasants with a modest life. However, increasingly both drought and pollution, together with soil erosion, are making it more and more difficult for Chinese farmers to make ends meet.

A far bigger bone of contention is that local peasantries across the country are constantly besieged by local government officials that heavily tax them. This heavy tax burden would be bad enough if the revenues were used to provide services to the taxpayers, but more often than not, these revenues are used to finance the extravagant lifestyles of local party officials.

While peasants break their backs in the hot fields, party officials ride around in limousines, enjoy lavish banquets, meet their mistresses in upscale hotels, and send their "Little Emperor"[26] offspring abroad for schooling—all the while dissipating China's wealth. As noted in the *Washington Post*, a fourth of all government revenues are diverted to the "upkeep of the country's 6 million officials at all levels."[27] Said peasant farmer Du Chongan of the situation: "We spend only 30,000 yuan to build our houses, but their homes cost 300,000 yuan."[28]

Much of this revenue stream—and the income from myriad other corrupt activities—finds its way into the vaults and safety-deposit boxes of officials in foreign banks. As noted in *Maclean's*, "with an estimated U.S.$60 billion stashed away each year in offshore accounts, corruption is not only undermining China's economic boom, but the ruling party's political legitimacy."[29]

Nor is this situation likely to improve any time soon. Although the central government has made a big show of cutting farm taxes, "the rural population remains bogged down in fees and taxes created by local governments to pay for ever-expanding bureaucracies."[30] Professor Jiang Wenran at the University of Alberta notes, "as soon as one tax is abolished, another is being invented. It's a game of survival."[31]

Arguably one of the ugliest by-products of the systemic dissipation of peasant income by corrupt bureaucrats has been reported by William Dobson of the *New Republic*. When the peasants do protest or riot, "it is not uncommon for police chiefs to hire local thugs or mafia heavies to crack down on protestors. Or, in a desperate effort to contain demonstrations, it isn't rare for local authorities to simply buy off protestors. Of course, this strategy only encourages more protests."[32]

An Eruption of Class Warfare

China's poor are growing ever more desperate and direction-less in the face of high unemployment and systemic corruption. While shimmering mega-cities and a rising middle class attest to China's newfound industrial might and burgeoning wealth, social tensions are on the rise, fuelled by a widening rift between rich and poor and a crumbling social safety net bowing under the strain of fast-paced change. The frustration percolating just below the surface is now rising to the fore, with a dramatic increase in violent protests that are arguably the greatest threat to the ruling Communist party's grip on power, and to the whole country's economic awakening.

—*Maclean's*[33]

In many ways, China's coming wars from within are not just a tale of a growing great urban-rural divide. They are also a tale of two very familiar Chinese warring coalitions.

On the one hand, there are the dirt poor peasants and oppressed proletariat labor who comprise most of China's enormous population and who provided Mao with his original power base. On the other hand, there is that very same coalition of wealthy corporate entrepreneurs and corrupt government officials that during the pre-Mao, Chiang Kai-shek era so thoroughly enriched themselves at peasant-proletariat expense. The perverse and peculiar twist here, however, is that the grand facilitator of the exploitation of labor by capitalists once described by Karl Marx himself is now paradoxically and tragically the Communist Party itself. As Lord Acton once noted, power does corrupt and absolute power does indeed corrupt absolutely.

The Corrosion of Corruption and the Allure of Quanxi

One percent of China's population owns 40% of its wealth, much of it built up through corrupt acts.

—Ross Terrill, *The New Chinese Empire*

The plunder of the general population by a small entrepreneurial and government elite that has taken place since China's economic awakening is every bit as extreme as that which occurs in every banana republic of South America and every dictatorial regime in Africa. The great difference is the very, very short time within which this redistribution of wealth has taken place—transforming what was a putatively egalitarian society without property rights just a few short decades ago into a plundering playground for the rich.

The following sidebar is based on one of the most fascinating books written about contemporary China, *Corruption and Market in Contemporary China*. The book summarizes the many and varied corrupt acts that plague China and, in doing so, suggests just how deeply the problem of corruption is embedded in the Chinese culture.

More broadly, in example after example, city mayors, provincial government officials, and high-ranking party members across the length and breadth of China have all been caught with their hand in the till. Whether it is gold bars smuggled out to Swiss bank accounts, free tuition for party offspring, or simply the dissipation of wealth through extravagant lifestyles, corruption is so rampant among many thousands of Chinese officials that together it makes the infamous U.S. Congressman Duke Cunningham, with his fancy yachts and homes, look like the beggar of small change.

Bribery (*shouhui*) is defined as payments in exchange for some type of favor. Examples include the receipt of commission payments as rewards, hiring of officials or family members as "consultants," "loans" that will not be paid back, and special-occasion gifts at holidays, weddings, and funerals.

Embezzlement (*tanwu*) refers to the theft of public funds through accounting fraud. Examples include fictitious payments and receipts or when a manager of a state-owned enterprise contracts a construction project to an independent builder at a percent higher than normal and receives shares in the project.

Illegal earnings (*feifa shouru*) is a *de facto* crime found when a government official cannot account for the gap between possessed assets and all possible incomes. Such illegal income usually comes from bribes, embezzlement, profiteering, or smuggling.

Misappropriation (*nuoyong*) refers to the illegal use of public funds that are meant to be paid back at some point. Examples range from loans for legal uses such as businesses or stocks and the diversion of "relief funds" to loans for illegal enterprises such as smuggling or drug trafficking.

continues

Moral decadence (*diode duoluo*) refers to personal lapses by government officials that go unchecked. These range from slander, rape, and patronizing prostitutes to spreading pornography, domestic abuses, and sheltering mistresses.

Negligence (*duzhi*) is a form of corruption that occurs when people are hurt or property is damaged because an official fails to perform his or her duty. Typically, such negligence involves other forms of corruption such as bribery to ensure that bureaucrats do not enforce health or safety regulations or fail to supervise product safety.

Privilege seeking (*yiquan mousi*) refers to seeking favors for relatives, friends, and oneself. Examples include allocating regulated goods to relatives and friends for profiteering and tuition for children paid by a subordinate agency.

Squandering (*huihuo langfei*) refers to the wasting of public funds on extravagances. Typical offenses range from feasting, gift giving, and sightseeing in fancy limousines to the use of luxury amenities such as imported cars and fancy offices.

Smuggling (*zousi*) involves the trafficking of illegal or legal goods, as well as the evasion of tariffs, quotas, or entry inspection.

Violation of accounting procedures (*weifan caijing jilu*) occurs through fraudulent accounting that transfers assets or hides illegal use of revenues. Examples include cheating the state out of its revenue allocation through false reporting and the illicit use of public funds.

At the root of China's all-pervasive corruption is a practice known as *quanxi*. This word describes a process in which business gets done in China not on the basis of *what* you know but *who* you know. *Quanxi* is all about connections and, as a practical matter, entrepreneurs must connect with Chinese government officials and party members because they have the power to seize lands and grant favors.

The result is a growing anger at the "flourishing alliance of Communist Party officials and well-connected businessmen" and, more broadly, the "increasingly intimate connection in modern China between big money and Communist government." [34] The results are spontaneous eruptions of anger that, in an age of cell phones and instant messaging, can rapidly evolve from a small incident to a huge riot.

Every Chinese Individual's Duty to the Revolution

If ordinary people in China don't make trouble, nothing is resolved. But if everyone thinks problems can only be resolved with violence, that's a very dangerous situation.

—Professor Lang Youxing, Political Scientist, Zhejiang University[35]

To truly grasp why China's rising wave of protests and riots pose such a threat to the stability of China's Communist government and society, it is essential to understand at least one small sliver of Chinese history and its profound implications. The Maoist revolution, which began with the founding of the Chinese Communist Party in 1921 and which was completed in 1949, was, at its roots, a prairie rebellion by rural peasants against the corrupt urban and government interests represented by Chiang Kai-shek's Nationalist Party. In fact, in China's cultural history, *the people not only have the right but also the "duty" to rise up against the ruling regime when it fails to represent the people's interest.*[36]

The duty to rise up is no trivial matter. The paramilitary People's Armed Police and other jackboots of China's central government are fully capable of repressing dissent in China's major cities—as the Tiananmen Square tank massacre of 1989 clearly illustrated. Effectively policing the rural peasantry is another matter entirely. Any effort by the central government to police its rural areas depends heavily on both local government officials and a highly decentralized military. To the extent that growing water shortages and pollution,

corrupt local government officials, forcible evictions, a rapidly widening income gap, and other forces are sowing dissent in rural areas,
they are contributing to a major source of social and political unrest.
As noted by the *American Thinker*:

> *The fact that China's government is repressive often leads*
> *foreign observers to assume that it is strong. In fact, China's*
> *rulers know very well that their hold on power is tenuous,*
> *and that the threat of popular discontent boiling over into*
> *rebellion and even disintegration is very real. China's history*
> *has many cycles of political fragmentation, alternating with*
> *cycles of centralization, and this is familiar to all.*[37]

Muslim Separatism and Ethnic Strife

As Muslim ethnic minorities chafe under Chinese rule, a sim-
mering revolt and seething ethnic conflict have turned much
of Western China into a heavily armed garrison ready to
crush sporadic, spontaneous and seemingly futile acts of
rebellion.

—*The New York Times*[38]

Within China, it is not just the specter of a civil war pitting Han
"brother against brother" that now haunts. There is also the possibility of ethnic strife and a separatist rebellion breaking out against the
ruling Han ethnic group. More than 50 different "minority nationali-
ties" (*shaoshu minzu*) are officially recognized in China. However,
almost 95% of the population is classified as "ethnic Chinese" or
"Han."[39] Ground zero for this ethnic strife is the northwest and primarily Muslim province of Xinjiang.

Xinjiang is China's largest province geographically but, with its
extremes of heat and cold and desert climate, it is also one of its most
sparsely populated. This province was formally annexed to the
Manchu Qing Empire as early as 1759 but, for all practical purposes,

it remained under the control of provincial warlords until the ascendancy of the Communist Party in 1949. That was when one of the most interesting, and possibly most ruthless historical events was ever perpetrated—one that allowed China to bring Xinjiang under its iron-fist control.

During the immediate post-World War II period, Xinjiang was controlled by Stalin and the Soviet-backed East Turkistan Republic. Reluctant to support a nationalist Muslim regime on the border of the then-Soviet Central Asian republics, Stalin brokered what appeared to be a peaceful accommodation between the Muslim leaders of East Turkistan and Mao's government. However, the plane carrying the East Turkistan leadership to Beijing to negotiate the peace agreement mysteriously—and all too conveniently—crashed and killed all aboard. In the ensuing leadership vacuum, Mao's forces stepped in and assumed control of Xinjiang, an "autonomous province" in name only.

From an agricultural point of view, much of Xinjiang is a virtual dustbowl[40] in no small part because of overgrazing, deforestation, overplowing, and the failed efforts of the central government to turn grasslands into farmland.[41] However, beneath Xinjiang's dusty soil and mountainous steppes[42] lies buried 40% of China's coal reserves.[43] Equally abundant and far more precious to the central government are oil and natural gas deposits[44] that total the equivalent of about 30 billion tons of oil and represent one fourth to one third of China's total petroleum reserves.[45]

Xinjiang is not just one of China's best bets for energy resources. Bordering eight countries in Central Asia and the Russian Federation, Xinjiang also has important strategic value. Central Asia can serve as a transshipment area for Middle East oil should war ever break out over Taiwan or China's various imperialist claims for oil reserves in the South China Seas. Central Asia republics such as Kazakhstan and Kyrgyzstan also have large petroleum reserves of their own that can help lessen China's Middle East oil dependence. For these reasons, China is building a vast network of modern infrastructure that includes railways, roads, and pipelines linking Xinjiang eastward to China's petroleum-thirsty industrial heartland and west and north to Central Asia and Russia.

Separatists or Terrorists?

[The Chinese military in] Xinjiang will always keep up the intensity of its crackdown on ethnic separatist forces and deal them devastating blows without showing any mercy.

—Xinjiang Party Secretary Wang Lequan[46]

In Xinjiang, the majority of the population consists of Uighurs, a Muslim Turkic people who face some of the harshest and most repressive government measures in the world. Activists are regularly arrested and tortured and often executed. Xinjiang "leads the nation in executions for state security 'crimes'."[47]

Any independent religious activity can be equated to a "breach of state security" and is often prosecuted. Celebrating religious holidays or studying religious texts is forbidden within state schools and the government has even "instituted controls over who can be a cleric, what version of the Koran may be used, where religious gatherings may be held, and what may be said on religious occasions."[48]

The repression has become only more intensified in the wake of the 9/11 terrorist attacks on the United States. The Chinese government seized upon this American tragedy as a golden opportunity to cut a very clever deal with the United States. China would support the U.S. war on terrorism if the United States would agree that the separatist activities of the majority Uighur population represented not simply an indigenous rebellion against autocratic rule but rather a legitimate terrorist threat with ties to Al-Qaeda and Osama Bin Laden. Under this cloak of terrorism:

China now defines a terrorist in Xinjiang as anyone who thinks "separatist thoughts." Under this pretext, China has over the past two years detained tens of thousands of people in Xinjiang—and executed many of them . . . [while] the authorities in Beijing recently said that this crackdown would continue indefinitely.[49]

Although such iron-fisted repression borders on the unbearable for much of the ethnic population, what sticks most in the craw of many Uighurs is the ongoing "Hanification" of Xinjiang. As a matter of policy, for decades the Chinese government has sought to pacify Xinjiang by importing large portions of its Han population from other, primarily poor areas. Today, the Han population is rising at a rate twice as fast as that of the Uighur population.

Rather than being pacified or tamed by the growing Han population, the Uighurs are just becoming more and more radicalized. There is a very bitter and dangerous irony in this ethnic strife. Whereas the Uighurs historically have been "among the world's most liberal and pro-Western Muslims, fundamentalist Islam is gaining sway among young Uighur men."[50] Today, "Uighurs report that small-scale clashes break out nearly every day between Chinese and Uighurs in Xinjiang's western cities."[51]

It is unlikely that a true guerrilla movement will emerge in Xinjiang to engage Chinese forces in an Algerian- or Vietnamese-style revolt. The populace is simply too small, and Chinese security forces are too big and powerful. However, in an age of "suitcase" nuclear bombs and biological terrorist weapons, China is exposed to terrorist threats at soft target points such as the Three Gorges Dam or in its teeming cities. Any such terrorist incidents could possibly help fuel conflicts in any one of a number of China's other "wars from within," making the severe repression of the Uighurs a risky strategy indeed.

10

Of "Bloodheads," Gray Dragons, and Other "Ticking Time Bombs"

In the old days, 25 years ago, life was straightforward in China. If you lived in a town, you worked in a state-owned factory or office. If you lived in the countryside, you worked on a collective farm. You didn't earn much, but that didn't really matter because there wasn't much to buy. Clothing options were largely limited to a choice of a dark gray Mao suit or a dark blue Mao suit. Only party officials got to use cars. For everyone else, private transport meant waiting months for the chance to buy a scarce Flying Pigeon bicycle.

In return for living the life of fathomless drabness, people's basic needs were reasonably well looked after. Health care (though it was, in truth, often seriously basic) was provided across the country by the state. Adequate pensions were provided in the same way. Housing was heavily subsidized, schooling was free.

—The Economist[1]

For centuries and centuries, a ghost has haunted Chinese history: that Ghost in Chinese is called Luan. *Luan is disorder or rather chaos. Luan is the moment when a society experiences a kind of collapse, a kind of flaw, where nothing works and where catastrophes are linked together. Chinese history has known this many times. . . .*

—Jean-Luc Domenach, *L' Asie et Nous*[2]

China is a nation rapidly graying. Looming dead ahead is a pension crisis the severity of which will make the Social Security woes of equally graying countries such as the United States, Japan, and Germany look like strolls through the park.

China is also a nation that is getting increasingly sick. Environmental pollution is proving to be an all too deadly catalyst for an explosion of a myriad of cancers and an epidemic of respiratory and heart diseases. This rapid rise in ill health is coming precisely when China's once-vaunted public health-care system has totally unraveled under the weight of China's ongoing privatization of social services and a host of other sweeping economic reforms.

Adding to the extreme pressures on its health-care system now comes an HIV/AIDS epidemic that many experts believe will become the worst in the world. This is an epidemic that began with *the* worst HIV/AIDS blood-donor scandal on the planet. It is now being rapidly fueled by rampant and rising intravenous drug use, a late-blooming 1960s-style sexual revolution, and the reemergence of China's once-infamous flesh trade.

For all of these reasons, no one in China's central government needs an abacus to calculate that time is running out on the Communist Party, and perhaps even the Chinese economic miracle. Any one of these ticking time bombs—pension deficits, a shredded health-care net, and an impending HIV/AIDS catastrophe—is capable of triggering severe bouts of economic, social and political instability. Taken together with the various wars from within analyzed in the preceding chapter, these ticking time bombs threaten to trigger what ultimately the Chinese fear most—chaos or *luan*.

The Gray Dragons—Where Have All the Pensions Gone?

The number of retirees in China's cities will soar from 48.2 million last year to 70 million in 2010 and 100 million by 2020, according to the Ministry of Labor and Social Security. Unlike the United States and Europe, which prospered before their elderly populations expanded, China is in danger of growing old before it gets rich.

—*USA Today*[3]

The senior citizens of China are not (yet) as well organized as vaunted political groups such as the *American Association of Retired Persons* (AARP) and the Gray Panthers in the United States. However, they do have far more to be angry about.

China's shattering of the iron rice bowl has not only helped create a staggering unemployment problem but also has left hundreds of millions of Chinese workers approaching retirement without the prospects of either an adequate pension or health care. During the "good old" iron rice bowl days, pensions were particularly generous, with workers receiving about 80% of their final salary. Today, current pension obligations are creating intense pressures on the existing system. These pressures are being further intensified by the fact that most workers still retire relatively early, by the age of 60 for men and 55 for women.

As in the United States and Japan, the underlying problem is that China's pension system is "pay as you go." Today's workers make contributions to the pension fund to support all of those in the retired pool. However, as China rapidly ages, that retirement pool will grow sharply at the same time the active worker base funding them shrinks precipitously. There is a big difference between China's situation and that of more developed countries such as the United States and Japan that are in a similar demographic crunch. China's per-capita income is much lower and therefore there are fewer resources to support the system. This is the inexorable demographic result of China's controversial "one-child" policy instituted back in 1979. Although attacked by conservatives and liberals alike, this policy was arguably needed to control China's burgeoning population. However, this policy undeniably has led to all sorts of economic and social perversions.

For starters, there is the widespread problem of female infanticide and a dramatic rise in aborted female fetuses, which has created a shortage of females in the segment of China's population that has now reached prime reproductive age. In a perverse variation on the "law of unintended consequences," the shortage of females has, in turn, increased the rate of prostitution and the spread of venereal disease and HIV as a large class of young male "unmarrieds" are forced into brothels to satisfy their carnal needs.

The one-child policy has also helped fuel the underground labor market because many couples choose to simply leave their villages and towns rather than be fined and punished or forced into sterilization by the local party apparatchiks. It has even increased the rate of child kidnapping as young male offspring are being snatched and sold to infertile couples.

Economically, however, the biggest long-term implication of the one-child policy has been a financially perverse demographic skew to China's population. In particular, the working-age population will be peaking somewhere around 2010. After that, there will be fewer and fewer workers to support more and more retirees.

Looming ahead is what is referred to in China as the "1-2-4 problem." Soon, there will be only one worker to support two parents and four grandparents. This problem is further compounded by the increasingly mobile nature of Chinese society. In the past, all players in the 1-2-4 game might live under the same roof, and the younger would take care of the older. Increasingly, workers may now live far from their parents and grandparents. This raises the cost of living because of the need to finance several households. It also creates particularly severe problems for China's rural poor, who do not receive any social security at all.

The longer-term economics of this situation do not bode well. With the smashing of the iron rice bowl and the collapse of many state-owned enterprises, the major economic and jobs-growth driver is the private sector. However, many private companies are ignoring or evading China's new social security system because the required contributions are so onerous—"a steep 24% of wages," which is "twice the level of U.S. social security payroll taxes."[4] As a consequence, "barely 10% of the urban work force is covered by the new system."

One obvious part of any solution to this crisis is to raise the retirement age, but that would anger large blocs of senior citizens. It would also make it even more difficult for China to provide enough jobs for its vast army of the unemployed and farmers pouring into the cities looking for work.

As noted by Richard Jackson, senior fellow at the Center for Strategic and International Studies, "Ultimately, the pension issue becomes an issue of social instability. The government sees that— they can't help but see that. But they don't know what to do."[5]

This is all a bitter, bitter irony for many loyal Communists who stoically endured the ravages of both the Great Leap Forward and the Cultural Revolution. After all, for much of their life, they worked commune style for modest wages under what they thought was an ironclad Maoist social contract that they would have lifetime security. Now, the Communist Party has abandoned these senior citizens at the most difficult time in their lives, and their rage continues to build as the reality of a shredded "safety net" hits with full force.

China's Pay Up or Die Health-Care System

Getting your appendix out is like a year's farming up the spout.

—A jingle in China[6]

Of all the challenges facing the PRC government, few are as important—or daunting—as fixing the national healthcare system. Not only do the health and welfare of the nation's 1.3 billion people depend on it, but in very real and direct ways, the rest of the world's health depends on it too.

—*China Business Review*[7]

On the day she arrived at the Number Three People's Hospital to seek treatment for HIV, Cai had no symptoms. But she did have a little bit of money, and that gets quick attention in the modern-day Chinese health care system: The doctors pressured her to check in and begin a regimen of expensive intravenous drugs, warning that the alternative was a swift death. . . . When she asked for the free anti-AIDS drugs the central government has begun providing to the poor, the doctors rebuffed her . . . until she agreed to pay for costly tests. And when she ran through her money and all she could borrow—her 45-day hospital stay exceeding $1,400, nearly triple her annual income—the doctors cast her out. "The director told me to go away and wait until I had some money. . . ."

—*The Washington Post*[8]

As bad as China's pension crisis may be, its health-care problems may be worse. China spends only about 6% of its GDP on health care. This compares to about 8% percent in Japan and fully 14% in the United States.[9]

There is a shortage of doctors, and sick people are forced to pay for their health care upfront. Those lacking the means to pay are cast out of hospitals and left to die an often slow and painful death. A big part of the problem is the cost of medical insurance—$50 to $200 per year[10]—in a country where the annual per-capita income for the vast majority of the population remains well below $1,000.

The situation has not always been so. During the first three decades after Mao assumed control in 1949, China developed a low-cost model of state-provided health care. It was a system that relied heavily on both state-funded hospitals and the so-called barefoot doctors who traveled from village to village and ran rural clinics.

In the so-called *Danwie* system, state-provided health care for civil servants (*gongfei yiliao*) was funded by taxation. Workers and their families in China's industrial sector were provided for by the state-run enterprises, and rural cooperatives financed their own plans. Thus, "the providers were the employers—the civil service, enterprise or cooperative—and they had a continuing duty of care for the worker after he or she had ceased work."[11]

The result of comprehensive health-care coverage was one of Mao's few great triumphs—a dramatic drop in infant mortality from 200 to 32 per 1,000 live births, and more than doubling life expectancy, from 35 to 71. The *Danwie* system also helped to limit measles and tuberculosis and eradicate other diseases such as schistosomiasis and syphilis.[12]

Today, however, this system has been totally shredded by China's economic reforms. The shredding began in the 1980s, and it has been as swift as it has been brutal. For starters, the decollectivization of farming abruptly ended the rural cooperative system. Almost immediately, the 90% of the rural peasantry that had been covered by China's health-care system plummeted to 10%.[13] At the same time, state-run enterprises were turned into profit-making entities, some of which cut health care to survive; others simply went bankrupt.

Between 1980 and 2004, the central government slashed funding for health care by more than half, from 36% to 17%. More significantly, however, under China's privatized model, doctors, hospitals, and pharmacies have been turned into "profit centers" expected to finance their activities through patient fees.

As part of the "reforms," the government continued regulating fees for basic health-care services and instituted price controls on selected drugs. Now hospitals are allowed to make whatever profits they can on the sales of both new drugs and high-technology tests.

The basic economic result has hardly been surprising: As hospitals have turned their pharmacies into profit centers and shared gains with the compliant physicians, doctors have been radically overprescribing drugs not covered by the price controls. Today, after hospitals and distributors mark up the prices of medicines, the retail price "can be 20 times higher than it is at the factory gate." That is why more than half of what Chinese patients pay for health care is devoted to pharmaceuticals, an astonishing statistic when compared to the roughly 15% average in most of the developed world.[14]

Doctors are also overprescribing new specialized treatments and tests that are not covered by price controls. Adding insult to injury, many Chinese find that the only way to get proper care, even if they can afford to enter a hospital, is by offering so-called red-envelope bribes.[15] Most heinously, according to China's own State Council Development Research Centre, some unscrupulous doctors have even "made patients more sick so they would buy more treatment."[16]

Not surprisingly, infant mortality in some of China's poorest regions is again on the rise[17] as the immunization rates for diseases such as TB, diphtheria, tetanus, and polio are steadily falling from levels that were close to 100% during the 1980s.[18] TB is again surging.[19] Add a rapidly expanding HIV/AIDS crisis (discussed later in the chapter) and the specter of exotic diseases such as bird flu and SARS and you have all the ingredients of a health-care meltdown.

The Environmental Protestors and Beggar Thy Neighbors

Choking on vile air, sickened by toxic water, citizens in some corners of this vast nation are rising up to protest the high environmental cost of China's economic boom.

—Knight Ridder Newspapers[20]

[China's] leaders are now starting to clean up major cities, partly because urbanites with rising incomes are demanding

*better air and water. . . . By contrast, the countryside, home
to two-thirds of China's population, is increasingly becoming
a dumping ground. Local officials, desperate to generate jobs
and tax revenues, protect factories that have polluted for
years. Refineries and smelters forced out of cities have moved
to rural areas. So have some foreign companies, to escape regulation at home. The losers are hundreds of millions of peasants already at the bottom of a society now sharply divided
between rich and poor. They are farmers and fishermen who
depend on land and water for their basic existence.[21]*

—*The New York Times*[22]

China's health-care crisis is rapidly being compounded as China
becomes much more polluted than Western nations such as the
United States. All manner of cancers are on the rapid rise along with
emphysema and respiratory-related diseases. It is not just fisherman
and farmers in the rural heartlands who are angry over the devastation that China's severe pollution brings to their crops and catches
and health. Increasingly, city dwellers across China, particularly in
the wealthier cities, are protesting foul air and filthy water.

One perverse result is that the more politically powerful and
richer coastal areas—from Guangdong in the south to Shanghai on
the northeast coast—have begun to push the most polluting types of
development out of their areas and deeper and deeper into the countryside. In effect, these rich cities are doing exactly what Korean and
Japanese and Taiwanese and U.S. corporations have been doing in
China—exporting their pollution.

As Elizabeth C. Economy has noted about China: "No doubt
there is an economic food chain, and the lower you are, the worst off
your environmental problems are likely to be."[23] Environmental
dumping and "industrial sprawl" development are only serving to fan
further the flames of the rural peasantry's rebellious passions.

The anger over environmental degradation is as palpable as it is
complex. One villager astutely and succinctly explained his willingness

to fight the police: "They are making poisonous chemicals for foreigners that the foreigners don't dare produce in their own countries. It is better to die now, forcing them out, than to die of a slow
suicide."[24]

The complexity of the rural peasantry's anger over the onslaught
of development is aptly illustrated by the following sidebar.

The Angry Chinese Blogger

*Huaxi is a village in Zhejiang Province near the Yangtze River
Delta. In an event widely covered by the international press, a
protest begun by a few hundred elderly women exploded into a
full-scale riot involving 30,000 people and thousands of police.[25]
This abridged and edited excerpt from the "Angry Chinese
Blogger"[26] illustrates how an explosive mix of environmental problems, forced evictions, and government corruption are creating a
thousand such points of conflict across China:*

The betrayal of Huaxi began one morning when many of the village's farmers woke up to find that the land that they had been
farming suddenly belonged to someone else. Their Village Committee had signed a lucrative deal to hand the land over to authorities in Dongyang, a city close to the village.

When pressed on the issue, Chen Qixian, a spokesperson for
authorities in Dongyang, said the land deal was completely above
board and, indeed, it was. These Village Committees are Communist controlled and they have the right to act on behalf off the villagers without their consent.

Soon after the deal was sealed, developers began the construction
of 13 chemical factories, some privately owned, other's owned by
the state. Despite the value of the land and the profitable factories
that were built on it, villagers saw little in the way of compensation.
The likely reason: The monies had been siphoned off by corrupt
local government officials in collusion with the Village Committee.

Though the seizure of land was a setback, some villagers believed
the factories might be beneficial, bringing the village jobs and

infrastructure such as the concrete roads needed to bring supplies into the area to feed the factories. Any such benefits, however, were soon to be outweighed by the costs.

The problems began with the local plant life: trees, grass, and other vegetation near the chemical plants started to die. Soon thereafter, farmers living further from the factories found that their crops were either dying in the fields or becoming inedible.

Next it was the turn of villagers themselves. Many began to experience health problems, babies began to be born with unusual birth defects and others were stillborn. Meanwhile, the Huashui River, used by villagers for watering animals, washing clothes, and irrigation, turned the color of low-grade diesel fuel, a sick and dirty brown.

As problems mounted, villagers complained to local authorities, but their concerns were dismissed. In desperation, residents sent a party to petition Beijing for assistance directly, but their petition was unceremoniously ignored.

The final straw came when Tan Yong, the mayor of Dongyang, barred the villagers from attending a supposedly open "meet-the-public" forum that would have allowed them to air their grievances. Shortly thereafter, around 200 people, mostly elderly women from the village's "old people's association," erected a blockade on the road leading up to the industrial compound that housed the offending factories. Their aim: to starve the factories out of commission by preventing supplies from being delivered.

The government responded by bussing in thousands of police armed with cutlasses, clubs, and tear gas canisters. The protest soon mushroomed into a huge riot involving more than 30,000 people.

Although tragic, the story of Huaxi is hardly unique. Annually, thousands of acres of farmland are being lost to urban and industrial development. There is also little or nothing that peasants can do to stop it because the Chinese system is weighed against them and because corruption involving the redistribution of agricultural land is rampant.

The Ticking HIV/AIDS Time Bomb

HIV/AIDS is a disease at once amazingly virulent and shockingly new. Only a generation ago, it lay undetected. Yet in the past two decades, by the reckoning of the Joint UN Programme on HIV/AIDS (UNAIDS), about 65 million people have contracted the illness, and perhaps 25 million of them have already died. The affliction is almost invariably lethal: scientists do not consider a cure to be even on the horizon. For now, it looks as if AIDS could end up as the coming century's top infectious killer.

—*Foreign Affairs*[27]

Today, the most serious HIV/AIDS crisis is unfolding not in China but in sub-Saharan Africa. This is an area where high-HIV-risk anal sex is commonly used as a birth-control mechanism, and the use of condoms is as rare as the availability of drug treatment. Here, more than 28 million people have been infected with the virus, with infection rates topping 30% in many countries and close to a mind-numbing 40% in Botswana.[28] As tragic as this crisis is from a humanitarian point of view, it remains a fairly small and isolated crisis from a global economic perspective. This is because the countries of sub-Saharan Africa contribute relatively little either to global commerce or military affairs.[29]

Note, however, that over the next several decades, the most serious HIV crises will be unfolding with brute force and far-reaching global economic implications in three powerhouse nations of Eurasia—India, Russia, and China.[30] Because of the long incubation periods associated with the disease (7 to 10 years), this epidemic is not scheduled to hit with full force until the period 2010 through 2020.

At present, it is India, not China, vying most ignominiously and successfully for the world reputation of worst future HIV crisis. Already, more than five million people have become infected in India. Because of a thriving heterosexual prostitution trade, strong cultural taboos against basic sex education, and widespread ignorance about prevention such as condom use, the epidemic is projected to grow even more serious over time.

Meanwhile, Russia has taken a different route. Because of an explosion of drug trafficking and IV drug use, a dramatic rise in promiscuity (as measured by a soaring number of out-of-wedlock births), an exponential rise in the sex trade, and a brutal prison system that serves as a giant rape room and incubator for the spread of the virus, Russia faces what may be the world's most serious economic crisis from HIV/AIDS.[31] Indeed, Russia's HIV/AIDS population has already soared past the one million mark, and it continues to grow rapidly. According to an analysis in *Foreign Affairs*, even a small epidemic will render the Russian economy stagnant, and a more severe epidemic would lower growth by an astonishing 40% by 2025.[32] It is worth understanding just how HIV/AIDS can have such a devastating impact on any economy, because the same type of HIV/AIDS braking system may soon be applied to the Chinese "economic miracle."

The Macroeconomics of HIV/AIDS

The emerging economic literature on the subject has identified some of the potential macroeconomic repercussions of AIDS-related illness and death. Population growth, labor supply, and savings rates all will be hurt—indeed the more comprehensive the framework employed, the more negative the conclusions seem to be.

Even so, a number of important potential economic ramifications of an HIV/AIDS epidemic in a low-income setting have as yet received little consideration. . . . First, by curtailing adult life spans, a widespread HIV epidemic seriously alters the calculus of investment in higher education and technical skills—thereby undermining the local process of investment in human capital. Second, widespread HIV prevalence could affect international decisions about direct investment, technology transfer, and personnel allocation in places perceived to be of high health risk. These factors suggest that an HIV breakout could have lasting economic consequences—in effect, cutting afflicted countries off from globalization. The long-run economic impact of these effects could be even more significant than the constraints the epidemic could impose on local labor supplies or savings.

—*Foreign Affairs*[33]

The grimmest economic reality of HIV/AIDs is that it strikes the most productive people in the work force—those between the ages of 20 and 40. The reason, of course, is that within this age bracket, people are most sexually active. Cut a big chunk of them out of the work force—or simply sicken many of them—and you have a direct hit on worker productivity.

Economists who have closely studied this problem have identified three particular types of costs of HIV/AIDS to employers and the broader economy. *End-of-service costs* include the payment of benefits and severance pay as well as funeral expenses. *Turnover costs* include increased job vacancies and the collateral costs of more recruitment and training. Plus, as higher-skilled workers are lost to the disease, companies and institutions lose the "know-how" of key employees who often cannot easily be replaced. Meanwhile, as already is being experienced in many African nations, healthier people have to work more overtime, causing stress and reduced efficiency.

Finally, there are *sickness-related costs*. These include obvious problems such as absenteeism, reduced productivity, increased management time to deal with HIV/AIDS-related problems, and medical care. There are also more subtle costs such as the productivity losses associated with attendance at funerals by co-workers and the lowering of morale. Numerous academic studies have shown a dramatic drop in worker productivity from HIV/AIDS. And, even if a worker is healthy, he or she may have to take time off to care for family members who are not.

At a macroeconomic level, HIV/AIDS does not just hit the factory floor and office buildings hard. It also hits the shopping malls, because HIV/AIDS lowers income and saving rates and thereby drives down the level of consumer spending—a key stimulus to GDP growth. Governments face a loss of tax revenues at the same time they face higher medical and social-service costs.

Many analysts believe that ultimately it will be China and not India or Russia that will face the most wrenching HIV/AIDS crisis and that the economic effects of this crisis will spill over most violently both into Chinese society and the broader world economy. In this grim scenario, total deaths from HIV/AIDS in China are projected to reach 40 million by the year 2025 in an "intermediate" scenario, and the epidemic will conservatively shave anywhere from 1% to 3% off China GDP growth rate.[34]

The question now to ponder is this: In a country not particularly noted for either homosexual activity or the same degree of sexual promiscuity as Brazil or Thailand, why is China emerging as the world's "factory floor" for the spread of HIV/AIDS? The answer to that question provides one of the most tragic and shameful tales in the annals of economic history because this is an epidemic that started out with all the best intentions—as a "poverty program" to lift the rural peasantry up by its bootstraps.

Of Bad Blood, Dirty Needles, and China's Sexual Revolution

Reports on HIV/AIDS in the official Chinese media tend to highlight intravenous drug use and unprotected sex as the main causes for the spread of the virus. A less well-publicized factor has been the operation of blood-collecting stations in many parts of China during the late 1980s and 1990s, particularly in several villages in Henan and other central provinces. Many of these were run by local government health departments, while others were illegal blood banks known as "bloodheads" (xuetou). They were established rapidly due to a highly profitable global demand for blood plasma. The blood-collection centres failed to implement basic safety checks in handling the blood, and as a consequence of the centres' poor practice, infections soared. . . . Estimates on the number of people infected in Henan Province alone through their use of such facilities range from 150,000 to over one million.

—Amnesty International[35]

In scientific terms, there are numerous "vectors" for the spread of HIV/AIDS. In most countries, sex and drugs top the list. However, a surprisingly large "conveyor belt" in China is that of former blood and plasma sales.[36] This vector involves one of the most tragic stories ever told in human history. It is a story about good intentions gone as bad as they can possibly go because of a volatile mix of bureaucratic foolishness, peasant ignorance, and entrepreneurial greed.

Vector One: "Poverty Relief" Kills

Donating blood is glorious.

—Propaganda material for blood donors

We all sold our blood to make money. We sold blood to pay the local taxes, to support our kids through school, and to make a living. By working on the farm we can't make money. We actually lose money. They paid us 40 RMB (5 USD) each time we sold them blood.

—A middle-aged female peasant from Henan Province[37]

They line the dusty roads outside the tiny villages of China's Henan Province, several hours' drive from Beijing—mounds of dirt funneled into crudely shaped cones, like a phalanx of

> *earthen bamboo hats. To the uninitiated, they look like a clever new way of turning over fields—an agricultural innovation, perhaps, meant to increase crop yields. But the locals know the truth. Buried under the pyramids, which now number in the thousands, are their mothers and fathers, brothers, sisters and cousins, all victims of AIDS. Like silent sentries, the dirt graves are a testament to China's worst-kept secret.*
>
> *—Time*[38]

The story of the "bloodheads" begins in China's heartland in the early 1990s, in some of the most desperately poor rural provinces in the country—Anhui, Hebei, Hubei, Shandong, Shanxi, Shaanxi, and, as we shall see, worst of all, Henan. Together, these seven provinces are home to more than 400 million people, and per-capita annual income hovers well below $500.

As part of China's economic reforms, bureaucrats hatched a plan to address rural poverty by capitalizing on high demand in both the domestic and international markets for blood and blood plasma. Economically, this seemed to be a stroke of bureaucratic genius.

China's hospital system faces a chronic shortage of blood because of the absence of any "donor culture" that motivates the numerous "blood drives" in places such as the United States. Globally, some 60% of the world's blood supply goes to less than 20% of the world's population, and "with an aging population, advances in medical treatments and procedures requiring blood transfusions, the demand for blood continues to increase in wealthy countries."[39]

Chinese entrepreneurial bureaucrats hoped to make a killing in this market by mobilizing the peasantry to give blood on a for-hire basis. Initially, the government's efforts focused on simply collecting just blood, but they quickly realized that frequent donations dramatically increase the risk of anemia. To maximize profits—and to best boost peasant incomes—they discovered the best business model involved extracting the plasma from the peasants' blood, then re-injecting the red and white blood cells and corpuscle material back

into the peasants. This prevented anemia, allowing peasants to contribute plasma much more frequently—as often as four to six days in
a row with a few days rest in between.[40]

The problem with the plan was the way doctors and nurses
returned the peasants' blood after the plasma extraction. In Western
hospital clinics, the plasma extraction can be done on an individual
basis in a single pass. In China, however, it was a two-stage process in
which blood was first drawn and the plasma separated.

In the deadly second stage, doctors would *combine* the plasma-
less blood into a common pool based on blood type. They would then
draw from this common pool to re-inject blood back into their
donors. *No more efficient way of spreading HIV, Hepatitis C, and
other viruses has ever been created.*

This trauma was further compounded by the regular reuse of
dirty needles, contaminated transfusion equipment, and blood containers. This "medical waste" was supposed to be disposable and dis-
posed of, but scavengers quickly learned to root the contraband out
of the trash and resell it. Penny-pinching hospital administrators
learned a similar lesson. This type of recycling was particularly deadly
because it led to the spread of the virus even faster across the donor
pool. At the same time, recipients of the donated blood were being
rapidly infected both through dirty blood transfusions and the use of
contaminated needles and equipment.

Now here is the even greater tragedy: When the Chinese bureaucracy figured out it was mass-producing HIV/AIDS victims as part of a
poverty program, it stopped. However, into the vacuum stepped a cadre
of entrepreneurs who had become, like the leaches of nineteenth-
century medicine, part of the whole plasma business. These were the
so-called bloodheads (*xuetou*). As the Chinese bureaucracy rapidly
retreated from its program, the bloodheads stepped in—and stepped
up—the production of plasma and further accelerated the spread of the
virus. This went on for *years* after the Chinese government outlawed
the practice.

In typical Chinese fashion, the government has refused to divulge the extent to which HIV/AIDS has spread as a result of these activities. Estimates place the number of fatalities in Henan Province alone at more than one million.[41] In addition, tens of thousands of children live as orphans in these provinces. To this day, the central government refuses to come clean on this scandal—and has even promoted many of the bureaucrats who originally ran the program.[42]

Adding insult to injury, there have "been reports of corruption and embezzlement of funds earmarked for Henan's AIDS catastrophe."[43] As AIDS activist Wan Yanhai has put it: "We are concerned that some Henan Province officials who made money for years selling blood will now have the chance to make fortunes for themselves on AIDS prevention."[44]

Vectors Two and Three—Drug Use and Prostitution

As Beijing has boosted trade links with Southeast Asia, the frontiers between Yunnan, Burma, and Laos have become porous—in some places, the border is just a low fence used primarily by heroin addicts, who lean on it as they shoot up with some of the most potent "China White" smack in the world.

—*World Policy Journal*[45]

Ruili stands on the border with Myanmar, which provides a constant supply of drugs. Also pouring over the border are the Burmese prostitutes who work in the salons and massage parlours close to the lorry park [truck stop] by the crossing-point. These girls are poor, and cheap; some earn as little as 5 yuan (about 60 cents) per customer. Many carry sexually transmitted diseases, and some are HIV-positive. They may have read the sign by the frontier post that shows a tightly furled condom, held in a delicate female hand, with a message recommending its use for health, happiness and protection against AIDS, but the girls are often too poor, or too intimidated, to refuse a client, often a truck-driver, who insists on unprotected sex.

—*The Economist*[46]

[Ruili is] the wildest place in China, and the girls are even more liberated than Americans.

—A Guangdong businessman[47]

It is an interesting question as to how the HIV virus originally found its way to contaminate blood supplies in remote farming provinces such as Henan and Anhui. The answer lies in the second and third major vectors for HIV/AIDS transmission in China. These vectors are found at the nexus of drug addiction and sexual promiscuity in Yunnan and Xinjiang Provinces in the morally weak southern and western underbelly of the Chinese drug and sex economy.

Yunnan is China's fourth-largest province and has a well-deserved reputation for renegade activity and resistance to central-government authority. Yunnan is also one of China's poorest provinces and a major gateway for Southeast Asian opium and heroin from the Golden Triangle, bordering as it does the major opium producer in Southeast Asia, Burma (Myanmar).

As with the bloodhead scandal, official Chinese government policy has played a key role in creating not just a drug monster but also an effective HIV/AIDS incubator in Yunnan. In an effort to boost that province's fortunes, in 1992, the central government assigned special privileges to investors along the border area. It also built an improved highway system to facilitate cross-border trade.

The result has been the emergence of boom towns such as Ruili that make the United States gold rush towns of Dodge City and Deadwood look tame. It was in Ruili in 1989 that the "first known epidemic of HIV in China was discovered among injecting drug users"[48] Since that time, "the drug trafficking route that started in

Yunnan has extended north along the impoverished and predominantly ethnic western provinces to Xinjiang, with HIV transmission following in its wake."[49]

It should certainly be no mystery why HIV/AIDS is spreading like wildfire along China's new opium roads—and moving deep into China's heartland. Drug addicts are sharing needles. Rates of infection are estimated to be as astonishingly high as 70% in the border areas.[50] Prostitutes infected by a customer or their own drug habit pass the virus on to truckers. Then, on an HIV/AIDS conveyor belt almost as efficient as the bloodhead scandal, Yunnan's truckers— some 400,000 of whom pass through Ruili a year—travel the length and breadth of China passing the virus on to other prostitutes, girlfriends, or wives. Faithful wives, infected by their spouses returning from the frontier towns, then pass the virus on to their fetuses.

Meanwhile, China's Triad gangs import more and more drug product into major cities of China such as Shanghai and Beijing where affluent middle- and upper-class "Little Emperors" engage in risky sexual and drug-injection practices. In these big cities, there is also a 1960s-style sexual revolution in full bloom—both straight and gay.[51] Sexually transmitted disease rates have soared more than a hundred-fold since the 1980s economic reforms.[52]

On top of all this, there is an astonishing ignorance of the dangers. Almost 20% of Chinese have never heard of HIV/AIDS,[53] and more than 80% of those infected with the HIV virus do not even know that HIV/AIDS is their problem.[54] In addition, close to 80% of Chinese do not realize that condoms can help prevent its spread.[55]

Surveys suggest that almost half of IV drug users share needles, almost 90% of sex workers are unaware of the risks of contracting HIV, and more than half of the sex workers do not always use condoms.[56] On the demand side of the equation, sex-trade clients will often offer a high premium for unprotected "bareback" sex because of an aversion to the desensitizing effects of condoms. Only a small fraction of gay Chinese men use condoms at all.[57]

As if all of these vectors and catalysts for an HIV/AIDS epidemic were not enough, several additional "conveyor belts" for the disease pose dangerous threats in the next wave of the virus transmission. One such conveyor belt is the existence of the "floating population" (*liudong renkou*) of migrant workers discussed in Chapter 1, "The 'China Price' and Weapons of Mass Production." This floating population numbers more than 100 million, and more than 80% are "between 15 and 45 years, with more than half of them between 20 and 30 years"—prime sexually active periods.[58]

A second HIV/AIDS conveyor belt is China's large group of "unmarriageable males."[59] These are the "surplus" men who have resulted from China's one-child policy and a resultant highly skewed male-female ratio. Millions of these "unmarriageable" men will fall back on either high-risk prostitution or even higher-risk homosexuality to satisfy their sexual needs.

For these reasons, many experts believe that it will be China rather than either India or Russia that ultimately suffers the worst AIDS epidemic. At present, because of repression by the Chinese government, reliable statistics on the scope of the problem are impossible to find. Nonetheless, one thing is clear: Within a decade, unless the government and populace radically changes course, China will have more HIV/AIDS victims than any other nation save perhaps India—as many as 10 to 15 million by 2010, according to estimates by the United Nations[60] and U.S. Intelligence Council.[61] This HIV/AIDS crisis will put a tremendous strain on a health-care system that is already far from adequate. It will hit China's work force and consumer cadres right where it hurts—in the prime-age worker and spender demography. Moreover, it will do so at a time when China will already be struggling with the need to finance a pension system severely in the red.

11

HOW TO FIGHT—AND WIN!—THE COMING CHINA WARS

If I tell you how things are, I've told you why things cannot change.

—Professor Edward C. Banfield[1]

This sobering observation from one of Harvard's great conservative professors would suggest that there is little or nothing that can be done to prevent the coming conflicts with China. Although I am a realist, I do not share this "council of despair."

Instead, I believe this: If all the major stakeholders in the Coming China Wars come to understand the high stakes involved, appropriate steps can be taken, all of which are difficult.

What is missing from the current political and policy calculus is any real sense of urgency about this mission. Instead, we as consumers and corporate executives and government policy makers and voters blithely go about our business as if no storm clouds are on the horizon—much less the prospect of a series of potentially devastating economic, ecological, and military conflicts with, and within, the world's most populous nation. The primary purpose of this book has been to raise the level of economic and political awareness sufficiently to a level that will allow all of us—including the Chinese—to begin to think much more deeply about how to stop the Coming China Wars and to participate in the set of hard choices that must be made.

There remains the question of what exactly the appropriate steps are. After a lengthy survey of the policy landscape, I believe the problem is not so much that of knowing what the "policy prescriptions" are. They are, in fact, well known. Rather, it is having the political will to adopt them. It is to these two issues and the inexorable tension between policy prescriptions and political will that this book now addresses.

The Policy Prescriptions

The Bush administration declared Tuesday that the United States has entered a new phase in its economic relationship with China and promised "rigorous enforcement" of laws aimed at curbing unfair trade practices. The pledge was contained in a 29-page administration review of America's economic relationship with China that was released four days after the government reported that the United States recorded a $202 billion trade deficit with China last year. That's the highest ever recorded with a single country and up 25 percent [from the previous year].

That deficit has brought renewed pressure from Congress for President Bush to be more forceful in cracking down on what China's critics see as blatant unfair trade practices in currency manipulation, theft of intellectual property and China's refusal to honor all the market-opening commitments it made when it became a World Trade Organization member in 2001.

U.S. Trade Representative Rob Portman, whose office prepared the new review, said the administration intended to use "all options available" to address various problems with China. "Our U.S.-China trade relationship lacks equity, durability and balance," Portman said at a news conference. "As a mature trading partner, China should be held accountable for its actions and required to live up to its responsibilities."

—*The Seattle Times*[2]

Many of the policy prescriptions to fight the Coming China Wars are straightforward. They have been discussed in numerous policy circles and featured in debates and negotiations in the U.S. Congress, both Asian and European parliaments, and bilateral negotiations between the Chinese and many other countries.

Consider, for example, the problem of rampant Chinese counterfeiting and piracy. The obvious "hard line" policy here is for the United States, the countries of Europe, and other nations of the world to adopt a "zero-tolerance" policy toward intellectual property theft. Any countries that violate this policy should be held to full account in bodies such as the World Trade Organization and punished accordingly.

The international tightening of border security to more effectively interdict pirate and counterfeit goods would synergistically serve other goals, too, particularly in the United States. Such goals range from reducing the risks from terrorism and interdicting illegal drugs to clamping down on the trade in "precursor chemicals" from China (and elsewhere), which are used to produce the "hard-drug four": cocaine, Ecstasy, heroin, and speed.

In a similar way, consider the spillover of Chinese environmental pollution onto the broader global stage. One solution is to set minimum environmental (and health and safety) standards in every multinational and bilateral trade agreement. This was done, albeit with some limited success, in the *North America Free Trade Agreement* (NAFTA). By adopting—and enforcing!—such standards in a free-trade framework, all nations of the world, not just China, would be forced to compete on a level playing field. The environment and people's health would be much the better for it.

To further combat China's global pollution, the governments of countries that have large foreign direct investments in China, such as the United States, Japan, Korea, and Taiwan, should not tolerate it when their own business enterprises set up shop in China simply to avoid more stringent restrictions in the home country—and nor should the Chinese! Such environmental "beggaring of thy neighbor" not only has significant ecological effects; it also costs the "home countries" domestic jobs and hollows out manufacturing capabilities necessary for longer-term economic growth *and* national security.

China's immoral and opportunistic use of its U.N. veto as a diplomatic shield for all manners of outrage is nothing short of reprehensible and intolerable. China's actions in countries ranging from the Sudan and Zimbabwe to Iran have not only led to the mutilation, death, and repression of millions of people but also have raised dramatically the stakes in the global arms race. This maneuver threatens the very viability of the United Nations itself and questions its viability as anything remotely resembling a cohesive world organization capable of bringing the rule of law and the cause of peace to far corners of the world.

The obvious step is for the United States, Europe, and key Asian nations to condemn China's actions in the strongest of terms and, if China's abuses of power continue, seek to strip China of its permanent veto. Thus far, however, key members of the United Nations have only been able to limply wring their hands or look the other way.

There is also the matter of the world's heavy and ever-increasing dependence on foreign oil. In a world where $100-a-barrel oil may soon be a floor rather than a ceiling, China's highly confrontational "energy diplomacy" is likely to become a major flash point, particularly in Sino-U.S. relations. A "Manhattan Project-style" commitment to reducing oil-import dependence in both the United States and Europe, through the full-scale development of alternative fuels and through increased, technology-mediated conservation, would go a long way toward reducing tensions with China. In addition, as with tightening border security, the ending of what President George Bush once called "an addiction to oil" would synergistically serve numerous other goals, too, from reducing military and political conflict in the Middle East to slowing the process of global warming.

What virtually all these policy prescriptions share in common—and why they represent "hard choices"—is that they require the economic and political will to stand up to China, along with the military might to back up the prescriptions. The policies also, in many cases, entail significant short-run economic costs. For example, raising global environmental standards will raise the cost of manufacturing goods, tightening border security puts further pressure on an already strained budget, and reducing oil import dependence would require a fairly massive industrial realignment.

A Mutually Parasitic Economic Codependence

There is surely something odd about the world's greatest power [the United States] being the world's greatest debtor. In order to finance prevailing levels of consumption and investment, must the United States be as dependent as it is on the discretionary acts of what are inevitably political entities in other countries?

It is true and can be argued forcefully that the incentive for Japan or China to dump treasury bills at a rapid rate is not very strong, given the consequences that it would have for their own economies. That is a powerful argument, and it is a reason a prudent person would avoid immediate concern. But it surely cannot be prudent for us as a country to rely on a

kind of "balance of financial terror" to hold back reserve sales
that would threaten our stability.

—Former U.S. Secretary of the Treasury Lawrence
Summers[3]

Nowhere is the problem of a lack of political will to confront China more problematic than in the United States—the continuous shrill chatter of "tough talk on China" notwithstanding. The sad irony is that although the United States is the world's best hope for challenging China's strong bid for world economic hegemony, it has also been the world's greatest failure in doing so. The underlying problem for both the United States *and* China is the highly destructive economic relationship each country now has with the other, a relationship driven by political pandering within each country and founded on a mutually parasitic economic codependence.

Far too many U.S. politicians, from the White House and Capitol Hill to the Federal Reserve and Treasury Department, do not have the courage to embrace either fiscal restraint or monetary responsibility. Instead of living within its means, the United States and its politicians have used large and chronic budget deficits together with ultra-"easy-money" policies to keep American consumers and voters happy—or at least pacified. The results in the United States are chronic budget and trade deficits. In the short run, these "twin deficits" allow Americans to enjoy a higher standard of living, but they do so only by hocking the country's longer-term future.

Of course, the biggest beneficiary from America's fiscal and monetary irresponsibility is China—for one obvious reason and for another reason far more subtle. The obvious reason comes from the fact that tax cuts and easy money and a lack of fiscal restraint have left Americans flush with cash to buy more Chinese products and thereby create more Chinese jobs. (Never mind that this "cash" is often borrowed and these profligate ways have left far too many Americans with unmanageable debt loads.)

The more subtle reason comes from the numerous opportunities for "financial blackmail" by China that the lack of fiscal restraint and monetary irresponsibility of the United States now are bringing. Such blackmail is alluded to in the preceding "balance of financial terror" excerpt from former Treasury Secretary Lawrence Summers and can only be understood by first understanding how the United States is financing its budget and trade deficits.

For the United States to run large budget deficits, there must be someone willing to buy U.S. government bonds. That's where China comes in. In less than a decade, China has vaulted to the top of the U.S. creditor heap and will soon surpass Japan as the single largest holder of U.S. debt. By buying so much of American debt, China is able to maintain a huge trade surplus with the United States—and thereby contribute mightily to chronic U.S. trade deficits. This result occurs because the recycling of U.S. dollars from China back into U.S. financial markets artificially suppresses the value of China's currency, the *yuan*, relative to the dollar. That helps keeps Chinese exports relatively cheap and U.S. exports to China relatively expensive.

The concept of "mutually parasitic economic codependence" comes in when China runs the dollar-recycling shell game on the United States because China's own pandering leaders do not want to run the political risk of the slower economic growth that a fairly valued Chinese currency would bring. From the Chinese government's perspective, the clear danger is a revolt of the masses. Slower growth also poses a clear threat to China's policy of rapid urbanization to address politically volatile rural poverty. Similarly pandering U.S. politicians allow this shell game to be run because they want to keep consumers and voters fat, dumb, and happy—and themselves in power. As a result, the game between the United States and China goes on and on.

Here, however, is the blackmail part and the increasing danger: As China acquires more and more U.S. securities, it has an increasing ability to destabilize U.S. financial markets and plunge the United States into recession. All China has to do to send U.S. interest rates

and inflation soaring is to stop buying new U.S. government securities. If China wants to trigger a crash in the U.S. stock and bond
markets—say, to back off the United States from protectionist tariffs
or to lessen its political will toward protecting Taiwan—all China has
to do is to start dumping large amounts of its current U.S. holdings.

From this discussion, it should be obvious why the United States,
over time, is becoming increasingly unable to stand up to the Chinese
on everything from piracy and counterfeiting to currency manipulation and unfair trade practices. To put it most simply, the balance of
financial terror that Summers refers to in the preceding excerpt is
rapidly shifting in favor of the Chinese to an imbalance of blackmail-
ing clout.

From this discussion, it should be equally obvious that the United
States will never be able to credibly and effectively challenge China
until it gets its own house in order. It should also be obvious that
every U.S. citizen—as well as consumers and voters around the
world—will have to understand the real and dangerous hidden costs
that are embedded in the purchase of cheap Chinese goods. This
book has directed its primary focus toward raising the level of awareness of the complexity and reach of the Chinese threat.

Will It Be the Hungry Dragon or Huggable Panda?

*Against a background of rising rural unrest, China has
unveiled ambitious plans to help its 800 million citizens living
in the countryside catch up economically with people in the
cities. More rural investment and agricultural subsidies and
improved social services are the main planks of a policy to
create a "new socialist countryside," which the president, Hu
Jintao, says is a priority. . . . But the ability of the central government to implement the policy is unclear. President Hu has
been promising "harmonious development" for three years,
but many profit-focused local authorities have balked at the*

cost of measures to protect the environment and improve industrial safety.

—*The Guardian* (London)[4]

A shift in China's economic discourse has begun, with the emphasis on high GDP rates moving to the very nature of growth itself—the nation's economic focal point has now focused on the importance of "sustainable growth" and "balanced development."

—*China & the World Economy*[5]

Just as the United States must get its own political and economic houses in order to fight the Coming China Wars, so, too, must the Chinese, particularly if they are to deal with their many wars from within. At least there are some signs of progress.

China's latest Five-Year Plan, unveiled in 2006 with great fanfare by President Hu Jintao and Premier Wen Jiabao, marks a significant evolution, if not altogether dramatic shift, from its "Adam Smith on steroids" growth-at-any-cost approach. The centerpiece of this plan is a strong commitment to "sustainable growth" and "balanced development," and it hits many of the right notes.

For example, the plan promises to shift spending priorities away from huge public-works projects such as dam building and water-diversion projects to more bread-and-butter issues such as additional funding for rural health care, better roads and communications networks, safe drinking water, methane facilities to power rural villages, and free compulsory education and textbooks for peasant children.[6]

The plan also seeks to cut the country's use of energy per unit of GDP output by 20% by 2010. More broadly, President Hu has declared that "saving energy and protecting the environment should also be considered a basic state strategy," and he has recommended "the country should promote recycling and the comprehensive use of resources."[7]

To combat rural poverty, the plan seeks to abolish the hated farm taxes and raise farm subsidies and promises to crack down hard on polluters, build more "green buildings," and impose environmental taxes on everything from golf balls and yachts to chopsticks.

On the surface, the chopsticks tax seems comical. It is, however, a serious environmental step. As noted in the London *Independent*: "The tax on chopsticks will come as a shock to a nation which uses them for breakfast, lunch and dinner, and where many people have never used a knife and fork. The Chinese use 45 billion pairs of disposable chopsticks every year, which adds up to 1.7 million cubic metres of timber or 25 million fully grown trees."[8]

More broadly, on the international stage, Chinese leaders now routinely promise currency readjustments and the lowering of tariffs and trade barriers. They also have made repeated big shows about cracking down on piracy and counterfeiting.

On the surface, all of these commitments, both to the Chinese people and the rest of the world, would seem to provide cause for optimism. The question is whether these commitments will be little more than the usual lip service from stonewalling Beijing bureaucrats, while the economic juggernaut continues to spin out of control. Consider this passage from the *Christian Science Monitor*, which represents a microcosm of China's lack of real policy commitment. It highlights the internal contradiction between China's ability to "talk a green streak" while failing abysmally to "walk the talk."

> Since China began seeking the Olympics and foreign investment in the 1990s, its leaders and city planners have talked a great "green" game that has left many foreign-based environmentalists swooning. On March 7, as part of the newest five-year plan, the construction ministry issued a new edict requiring that by June all new construction be 50 percent more energy efficient.
>
> But the actual record on energy- and resource-friendly construction in China remains mixed at best. The green visions of

ecology-minded policymakers vie with the realities of a nation rebuilding its urban centers day and night, with aggressive developers, impatient construction firms, quick money, and a floating population of as many as 400 million workers needing housing in coming decades.

Few Chinese developers or experts feel the nation will match the March 7 edict for energy efficiency. "We can't enforce it," explains a knowledgeable government source in Beijing.[9]

That's why in dealing with China, it always much more important for often surprisingly naïve Westerners to watch carefully what China does rather than to listen to what it says. This points to a broader problem: Just how much reform can the central government impose on a country in which local and provincial governments hold the power of the purse, a tiny fraction of the country controls more than half of the wealth, corruption is deeply engrained in the social fabric, peasants and workers are growing increasingly restive, the ecology is already strained to the breaking point, as much as a third of the country's GDP relies on counterfeiting for its growth, the drug trade is becoming increasingly entrenched, an AIDS epidemic appears close to unstoppable, and foreign capital is gaining more and more control of the economic and political systems?

There is, of course, a bitter irony here. For even as China's state-subsidized companies roam the Earth imperialistically plundering in Africa and Latin America and elsewhere, foreign corporations are doing much the same now in China—with similar environmental degradation and worker exploitation.

One final comment on China's economic strategy is in order: China's rolling of the dice on a massive urbanization drive to lift the income of the rural peasantry is a very high-risk maneuver. As the United States and other industrialized nations of the world learned during the Great Depression, moving people rapidly off the farms and into the factories is a recipe for far greater economic volatility once an economic slowdown hits. The reason: Farmers can always fall back during hard times on subsistence living. However, factory workers, separated from their land, can only stream into the streets in protest.

Concluding Remarks and the Nuclear Elephant in the Room

While stateless terrorists fill security vacuums, the Chinese fill economic ones. All over the globe, in such disparate places as the troubled Pacific Island states of Oceania, the Panama Canal zone, and out-of-the-way African nations, the Chinese are becoming masters of indirect influence—by establishing business communities and diplomatic outposts, by negotiating construction and trade agreements. Pulsing with consumer and martial energy, and boasting a peasantry that, unlike others in history, is overwhelmingly literate, China constitutes the principal conventional threat to America's liberal imperium.

—*Atlantic Monthly*[10]

[T]he Pentagon has issued its annual assessment of China's military modernization . . . as an internal policy debate between panda-huggers and dragon-slayers rages. Is China an economic ally with dramatic internal challenges, or an economic rival with long-range goals it may someday seek to achieve through military power? One disturbing and consistent theme is the United States' curious lack of strategic planning as to how the United States approaches such challenges—beyond threats to unleash the world's most powerful military.

—*Defense News*[11]

I began my China journey more than 30 years ago during my days as a Peace Corps volunteer in Asia. At that time, the closest I ever got to a then very isolationist China was Taiwan, Hong Kong, and Macao. However, in traveling extensively through other countries ranging from Burma, Japan, and Korea to Laos, Malaysia, and Thailand, I came to learn much about the economics, politics, and culture of the region. I also came to understand the heavy influence that China has always exerted on Asia's development, particularly through its overseas Chinese communities, which control much of Asia's business and commerce.

Today, China is a country very much open to travel. However, in many ways, it still remains closed to any real scrutiny. Sadly, much of this lack of transparency in Chinese affairs is the result of a self-imposed self-censorship by various stakeholders. Many Chinese journalists are forced to toe the party line for fear of beatings and torture,[12] and at least some foreign correspondents voluntarily pull their punches for fear of losing what has become a plum posting.[13] Some foreign companies such as Google and Yahoo! willingly assist the Chinese government in silencing dissident voices, while other foreign companies mute their criticisms for fear of being denied access to China's lucrative markets.[14] Meanwhile, China scholars and more policy-oriented China watchers alike sometimes self-edit their analyses and critiques for fear of being denied a university job in China or, in the case of foreigners, merely access to the country.

Because many of the potential critics of China have come to constitute a new "silent majority" who remain tight-lipped out of self-interest, far too much of the current debate has become needlessly polarized. This shrill debate pits ardent supporters of China—derisively dubbed Panda Huggers or Sinopologists—against the so-called hard-line Dragon Slayers or China Bashers. The result of this polarization—and the abdication of any policy analytic responsibility by the silent majority—has been to generate far more heat than light and far too little real policy movement. This book is a carefully researched attempt to break free from the chains of repression and non-fact-based rhetoric that has characterized so much of the current debate.

In closing, I note that for the most part I have purposely avoided the topic of a possible "hot" *military* war with China. Instead, I have focused much more narrowly on the many impending *economic* conflicts with China. I have adopted this presentation strategy because I believe that any sharp focus on the specter of Chinese and U.S. military forces going bayonet to bayonet—with a real possibility of an exchange of nuclear weapons—would detract from the essence of this book, which is to explore, in detail, the underlying economic origins of the myriad conflicts now facing us. It is time now, however, to at least briefly acknowledge the nuclear elephant in the room and some of the hot-button issues that might trigger either a conventional or nuclear war.

To lay the foundation for this discussion, it is first useful to note that the rate of China's military spending is growing even faster than its economy. Between 2000 and 2005, the Chinese military budget *doubled,* and annually that budget is growing by more than 10% a year.[15] Most broadly, as a recent Pentagon report noted, China appears intent on developing a longer-range military reach capable of waging war on any continent in the world.[16] Toward this end, China maintains the largest standing army in the world—more than two million troops. As noted in Chapter 4, "The 'Blood for Oil' Wars—The Sum of All Chinese Fears," China is also well on its way to deploying a blue water navy capable of challenging the only real naval power in the world—the United States. Within the context of China's growing military might, it is useful to identify at least six major military war triggers.

Trigger 1: Taiwan Twists in the Wind

The United States has promised to defend Taiwan against a Chinese invasion, and China has promised to invade if Taiwan declares its independence. Meanwhile, close to a half million Chinese troops stand at the ready to invade Taiwan, and each year China adds another 100 or so low-range ballistic missiles to its arsenal pointing at Taiwan. This arsenal already totals close to a thousand missiles.

Trigger 2: The Rising Sun Versus the Red Star

Economic relations between China and Japan have never been better. Japan's economy is growing again after more than a decade of economic stagnation, largely because of its burgeoning trade with China. China has benefited greatly from importing sophisticated Japanese technologies and Japanese management skills.

However, even as mutually beneficial economics unites the two countries, cold-steel politics and harsh rhetoric are driving them apart. As one flash point and long open wound, China continues to object to Japan's revisionist history of the Rape of Nanjing and other Japanese atrocities during the 1930s occupation of China. China has never forgotten that it was Japan that once turned Taiwan into a colony. There is also the close relationship Japan maintains with the United States, which is now strongly encouraging Japan to remilitarize as a way of providing countervailing power in the region. As noted in Chapter 4, one option now on the table is for Japan to join the ranks of the world's nuclear powers, which China would surely interpret as a very significant threat.

Japan, for its part, resents China's opposition "over what it views as China's attempts to use history as a weapon to keep Japan humiliated and subjugated as China rises," while "Japanese public opinion is at a historic low, fueled by a number of perceived provocations, such as the incursion of a Chinese nuclear submarine off the Okinawan coast in 2004, Beijing's opposition to Japan's bid for a permanent UN Security Council seat, Japan's own military build-up, and periodic anti-Japanese populist violence on the mainland." [17] Japan also rightly fears that once China reaches a higher level of economic development, Japan will become expendable and China will become far more of a dangerous competitor than a consumer of Japanese products.

Trigger 3: Pyongyang—Still Crazy After All These Years

As a charter member of the Bush administration's "axis of evil," North Korea's renegade regime of the dictator Kim Jong-Il provides a

constant irritant to the United States. It counterfeits millions of dollars
in U.S. currency, is a major conduit for the world's drug and arms trades,
and periodically threatens South Korea with a blitzkrieg-style invasion.

China currently provides the Pyongyang regime with two thirds
of its fuel and one third of its food.[18] In exchange, China is able to
exert at least some influence over North Korean policies. Yet in its
dealings with Pyongyang, China remains schizophrenic. On the one
hand, it wants the regime to remain in power because it fears Korean
unification would bring U.S. troops closer to its borders. On the other
hand, China views North Korea in much the same way as the West, as
a loose nuclear cannon with the potential to destabilize the region.

The one certainty in this relationship is its lack of any certainty.
This translates into high risk—the proverbial nuclear joker in the
deck—should famine or whim or any number of random events trigger a North Korean military outburst and force China to take sides.

Trigger 4: "'China Si', Yanqui No!"

In Latin America, China has brazenly sold arms and missiles to Cuba and
uses an old Soviet base of operations in Cuba to eavesdrop electronically
on the United States for both military and commercial espionage purposes. Equally troubling to U.S. defense analysts, China is helping Brazil
develop sophisticated satellite and satellite-tracking technologies. Such
capabilities can be used to track U.S. satellites and, in time of war, could
assist China in knocking the U.S. military satellites out of the skies.

There is also the "Panama Connection." After the United States
returned the Panama Canal Zone to Panama in 1999, a Chinese company, Hutchison Whampoa, with close ties to Beijing, successfully bid
to run canal operations. Under this Chinese oversight, the Panama
Canal has become a major transit point for everything from illegal
drugs and the precursor chemicals used to make them to weapons
and counterfeit goods.

Then there is China's dangerously provocative tango with the
populist anti-American president of Venezuela, Hugo Chavez.

Venezuela is the fourth-largest supplier of oil to the United States. It is also the United States' biggest Latin American antagonist. Even as the United States has sought to impose an arms embargo on Venezuela for its assistance to terrorist regimes, an ever-opportunistic China has stepped into the breach in the hopes of trading weapons for oil. An unrepentant Chavez taunts the United States with threats of turning over some of Venezuela's U.S. F-16 fighter jets to Cuba or Iran while China orchestrates a Latin American arms buildup of unprecedented proportions.

Common to each of China's Latin American forays is an increasingly antagonistic Yanqui-baiting. What China preaches quite effectively to Latin America's many populist leaders is a "multipolar world" in which China is a strategic partner against the "unipolar" domination of the United States. In its quest for oil and raw materials and arms sales, China continues to raise the stakes in a very dangerous poker game right in America's backyard.

Trigger 5: Mao of Arabia

As another key facet of its energy "diplomacy," China's extended courtships of Iran and other countries of the Middle East are now setting off alarm bells from Capitol Hill and the CIA to the Department of Energy and the Pentagon. China's attempt to drive a wedge between the long-standing close relationship between the United States and Saudi Arabia is particularly incendiary given the United States' large thirst for oil and the Saudi's standing as the largest global oil producer.

China's diplomatic shielding of Iran from sanctions by the United Nations for its attempts at nuclear proliferation moves the region closer and closer to a nuclear capability and a Middle East arms race. It has become an open, festering wound in the U.S.-China relationship.

Yet another wild card is Israel. With Iran's president promising to destroy Israel, Israel is moving toward a preemptive bomb strike on Iran's nuclear facilities—as Israel once did in Iraq when it crippled the Osirak light water reactor facility of Saddam Hussein in 1981.[19] By thrusting itself into the world's hottest hot spot, China is courting, rather than seeking to avoid, military conflict.

Trigger 6: The China-Russia Connection

For a ten-year period following the establishment of the People's Republic of China in 1949, China and the Soviet Union worked together in a close alliance. During this ever-so-brief Sino-Soviet thaw, China, aided by a large army of Soviet advisors, adopted the Stalinist model of heavy industrial economic development.

By 1959, what was to become a very deep "Sino-Soviet split" began. It was caused partly by sharp personal clashes between Mao and Soviet leader Nikita Khrushchev, partly by equally sharp conflicts over ideology and the direction of the Communist revolution, and partly by the natural enmity between Russia and China. Today, however, the Russian Bear and Chinese Panda are moving much closer together economically, militarily, and strategically.

Economically, China has become one of Russia's most important energy consumers, while Russia has become one of China's most important suppliers of sophisticated technologies and weaponry. Militarily, Russia and China launched their first joint military operation in 2005. Now, a new Chinese-Russian military alliance—once mercifully avoided during the peak of the Cold War era—is rising up to challenge the United States.

Strategically, the Defense Department has warily watched the emergence of Chinese-inspired, anti-American alliances such as the so-called Shanghai Cooperative Organization. This particular organization includes both China and Russia as well as the petroleum-rich Central Asian republics of Kazakhstan, Kyrgyzstan, Tajikistan, and Uzbekistan. It also includes India, Indonesia, Iran, and Pakistan as observers.

The Shanghai Cooperative Organization was originally formed to promote regional cooperation on the "three evils of terrorism, religious extremism, and separatism."[20] However, it is increasingly focused on ousting the U.S. military from its bases of operations in Central Asia. These bases have been critical in the war on terrorism, particularly in Afghanistan, and their loss would be a substantial blow to U.S. homeland security.[21]

✿　✿　✿

These six possible hot war triggers, together with the numerous cold economic wars documented in this book, add up to one of the most dangerous situations the world has ever faced. I hope to raise global awareness about the real risks looming before us. For the children's sake, let us all move forward now with the facts in hand and with all due speed toward the common goal of resolving the many differences both peacefully and prosperously.

ACKNOWLEDGMENTS

The book benefited greatly from numerous discussions and interviews conducted over a five-year period. I am particularly grateful to the many Chinese students in my business school classes at the University of California-Irvine from both the People's Republic of China and the Republic of China (Taiwan). Despite cultural barriers, many were willing to express and share their views candidly in both a classroom setting and private conversations.

The primary research for this book involved analyses of tens of thousands of pages of material from books, newspapers, magazines, scholarly journals, government agencies both within and outside China, international organizations such as the World Bank and World Health Organization, "think tanks," and numerous websites and blogs. On the *newspaper and magazine* front, one thing became abundantly clear during my China research. The vast majority of the print media is in full retreat when it comes to comprehensive international coverage. Faced with severe cost-cutting pressures from declining readerships and competition from the World Wide Web, international bureaus at major newspapers have been some of the first to feel the cuts. Perhaps because of this, certain newspapers and magazines clearly stand out above the rest in their China coverage, and I have found them useful in writing this book.

The *Economist* wins my own version of a Pulitzer Prize for its consistent and diverse coverage of China's many challenges. Only slightly less complete has been the coverage of *The New York Times*, with correspondents such as Joseph Kahn, Erik Eckholm, and Jim Yardley particularly noteworthy. *Reuters* provides an ongoing excellent stream of straight China news. British newspapers worth mentioning for their coverage include the *Financial Mail*, the *Guardian*, the *Observer*, and the *Times*.

Business Week's article on the "China Price" has proved to be an important event in the policy debate. The *Wall Street Journal* has added some interesting stories to the China oeuvre; however, the WSJ does not offer its archives as "open source" and available on the web but rather operates on a "pay-per-view" approach. As a result, the WSJ's impact on the China debate may be less than it otherwise might (and could) be.

Specific journalistic contributions worth noting include the hard-hitting articles of Joshua Kurlantzick and Stephanie Giry in *The New Republic;* the eloquent prose of Lindsay Hilsum and Moeletsi Mbeki in the London-based *New Statesman;* Vivienne Walt's fine piece in *Fortune* on Chinese imperialism in Africa; Mitchell Koss's pedal-to-the-medal vamp on methamphetamines in the *L.A. Weekly;* Edward Cody's insightful coverage for the Washington Post Foreign Service; Jane Bussey's and Glenn Garvin's journalistic jolt for the *Miami Herald* on the growing influence of China in Latin America; *Time* magazine's timely feature on AIDS in China; the data-driven and comprehensive AIDS coverage in *Foreign Affairs* in articles by Nicholas Eberstadt as well as co-authors Gill Bates, Jennifer Change, and Sarah Palmer; Andrea Mandel-Campbell's China coverage in

Canada's eminently readable news weekly *Maclean's*; James Nurton as well as Tony Chen and Pilar Woo on counterfeiting in the niche publication *Managing Intellectual Property;* and Jamie Doward's and Tony Thompson's eye-opening piece in the *London Observer* on the role of China in the international drug trade.

A number of English-language Chinese newspapers also deserve both mention and regular monitoring by any aspiring "China watcher." The *Asia Times Online* serves as a *de facto* international paper of record for much of what transpires in the PRC. The PRC-based and state-owned *China Daily* can provide useful information: however, it must always be taken with a grain of salt and independently verified because the paper is subject to significant censorship. The same must be said for the *People's Daily,* which is the official newspaper of the Communist Party of China and may be read to get the "official party line."

On Taiwan, three papers stand out: the *China Post,* the *Taiwan News,* and the *Taipei Times.* I also note the *Epoch Times,* which is the largest newspaper catering to overseas Chinese as well as one of the most controversial. This newspaper consistently provides hard-hitting stories about the PRC and is banned in the PRC. Because it clearly has an anti-PRC point of view, both its stories and facts must be carefully and independently verified. Nonetheless, the newspaper plays an important role in the ongoing debate and serves as a useful counterweight to the propaganda of the heavily controlled PRC press.

On the *government and organizational fronts,* the hearings and reports of the U.S.-China Economic and Security Review Commission represent valuable sources of both data and analyses as do, to a lesser extent, those of the Conference Board and the U.S. National Association of Manufacturers. The comments and candor of Pan Yue, the Deputy Director of China's State Environmental Protection Administration, have been particularly revealing, as have been those of numerous Chinese scholars, both within and outside the PRC.

Publications on various subjects relating to China by the World Bank, the World Health Organization, the World Dam Commission, and the U.S. Drug Enforcement Agency also proved useful to the research effort. Many of the international agencies do, however, appear to be somewhat constrained politically from fully assessing the situation fully.

In the *think tank* dimension, Stephen Johnson of the Heritage Foundation, Dan Blumenthal writing for the *Middle East Quarterly*, and Tashi Tsering writing for the Tibet Justice Center all deserve special accolades for their cogent analyses. The *Far Eastern Economic Review* and *China Business Review* also proved to be valuable *scholarly research* tools on a wide variety of subjects relating to China.

There are many fine *books* about China. Without a lack of respect for what is a vast literature, I want to note at least several books that would be a valuable part of any contemporary China watcher's bookshelf.

- John Bryan Starr's *Understanding China* quite lives up to its title. It is a wonderful guide to China's "economy, history, and political culture" that never gets too bogged down in the lengthy and often labyrinthine march through China's many dynasties.

- The wonderfully named Elizabeth C. Economy has set the gold standard in environmental reportage of China. Her *River Runs Black* should be required reading for every world leader and legislator and every Chinese citizen.

- Oded Shenkar's *The China Century* is a useful scholarly account of the impact of the Chinese economy on the world. His chapter on piracy and counterfeiting particularly shines. In a stylistic counterpoint, Ted Fishman's *China Inc.* is a useful kaleidoscope trip through the Chinese urban landscape and countryside.

- James McGregor's best-selling *One Billion Customers* provides an executive perspective on doing business in China with a totalitarian state and a corrupt bureaucracy. The little-read but equally compelling *Corruption and Market in Contemporary China* by Yan Sun should not be missed.

- *Regional Powerhouse* by Michael Enright, Edith Scott, and Ka-mun Chang is a long and often difficult slog, which also (unfortunately) has not yet sold many copies. However, the book's analysis of the Chinese economic model, particularly the use of so-called network clustering, is a sobering reminder to any politician or business person that beating China at its own low-cost manufacturing game will never be an easy task. It is also required reading for any businessperson seeking to open up shop in China.

In closing, I must offer my sincerest thanks and gratitude to Dr. Cynthia J. Smith, a lecturer in business and anthropology at Ohio State University, and author Russ Hall. Together with my editor Jim Boyd, they all dutifully read numerous drafts of the manuscript and provided constructive editorial and analytical remarks. Of course, any errors and omissions remain my own.

Peter Navarro
The University of California-Irvine
Merage School of Business
www.peternavarro.com

NOTES

Note to readers: Much of the research conducted for this book was done over the internet. For your convenience, I have provided the URLs of all references that were available at the time of this writing. I have also posted this "Notes" section of the book on my website at www.peternavarro.com/chinawars.html as a downloadable file. Each of the URLs appear in this file as hyperlinked text that you can click on and go right to the relevant page.

Chapter 1

1. Pete Engardio, Dexter Roberts, with Brian Bremner in Beijing, and bureau reports, "The China Price," *Business Week*, December 6, 2004. http://www.businessweek.com/magazine/content/04_49/b3911401.htm

2. Richard McGregor, *Financial Mail*, July 8, 2005.

3. See note 1 above.

4. The U.S. civilian labor force is roughly 150 million.

5. "China Confronts Problems of Growth," *Times* (London), September 30, 2003.

6. Jim Yardley, "Migrant Work Leaves Families Broken; The Great Divide/A Missing Generation," *International Herald Tribune/New York Times*, December 22, 2004.

7. Kim Peterson, "The Broken Iron Rice Bowl," *Dissident Voice*, August 18, 2003. http://www.dissidentvoice.org/Articles7/Petersen_ China-Growth.htm

8. "China: Quicken Urbanization Pace," *China Daily*, November 18, 1999.

9. Tong Xin and Lu Qingshuang, "China's Highly Dangerous Inverted T-Shaped Social Structure," *Epoch Times*, March 20, 2006. http://www.theepochtimes. com/news/6-3-20/39495.html

10. From 1988 to 1997, the average annual U.S. grain production was 395 million tons, but actual production ranged from 274 million tons (31% below the average) to 469 million tons (19% above the average). "Rail Officials to Participate in Grain Transport Conference." PR Newswire, July 23, 1998.

11. Joseph Kahn, "Chinese Girls' Toil Brings Pain, Not Riches," *New York Times*, October 2, 2003. http://www.international.ucla.edu/asia/rights/Chinesegirls031002.asp

12. By decree, there is only one "labor union" in China, and that is the Communist Party.

13. Joseph Kahn, "China's Workers Risk Limbs in Export Drive," *New York Times*, April 7, 2003. http://www.asria.org/ref/library/social/lib/031208_NYTimes_ sweatshops_inchina.pdf

14. R. H. McGuckin and M. Spiegelman, "China's Experience with Productivity and Jobs," The U.S. Conference Board, 2004. http://www.conference-board.org/ publications/describe.cfm?id=809

15. See note 1 above.

16. Michael Enright, Edith Scott, and Ka-Mun Chang, *Regional Powerhouse: The Greater Pearl River Delta and the Rise of China* (John Wiley & Sons, 2005), 57.

17. See generally Ibid.

18. Quoted in "Genuine Problem: Counterfeit Products from China Continue to Bedevil Makers of Legitimate Goods," *Journal of Commerce.* June 27, 2005.

19. "The Importance of Trade Remedies to the U.S. Trade Relationship with China," U.S.-China Economic and Security Review Commission, May 16, 2005.

20. The traditional economist's assumption of "holding other things constant" is critical here.

21. The Chinese claim to have changed to a more adjustable currency. However, little adjustment appears to be taking place, at least at the time of this book's writing.

22. Remarks by Commerce Secretary Donald L. Evans to the President's Export Council—American Chamber of Commerce in Beijing, China, June 23, 2004. http://hongkong.usconsulate.gov/uscn/trade/general/doc/2004/062301.htm

23. See note 19 above.

Chapter 2

1. Ted Fisherman, *China, Inc.* (New York: Scribner, 2005), p. 236.

2. Tim Phillips, *Knockoff: The Deadly Trade in Counterfeit Goods* (London: Kogan Page, 2005), 19.

3. "The Purse-Party Blues," *Time,* August 2, 2004.

4. Statement of Professor Daniel C. K. Chow, Congressional-Executive Commission on China, May 16, 2005. "Intellectual Property Protection as Economic Policy: Will China Ever Enforce Its IP Laws?" http://www.cecc.gov/pages/roundtables/051605/Chow.php

5. Oded Shenkar, *The Chinese Century* (Upper Saddle River, New Jersey: Wharton School Publishing), 88.

6. See note 2 above, quoted on pages 64–65.

7. Jeff Sanford, "Knockoff Nation," *Canadian Business,* November 8, 2004.

8. "China City Is Haven for Fake Fram, Bogus Bose," *Automotive News,* October 27, 2003.

9. "Counterfeiting Costs Auto Industry Billions," *Plastics News,* November 17, 2003.

10. Joann Muller, "Stolen Cars," *Forbes,* February 16, 2004. http://www.forbes.com/business/forbes/2004/0216/058.html

11. See note 8 above.

12. Tim Kraus (vice president, Heavy-Duty Market-Segment Association), "Counterfeiting: The 21st Century Crime," *Fleet Equipment,* March 2005.

13. See note 10 above.

14. James Nurton, "The New Battle Against Counterfeits," *Managing Intellectual Property.* October 2005.

15. Ibid.

16. See note 2 above, page 22.

17. See note 14 above.

18. Mathew Benjamin, "A World of Fakes," *U.S. News & World Report,* July 14, 2003.

19. See note 2 above, page 189.

20. See note 2 above, page 202.

21. See note 2 above.

22. See note 1 above, page 252.

23. Timothy P. Trainer, "The Fight Against Trademark Counterfeiting," *China Business Review,* November/December 2002.

24. "No End for China's Counterfeiting Contagion," *Women's Wear Daily,* October 11, 2004. http://www.betsylowther.com/counter1.html

25. "Vendors Step Up Efforts in Counterfeit War," *Women's Wear Daily*, April 11, 2005.

26. See note 5 above, page 90.

27. "Not All Is Fair in China's Booming Bike Business," *Bicycle Retailer & Industry News*, April 1, 2004.

28. See note 14 above.

29. See note 2 above, page 59.

30. See note 2 above, quoted on page 39.

31. See note 5 above, page 96.

32. See note 3 above.

33. "Fakes!" *Business Week*, February 7, 2005.

34. "Copyright Lesson," *Managing Intellectual Property*, April 2005.

35. See note 24 above.

36. See note 2 above, page 61.

37. Tony Chen and Pilar Woo, "China in 2004 and Beyond," *Managing Intellectual Property*. http://www.managingip.com/?Page=17&ISS=12730&SID=495719

38. Ibid.

39. "Toyota Lost a Lawsuit Against a Chinese Car Manufacturer," CCPIT Patent and Trademark Law Office. http://www.ccpit-patent.com.cn/News/2003123006.htm

Chapter 3

1. Peter Wonacott, "Polluters in China Feel No Pain," *Wall Street Journal*, March 24, 2004.

2. Gary Polakovic, "Asia's Wind-Borne Pollution a Hazardous Export to U.S.," *Los Angeles Times*, April 26, 2002. http://www.al.noaa.gov/ITCT/2k2/news.shtml

3. "Benxi is located in the eastern mountainous region of Liaoning Province. It is an important industrial raw material base of iron and steel, coal, building materials and chemical products. About 1.5 million people live in Benxi. During the past decades, Benxi has undergone drastic economic, social, and urban development, becoming one of the 17 largest cities in China." http://www.chinacp.com/eng/cpcities/cp_benxi.html

4. "Benxi to Experiment with Emissions Trading," U.S. Embassy in Beijing, June 2000. http://www.usembassy-china.org.cn/sandt/Benxiweb.htm

5. Joshua Kurlantzick. "Purple Haze," *New Republic*, August 30, 2004. http://www.tnr.com/doc.mhtml?i=20040830&s=kurlantzick083004

6. Matt Pottinger, Steve Stecklow, and John J. Fialka, "Invisible Export—a Hidden Cost of China's Growth: Mercury Migration," *Wall Street Journal*, December 20, 2004. http://yaleglobal.yale.edu/display.article?id=5058

7. "People in the felt-hat industry sometimes showed signs of mercury poisoning and came down with 'Mad-Hatter' syndrome. This is where the phrase 'mad as a hatter' originated and was the basis for the 'Mad Hatter' character in Lewis Carroll's book *Alice in Wonderland*." Quoted from "Get the MERCURY Out! The Effects of Mercury on the Nervous System," Neuroscience for Kids. http://faculty.washington.edu/chudler/merc.html

8. Carolyn Williams, "China: A Land Turned to Dust," *New Scientist*, June 4, 2005. http://www.newscientist.com/article.ns?id=mg18625021.400&feedId=earth_rss20

9. Jonathan Watts, "Satellite Data Reveals Beijing as Air Pollution Capital of World," *Guardian* (London), October 31, 2005.

10. "A Great Wall of Waste," *Economist*, August 21, 2004.

11. See note 6 above.

12. See note 6 above.

13. "Five Who Laid the Groundwork for Historic Spike in Oil Market," *Wall Street Journal*, December 20, 2005.

14. China's Acid Rain Pollution Worsens in 2003," *People's Daily*, March 25, 2004. http://english.people.com.cn/200403/25/eng20040325_138514.shtml

15. "Grapes of Wrath in Inner Mongolia," U.S. Embassy in Beijing, May 2001. http://www.usembassy-china.org.cn/sandt/MongoliaDust-web.htm

16. Ron Gluckman, "Beijing's Desert Storm," *Asiaweek*, October 13, 2000. http://www.gluckman.com/ChinaDesert.html

17. This is also spelled Mengzi or Meng-tzu.

18. Shi Yuanchun (professor and ex-president of China Agricultural University, and academician of the Chinese Academy of Sciences), "Reflections on Twenty Year's Desertification-Control in China." http://us.tom.com/english/2137.htm

19. "Asian Dust, Sand Storms Worsening, U.N. Says," MSNBC, March 31, 2004. http://www.msnbc.msn.com/id/4638243/

20. "Beijing Environment, Science and Technology Update for March 29, 2002," U.S. Embassy in Beijing. http://www.usembassy-china.org.cn/sandt/estnews032902.htm

21. See note 8 above.

22. Yang Youlin, Victor Squires, and Lu Qi, eds., "Global Alarm: Dust and Sand-storms from the World's Drylands," United Nations, Convention to Combat Desertification. June 2002. http://www.unccd.int/publicinfo/duststorms/menu.php

23. Lester R. Brown, "Deserts Invading China: From Ecological Deficits to Dust Bowl," in *The Earth Policy Reader* (New York: W.W. Norton & Co., 2002).

24. Peili Shi and Jintao Xu, "Deforestation in China." http://www.usc.cuhk.edu.hk/wk_wzdetails.asp?id=1290

25. Margaret Hsu and Laura Yee, "The Asian Brown Cloud," *Global Environmental Issues*. http://www.sfuhs.org/features/globalization/asian_cloud/

26. Michael Richardson, *South China Morning Post*, August 27, 2004.

27. "Warning by UN as Dust Storms Worsen," *Financial Times* (London), April 3, 2004.

28. Patrick Mazza and Rhys Roth, "Global Warming Is Here: The Scientific Evidence." http://www.climatesolutions.org/pubs/gwih.html

29. "World: Asia-Pacific China's Floods: Is Deforestation to Blame?" BBC, August 6, 1999. http://news.bbc.co.uk/1/hi/world/asia-pacific/413717.stm

30. See note 28 above.

31. "Global Warming," Natural Resources Defense Council. http://www.nrdc.org/globalWarming/f101.asp#1

32. Jim Yardley, "Rivers Run Black and Chinese Die of Cancer," *New York Times*, September 12, 2004. http://www.globalpolicy.org/socecon/develop/quality/2004/0912chinapollution.htm

33. "Bureaucracy: A Controversial Necessity," Democracy in America. http://www.learner.org/channel/courses/democracyinamerica/dia_8/dia_8_video.html

34. Victor Mallet, "Dirty Business: The Scale of China's Environmental Problems Defies an Optimistic Outlook," *Financial Times* (London), June 26, 2004.

35. See note 10 above.

36. Joseph Kahn, "Foul Water and Air Part of Cost of the Boom in China's Exports," *New York Times*, November 4, 2003.

Chapter 4

1. Patrick H. Donovan, "Oil Logistics: In the Pacific War," *Air Force Journal of Logistics,* Spring 2004. http://www.findarticles.com/p/articles/mi_m0IBO/is_1_28/ai_n6172425/print

2. Japan's incursions into what is now Indonesia also played a role while Great Britain joined in the boycott.

3. U.S.-China Economic and Security Review Commission 2004 Report to Congress, Washington: U.S. Government Printing Office, Chapter 6: China's Energy Needs and Strategies, 152.

4. R. L. Hirsch, R. H. Bezdek, and R. M. Wendling, "Peaking of World Oil Production: Impacts, Mitigation and Risk Management," *DOE NETL*, February 2005.

5. In 2005, China finished building its first tank farm in Zhenhai, which is located in the port city of Ningbo. This 33-million-barrel facility will hold about one third of China's planned reserves, but high oil prices have made it difficult to fill. (*China Daily,* September 2, 2005). Even when China's reserve is finished sometime over the next five years, it will only hold 20 days of consumption (102 million barrels versus the 700-million-barrel capacity of the United States).

6. In this regard, to noneconomists, it may seem counterintuitive to blame China for the kind of demand-driven oil price shocks that the world economy has

already begun to suffer from. After all, as just noted, it is the United States and not China that is by far the largest oil consumer. Economists, however, always look not at total consumption per se when determining price effects but rather at incremental consumption that occurs at the "margin." Viewed from this perspective, China's rapidly growing thirst for oil has been a highly disruptive influence on oil markets, which have had plenty of capacity to meet traditional U.S. and other world needs but now find themselves straining mightily to keep up with China's growing thirst at the market's margin.

7. "The Impact of Higher Oil Prices on The Global Economy," International Monetary Fund, December 8, 2000. http://www.imf.org/external/pubs/ft/oil/2000/oilrep.PDF

8. See note 4 above.

9. Mark Magnier, "China Stakes Claim for Global Oil Access," *Los Angeles Times,* July 17, 2005.

10. Stanly Lubman, "The Dragon as Demon: Images of China on Capital Hill," *Journal of Contemporary China,* 13(40), August 2004, 541–565. http://ejournals.ebsco.com/direct.asp?ArticleID=2U5A1VACL6K7BLPNC7WB

11. Joseph Kahn, "Chinese General Threatens Use of A-Bombs if the U.S. Intrudes," *New York Times,* July 15, 2005.

12. Constantine C. Menges, *China: The Gathering Threat* (Nashville: Nelson Current, 2005).

13. See note 3 above, page 151.

14. Dan Blumenthal, "Providing Arms: China and the Middle East," *The Middle East Quarterly,* XII(2), Spring 2005. http://www.meforum.org/article/695

15. The only condition that China has—and it's a very loose one—is that a country not officially recognize Taiwan.

16. "Forget Mao, Let's Do Business," *Economist,* February 7, 2004.

17. Daniel Byman and Cliff Roger, "China's Arms Sales: Motivations and Implications," Rand, 1999, 8. http://www.rand.org/publications/MR/MR1119/MR1119.chap3.pdf

18. See note 14 above.

19. "Iran Country Analysis Brief," Energy Information Administration, http://www.eia.doe.gov/emeu/cabs/iran.html

20. U.S. Department of State Office of the Coordinator for Counterterrorism, Country Reports on Terrorism 2004, April 2005. http://www.state.gov/documents/organization/45313.pdf

21. "Iran Makes Another Step Towards Nuclear Bomb Slovene Daily Says," BBC Monitoring International Reports, August 2005.

22. "China Signs $70 Billion Oil and LNG Agreement with Iran," *Daily Star,* October 30, 2004. http://www.dailystar.com.lb/article.asp?edition_id=10&categ_id=3&article_id=9713

23. "A New Scramble; China's Business Links with Africa," *Economist*, November 27, 2004.

24. As noted in U.N. documentation, "in accordance with the relevant provisions of the Charter of the United Nations, decisions of the Security Council are made by an affirmative vote of nine members of the Council including the concurring votes of the five permanent members (China, France, Russian Federation, United Kingdom of Great Britain and Northern Ireland, United States of America). If a permanent member casts a negative vote, the draft resolution being voted on is not passed." This veto power accrues to all permanent members of the United Nations Security Council.

25. Stephanie Giry, "China's Africa Strategy. Out of Beijing," *New Republic*, November 15, 2004.

26. "Global Trade, Local Impact: Arms Transfers to All Sides in the Civil War in Sudan," Human Rights Watch, August 1998. http://www.hrw.org/reports98/sudan/Sudarm988-03.htm

27. Other nations include Cuba, Iran, Libya, North Korea, and Syria.

28. Karby Leggett, "China Flexes Economic Muscles Throughout Burgeoning Africa," *Wall Street Journal*, March 29, 2005. http://www.howardwfrench.com/archives/2005/03/29/china_flexes_economic_muscle_throughout_burgeoning_africa/

29. Jean-Christophe Servant, "China's Trade Safari in Africa," *Le Monde diplomatique*, May 2005.

30. John McMillan, "The Main Institution in the Country Is Corruption: Creating Transparency in Angola," Center on Democracy, Development, and the Rule of Law, Stanford Institute on International Studies. http://iis-db.stanford.edu/pubs/20814/Corruption_transparency_Angola1_No36.pdf

31. "Time for Transparency," Global Witness, March 2004. http://www.globalwitness.org/reports/show.php/en.00049.html

32. Country Reports on Human Rights Practices, U.S. Department of State. February 25, 2000. http://www.state.gov/g/drl/rls/hrrpt/1999/223.htm

33. Steven Mosher, *Hegemon* (San Francisco: Encounter Books, 2000), p. 105.

34. Charles Wolf Jr. et al., "Fault Lines in China's Economic Terrain," Rand, 2003. http://www.rand.org/publications/MR/MR1686/

35. Ibid.

36. "Japan and China Face Off over Energy," Asia Times Online, July 2, 2005. http://www.atimes.com/atimes/Japan/GG02Dh01.html

37. "Japan's Provocation in East China Sea Very Dangerous," People's Daily Online, July 21, 2005. http://english.people.com.cn/200507/21/eng20050721_197493.html

38. "Oil and Gas in Troubled Waters," *Economist*, October 6, 2005.

39. See note 37 above.

40. Richard Rhodes and Denis Beller, "The Need for Nuclear Power," *Foreign Affairs*, January/February 2000.

Chapter 5

1. "Imperialism, the Highest Stage of Capitalism," http://www.marxists.org/archive/lenin/works/1916/imp-hsc/

2. "China Looms Large in the Global Mining Industry," *Asia Pacific Bulletin*, April 4, 2003. http://www.asiapacificbusiness.ca/apbn/pdfs/bulletin102.pdf

3. "Chinese and Builders Go Global," *Far Eastern Economic Review*, May 13, 2004.

4. Ibid.

5. Lindsey Hilsum, "The Chinese Are Coming," *New Statesman*, July 4, 2005. http://www.newstatesman.com/200507040007

6. Mao Tse-tung, "The People of Asia, Africa and Latin America Should Unite and Drive American Imperialism Back to Where It Came From," May 7, 1959. http://www.marxists.org/reference/archive/mao/selected-works/volume-8/mswv8_52.htm

7. "No Questions Asked," *Economist*, January 19, 2006. http://www.economist.com/displayStory.cfm?story_id=5425730

8. Samuel Wilson, "The Emperor's Giraffe," *Natural History* (101:12), December 1992. http://muweb.millersville.edu/~columbus/data/art/WILSON09.ART

9. Lindsey Hilsum, "We Love China," *Granta*. http://www.granta.com/extracts/2616

10. Ibid.

11. See note 5 above.

12. Karby Leggett, "Staking a Claim China Flexes Economic Muscle Throughout Burgeoning Africa," *Wall Street Journal*, March 29, 2005. http://www.howardwfrench.com/archives/2005/03/29/china_flexes_economic_muscle_throughout_burgeoning_africa/

13. Ibid.

14. Ibid.

15. Ibid.

16. "Exports by and Imports from Africa," Global Timer. http://www.globaltimber.org.uk/africa.htm

17. See note 12 above.

18. Stephanie Giry, "China's Africa Strategy. Out of Beijing," *New Republic*, November 15, 2004.

19. See note 9 above.

20. Vivienne Walt, "China's African Safari," *Fortune* (53:3) February 20, 2006, 58–63. http://money.cnn.com/magazines/fortune/fortune_archive/2006/02/20/8369153/index.htm

21. "Africa: China's Great Leap into the Continent," *Reuters*, March 23, 2006. http://www.alertnet.org/thenews/newsdesk/IRIN/acc4f61d2e9ccffcbb52abfb6cbf5e65.htm

22. "Made in China," *Business Africa,* July 1–15, 2005.

23. "China's Business Links with Africa, a New Scramble," *Economist,* November 25, 2004. http://www.economist.com/business/displayStory.cfm?story_id=3436400

24. See note 9 above.

25. See note 20 above.

26. Moeletsi Mbeki, "The Future Is to Follow China," *New Statesman,* March 14, 2005. http://www.newstatesman.com/nssubsfilter.php3?newTemplate=NSArticle_NS&newDisplayURN=200503140020

27. Henry Corbett Dillon, "China's Back-Door Energy Squeeze," *The Ornery American,* June 17, 2005. http://www.ornery.org/essays/2005-06-17-1.html

28. Tom Buerkle, "Ole China," Institutional Investor-International Edition (30:3), March 2005, 45–49.

29. Stephen Johnson, "Balancing China's Growing Influence in Latin America," Backgrounder #1888, The Heritage Foundation, October 24, 2005. http://www.heritage.org/Research/LatinAmerica/bg1888.cfm

30. Jane Bussey and Glenn Garvin, "China Exerting Regional Influence: Analysts Warn of Political, Strategic Challenges to U.S. in Latin America," *Miami Herald,* April 15, 2001. http://www.latinamericanstudies.org/cuba/china-influence.htm

31. David Sax, "A Hungry Dragon," *Canadian Business* (78:1), December 27, 2004, 27–28. http://www.canadianbusiness.com/managing/article.jsp?content=20041227_ 64453_64453

32. According to Stephen Johnson of the Heritage Foundation, "Radio China International signals originate from Cuba, as does interference with U.S. East Coast radio communications and air traffic control, according to Federal Communications Commission complaints." See note 29 above.

33. See note 29 above.

34. "China Goes Latin," *Economist,* February 14, 2005.

35. See note 29 above.

36. Paul Harris, "Chile Close on China FTA," *Reuters,* September 24, 2005. http://www.bilaterals.org/article.php3?id_article=2771

37. Geri Smith, "China and Chile: South America Is Watching," Business Week Online, November 18, 2005. http://www.businessweek.com/bwdaily/dnflash/nov2005/nf20051118_8302_db016.htm?campaign_id=rss_daily

38. See note 34 above.

39. See note 28 above.

40. See note 28 above.

41. See note 29 above.

42. See note 29 above.

43. See note 28 above.

44. "Falling Out of Love: Brazil's Affair with China Is Going Off the Boil," *Economist*, August 4, 2005. http://www.economist.com/world/la/displayStory.cfm?story_id=4249937

45. Ibid.

46. See note 29 above.

47. Melody Chen, "Taiwan, Grenada Set to Cut Ties," *Taiwan Times,* January 27, 2005. http://www.taipeitimes.com/News/taiwan/archives/2005/01/27/2003221117

48. Ibid.

49. See note 28 above.

50. See note 30 above.

Chapter 6

1. "Drug Intelligence Brief," U.S. Drug Enforcement Administration, Intelligence Division. February 2004. http://fas.org/irp/agency/doj/dea/product/china0204.pdf

2. "The Great Ecstasy Epidemic," *London Observer,* September 2003. http://mdma.net/club-drugs/global-ecstasy.html

3. The Golden Crescent also includes Iran and Pakistan. It is named for the "mountainous peripheries [that] define the crescent." Pierre-Arnaud Chouvy. "Drug Trade in Asia," Encyclopedia of Modern Asia (Chicago: Scribner's, 2002). http://www.pa-chouvy.org/drugtradeinasia.html

4. According to Wikipedia, "[I]t takes 10 kg of opium to make 1 kg of 90% pure heroin. The CIA states that impurities are introduced into the processed heroin before it hits the street, making the purity of the end consumer product about 40%. That implies that 10 kg of opium makes about 2.25 kg of 40% pure heroin." Assuming a street value of roughly $2 per gram, an equally rough estimate of the value of a ton of pure Afghan heroin (which commands a premium over lesser-quality Mexican heroin) exceeds $1 billion. This estimate is consistent with information from the U.S. Drug Enforcement Agency, which puts the street value of a ton of heroin at around a billion dollars. See http://www.dea.gov/pubs/states/newyork.html.

5. Kristianna Tho'Mas, "Opium War: Britain Stole Hong Kong from China," *Workers World,* July 10, 1997. http://www.serendipity.li/wod/hongkong.html

6. Frontline, "The Opium Kings." "The first to process heroin was C. R. Wright, an English researcher who unwittingly synthesized heroin (diacetylmorphine) in 1874 when he boiled morphine and a common chemical, acetic anhydride, over a stove for several hours." http://www.pbs.org/wgbh/pages/frontline/shows/heroin/transform/

7. According to Wikipedia, "'Realpolitik' is foreign policy based on practical concerns."

8. Tom Marzullo. "China's Western Expansion Strategy: Part Three," *Men's News Daily*, January 28, 2005. http://www.mensnewsdaily.com/archive/m-n/marzullo/2005/marzullo012805.htm

9. "Drugs, Oil, and War: Preface." http://ist-socrates.berkeley.edu/~pdscott/dowpref.html

10. "Heroin," Interpol, January 14, 2006. http://www.interpol.int/Public/Drugs/heroin/default.asp

11. "Globalization of the Drug Trade," Sources, April 1999. http://www.unesco.org/most/sourdren.pdf

12. Mitchell Koss, "Speed Sells: A tale of methamphetamine, drug cartels and an amateur chemist named Fester," *LA Weekly News*. February 11–17, 2000. http://www.laweekly.com/ink/00/12/news-koss.php

13. Bob Huff, "Speed Nation: Methamphetamine, HIV, and Hepatitis," *GMHC Treatment Issues*, July/August 2005. http://www.gmhc.org/health/treatment/ti/ti1978.html

14. "Methamphetamine," National Drug Threat Assessment, April 2004. http://www.usdoj.gov/ndic/pubs8/8731/

15. Lyrics by the Fugs. "New Amphetamine Shriek," 1966.

16. "Methamphetamine," Colorado North Metro Task Force, undated. http://www.nmtf.us/methamphetamine/methamphetamine.htm

17. See note 12 above.

18. See note 12 above.

19. "InfoFacts: Methamphetamine," National Institute on Drug Abuse, NIDA. http://www.nida.nih.gov/Infofacts/methamphetamine.html

20. See note 13 above.

21. See note 12 above.

22. "Amphetamine-Type Stimulants," U.N. General Assembly Special Session on the World Drug Problem, June 1998. http://www.un.org/ga/20special/featur/amphet.htm

23. Michael Scott, "Clandestine Drug Labs," Center for Problem-Oriented Policing. http://www.popcenter.org/Problems/problem-druglabs.htm

24. "Drug Intelligence Brief," U.S. Drug Enforcement Administration, Intelligence Division. February 2004. http://fas.org/irp/agency/doj/dea/product/china0204.pdf

25. "China Fights Surge in Illegal Narcotics Use," *Contra Costa Times*, March 2, 2004. http://six.pairlist.net/pipermail/burmanet/20040302/000378.html

26. See note 24 above.

27. Sally Apgar. "Isle 'Ice' Flows From California," *Honolulu Star-Bulletin*, September 9, 2003.

28. Rogue Pundit, "Random Nature #49," October 5, 2005. http://roguepundit.typepad.com/roguepundit/2005/10/index.html

29. "Chemically Synthesized Ephedrine Put into Mass Production in China," *People's Daily,* November 5, 2001. http://english.people.com.cn/english/200111/05/eng20011105_83931.html

30. "International Narcotics Control Strategy Report," U.S. Embassy in Moscow, 2003. http://moscow.usembassy.gov/embassy/section.php?record_id=report_narcotics

31. See note 24 above.

32. "Record Seizure of Ecstasy Stashed in Pineapple Tins from China." Australian Minister for Justice and Customs, Senator the Hon. Chris Ellison, Media Release, April 7, 2001.

33. "Utopian Pharmacology," BLTC Research, undated. http://www.mdma.net/

34. Ibid.

35. Ibid.

36. Ibid.

37. Ibid.

38. Ibid.

39. An article with this title originally appeared undated on the web in *Counselor Magazine.* http://www.counselormagazine.com/display_article.asp?aid=Agony_of_Ecstasy.asp

40. "MDMA (Ecstasy)," Executive Office of the President, Office of National Drug Control Policy, February 2004. http://www.whitehousedrugpolicy.gov/publications/factsht/mdma/

41. See note 39 above.

42. "The Great Ecstasy Epidemic," *Observer* (London), September 2003. http://mdma.net/club-drugs/global-ecstasy.html

43. Ibid.

44. Ibid.

45. Ibid.

46. "Efforts to Control Precursor Chemicals," International Office of National Drug Control Policy. ONDCP fact sheet, undated. http://www.whitehousedrugpolicy.gov/publications/international/factsht/precursor.html

47. International Narcotics Control Strategy Report, 1999. Bureau for International Narcotics and Law Enforcement Affairs, U.S. Department of State, Washington, D.C., March 2000. http://www.usconsulate.org.hk/uscn/narcotic/2000/incsr99.htm

Chapter 7

1. Tashi Tsering, "Policy Implications of Current Dam Projects on Drichu—the Upper Yangtze River," Tibet Justice Center, 2004. http://www.tibetjustice.org/enviro/Harvard_paper_drichu.pdf

2. Lubiao Zhang, "Social Impacts of Large Dams: The China Case," Chinese Academy of Agricultural Science, Contributing Paper, World Commission on Dams, undated. http://www.dams.org/docs/kbase/contrib/opt124.pdf

3. Ainun Nishat and Mahfuz Ullah, "Dammed or Damned," *Daily Star* (Bangladesh), December 22, 2000. http://www.dams.org/news_events/media235.htm

4. Henry Chu, "Yellow River Giving China New Sorrow. Asia: Overuse, Dry Weather Deplete Waterway Once Known for Flooding," *Los Angeles Times,* February 18, 1999.

5. "Confronting Pollution on the Yangtze River," *International Water Power & Dam Construction* (52:1) January 2000, 9.

6. Hai-Lun Zhang, "China Flood Management," WMO/GWP Associated Programmed on Flood Management. World Meteorological Organization and the Global Water Partnership. http://www.apfm.info/pdf/case_studies/syn_china.pdf

7. "Large Dams in China," Chinese National Committee on Large Dams, undated. http://www.icold-cigb.org.cn/icold2000/largedam.html

8. Ibid.

9. Antoaneta Bezlova, "Corruption Claims Rise Around Three Gorges Dam," *Asia Times,* July 26, 2000. http://www.atimes.com/china/BG26Ad01.html

10. Ma Jun, "China's Water Crisis," Norwalk Connecticut: Eastbridge, 2004. http://66.70.211.72/ChinasWaterCrisisMoreInfo.html

11. "China Floods Kill 120, Three Gorges on Alert," *Reuters,* September 7, 2004. http://www.mindfully.org/Water/2004/Three-Gorges-Dam7sep04.htm

12. Jasper Becker, "Part 1: The Death of China's Rivers," *Asia Times,* August 26, 2003. http://www.atimes.com/atimes/China/EH26Ad01.html

13. See note 1 above.

14. "Unsafe Dams Threaten 146 Million Chinese," *Epoch Times,* July 12, 2005. http://www.theepochtimes.com/news/5-7-12/30275.html

15. Ibid.

16. Ibid.

17. "30,000 Chinese Dams Unsafe," *Washington Times,* July 15, 2005. http://www.washtimes.com/upi/20050715-101040-9754r.htm

18. See note 1 above.

19. "Banqiao Dam," Wikipedia. http://www.answers.com/topic/banqiao-dam

20. Trần Tiến Khanh, "Death of a River: The Mekong River and the Chinese Development Projects Upstream," February 2003. http://www.vnbaolut.com/deathofariver.html

21. Sandra L. Postel and Aaron T. Wolf, "Dehydrating Conflict," *Foreign Policy,* September/October 2001, 60–67.

22. Fred Pearce, "Where Have All the Fish Gone? The Mighty Mekong Is Drying Up—and So Is the River's Rich Harvest. Vast New Dams in China Could Be to Blame," *Independent* (London), April 21, 2004.

23. Jane Perlez, "In Life on the Mekong, China's Dams Dominate," *New York Times,* March 19, 2005.

24. John Vidal, "Dammed and Dying: The Mekong and Its Communities Face a Bleak Future," *Guardian* (London), March 25, 2004.

Chapter 8

1. Prema Viswanathan and Florence Tan, "Troubled Waters," *Asian Chemical News* (10:456). August 16, 2004, 12–18.

2. Guang-Xin Zhang and Deng Wei, "The Groundwater Crisis and Sustainable Agriculture in Northern China," *Water Engineering & Management,* April 13, 2002.

3. "China Says Water Pollution So Severe That Cities Could Lack Safe Supplies," *China Daily,* June 28, 2005.

4. Tina Butler, "China's Imminent Water Crisis," Mongabay.com, May 30, 2005. http://news.mongabay.com/2005/0531-tina_butler.html

5. Ibid.

6. "China Economy: Water Crisis," EIU ViewsWire. New York, May 23, 2005.

7. See note 4 above.

8. Nicholas Stein, "Water, Water," *Fortune,* October 4, 2004.

9. "The Frequency of Offing Red-Tide Increasing," Xinhua Agency Report. http://monkey.ioz.ac.cn/bwg-cciced/english/warnings/warnings.htm

10. Joe McDonald, "China Has Another Environmental Disaster," *Associated Press,* December 22, 2005.

11. "Exposing a Dirty Secret; China's Pollution," *Economist,* July 21, 2001.

12. Peter Wonacott, "Polluters in China Feel No Pain; But Watchdog Seeks Changes by Holding Officials Accountable," *Wall Street Journal,* March 24, 2004.

13. "Toxic Chemicals to Be Phased Out," China.org.cn, November 11, 2004. http://www.china.org.cn/english/2004/Nov/111804.htm

14. See note 12 above.

15. See note 1 above.

16. Jianguo Liu and Jared Diamond, "China's Environment in a Globalizing World," *Nature,* June 30, 2005, 1179–1186. http://www.nature.com/nature/journal/v435/n7046/pdf/4351179a.pdf

17. "Study of Control and Management of Rural Nonpoint Source Pollution," Asian Development Bank, June 2002. http://www.adb.org/documents/tars/prc/R144_02.pdf

18. See note 16 above.

19. Hamish McDonald, "China's Unsafe Farming Practices May Be Breeding More Than Pigs," *Sydney Morning Herald,* April 7, 2003. http://www.smh.com.au/articles/2003/04/06/1049567564240.html

20. "China Needs to Recycle More," DC Consulting, May 8, 2002. http://www.dckonsult.com/news-envir-solidwaste.htm

21. Primary treatment involves the removal of floating and suspended solids, and secondary treatment uses biological methods such as digestion.

22. "Toxic Red Tide Spreads off China," PlanetArk, May 17, 2004. http://www.planetark.com/dailynewsstory.cfm/newsid/25118/story.htm

23. "China Reports Huge Losses Caused by Maritime Disasters in 2003," New China News Agency, February 15, 2004.

24. "Major Red Tides of Toxic Algae Found in China's Only Inland Sea," Xinhua News Agency, June 15, 2004. In 2003, China was hit by red tides 119 times, 40 times more than in 2002. Approximately 14,000 square kilometers were affected, devastating marine life, contaminating fish stock, and causing economic losses of more than $5 million. According to an official from the State Oceanic Administration, the increasing incidence of red tides is caused by rising pollution discharged into Chinese sea water in recent years.

25. "China Says Water Pollution So Severe That Cities Could Lack Safe Supplies," *China Daily,* June 7, 2005. http://www.chinadaily.com.cn/english/doc/2005-06/07/content_449451.htm

26. "Millions Face Water Shortage in North China, Officials Warn," *New York Times,* June 6, 2003.

27. Malin Falkenmark and Carl Widstrand. "Population and Water Resources: A Delicate Balance," Population Bulletin, Population Reference Bureau: Washington, D.C. 1992.

28. See note 6 above.

29. Henry Cho, "Yellow River Giving China New Sorrow; Asia Overuse, Dry Weather Deplete Waterway Once Known for Flooding," *Los Angeles Times,* February 18, 1999.

30. See note 6 above.

31. Lester R. Brown and Brian Halweil, "China's Water Shortage Could Shake World Grain Markets," Worldwatch Institute, April 22, 1998.

32. "An Unquenchable Thirst," *Economist,* June 19, 2004.

33. Water-technology.net, undated. "South-To-North Water Diversion Project, China." http://www.water-technology.net/projects/south_north/

34. Erik Eckholm, "China to Divert Waters at People-Moving Cost," *New York Times,* November 16, 2004.

35. Ibid.

36. H. Yang and A. Zehnder, "China's Regional Water Scarcity and Implications for Grain Supply and Trade," *Environment and Planning* (33:1), January 2001, 79–95.

37. "Beijing's Ground Sinks from Extraction of Ground Water," *Epoch Times.* August 6, 2004. http://www.theepochtimes.com/news/4-8-6/22750.html

38. "The Death of China's Rivers. Part 1," Jasper Becker, Asia Times Online, August 26, 2003. http://www.atimes.com/atimes/China/EH26Ad01.html

39. See note 2, page 4.

Chapter 9

1. Robert Marquand, "In China, Stresses Spill Over into Riots," *Christian Science Monitor,* November 22, 2004. http://www.csmonitor.com/2004/1122/p01s03-woap.html

2. Chris Buckley, "China to 'Strike Hard' Against Rising Unrest," Reuters, January 26, 2006. http://www.howardwfrench.com/archives/2006/01/27/china_to_strike_hard_against_rising_unrest/

   Jonathan Watts, "China Activists 'Vanish amid Protests,'" *Guardian,* February 25, 2006. http://www.guardian.co.uk/china/story/0,1717604,00.html

3. Eva Cheng, "China: New Protests and Riots Worry Beijing," *Green Left Weekly,* November 3, 2004.

4. John Chan, "China: Riot in Guangdong Province Points to Broad Social Unrest," World Socialist Web, November 2004. http://www.wsws.org/articles/2004/nov2004/chin-n30.shtml

5. "The Chizhou Incident," undated, EastSouthWestNorth website. www.zonaeuropa.com/200508brief.htm

6. See note 1 above.

7. "Quarrel over Toll Station Sparks Deadly Riot," *Taipei Times,* November 17, 2004. http://www.taipeitimes.com/News/world/archives/2004/11/17/2003211425

8. Kathy Chen, "Chinese Protests Grow More Frequent, Violent," *Wall Street Journal,* May 11, 2004. http://www.chinalaborwatch.org/en/web/article.php?article_id=50225

9. "Pakistan Denies Hand in China Riots," United Press International, February 12, 1997.

10. See note 1 above.

11. See note 8 above.

12. Wing-yue Trini Leung, "What Can Be Done for the Largest but Deadliest Manufacturing Center in the World?" Testimony before the Congressional-Executive Commission on China. November 2, 2002. http://www.cecc.gov/pages/roundtables/110702/leung.php

13. Ibid.

14. Ibid.

15. Ibid.

16. "Migrant Workers' Unpaid Wages A Nagging Problem," *China Daily,* August 17, 2005. http://www.china.org.cn/english/2005/Aug/138763.htm

17. "Does China Have 10m Slaves?" *Economist,* February 1, 2003.

18. Ibid.

19. Mao Tse-tung, "Report on an Investigation of the Peasant Movement in Hunan, March 1927," Modern History Sourcebook. http://www.fordham.edu/halsall/mod/1927mao.html

20. Carol Divjak, "Rural Protests in China Put Down by Riot Police," World Socialist website, September 7, 2000. http://www.wsws.org/articles/2000/sep2000/chin-s07.shtml

21. "Democracy Chinese-Style," *Economist,* October 13, 2005. http://www.economist.com/displaystory.cfm?story_id=5028611

22. "Desperate Measures," *Economist,* January 26, 2006. http://www.economist.com/world/displaystory.cfm?story_id=5436968

23. Ibid.

24. See note 20 above.

25. "Struggle for China's Farmers Endures, Despite Modernisation," *Asia Pacific News,* February 27, 2006. http://www.channelnewsasia.com/stories/afp_asiapacific/view/195259/1/.html

26. This is a term used in China to describe the spoiling of the single children of many families dictated by the one-child policy.

27. Edward Cody, "In Face of Rural Unrest, China Rolls Out Reforms," *Washington Post Foreign Service,* January 28, 2003.

28. See note 25 above.

29. Andrea Mandel-Campbell, "Ready for Revolution," *Maclean's,* August 29, 2005.

30. Ibid.

31. Ibid.

32. William Dobson, "Bad News for China's Autocrats," *New Republic,* December 14, 2005. http://www.tnr.com/doc.mhtml?i=w051212&s=dobson121405

33. See note 29 above.

34. Edward Cody, "A Chinese City's Rage at the Rich and Powerful Beating of Student Sparks Riot, Looting," *Washington Post Foreign Service,* August 1, 2005.

35. Lindsay Beck, "Violence Works Where Peace Failed for China Villages," *Reuters,* February 1, 2006. http://www.boston.com/news/world/asia/articles/2006/02/01/violence_works_where_peace_failed_for_china_villages/

36. This belief dates back as far as the era of the Chinese philosopher Mencius (372–289 B.C.). As noted on the web (Chinese Philosophy, Mencius) by Richard Hooker, "Mencius, like Confucius, believed that rulers were divinely placed in order to guarantee peace and order among the people they rule. Unlike Confucius, Mencius believed that if a ruler failed to bring peace and order about, then

the people could be absolved of all loyalty to that ruler and could, if they felt strongly enough about the matter, revolt." http://www.wsu.edu/~dee/CHPHIL/ MENCIUS.HTM

37. "China Riots: Silencing Protest Is Not the Answer," *The American Thinker*, April 13, 2005. http://frankwarner.typepad.com/free_frank_warner/2005/04/china_ riots_sil.html

38. Patrick Tyler, "In West China, Tensions with Ethnic Muslims Erupt in Riots, Bombings," *New York Times*, February 28, 1997.

39. David Theo Goldberg and John Solomos, eds., *A Companion to Racial and Ethnic Studies* (Oxford: Blackwell, 2002), 495–510. Frank Dikötter quoted.

40. Xinjiang does produce a large share of China's cotton, wool, sugar beets, grapes, and tomatoes.

41. "A decision in Beijing in 1994 to require that all cropland used for construction be offset by land reclaimed elsewhere has helped create the ecological disaster that is now unfolding. . . . The fast-growing coastal provinces, such as Guandong, Shandong, Xheijiang, and Jiangsu, which are losing cropland to urban expansion and industrial construction, are paying other provinces to plow new land to offset their losses. . . . as the northwestern provinces, already suffering from overplowing and overgrazing, plowed ever more marginal land, wind erosion intensified. Now accelerating wind erosion of soil and the resulting land abandonment are forcing people to migrate eastward, not unlike the U.S. westward migration from the southern Great Plains to California during the Dust Bowl years," Earth Policy Alert, International Erosion Control Association, 2005. http://www.ieca. org/Resources/Article/ArticleDustBowlChina.asp

42. Steppes are large, semiarid grass-covered plains.

43. Tang Fuchun, "Xinjiang, a Natural Reserve Bonanza," China.org.cn. March 12, 2005. http://www.china.org.cn/english/2005/Mar/122605.htm

44. Oil deposits are estimated at 20.86 billion tons and natural gas deposits at 10.3 trillion cubic meters. "Cleaner Production in China." http://www.chinacp.com/ eng/cpfactories/cpfact_lunnan_oilfield.html

45. "Xinjiang's Oil Output Tops 24 Mln Tons in 2005," Xinhua News Agency, China.org.cn. January 4, 2006.

46. Chinese news agency Zhongguo Xinwen She, Beijing, January 14, 2003.

47. "Devastating Blows Religious Repression of Uighurs in Xinjiang," *Human Rights Watch* (17:2c), 2005. http://hrw.org/reports/2005/china0405/china0405text.pdf

48. Ibid.

49. "China's Domestic 'Terrorists,'" Simon World, August 30, 2004. http://simonworld. mu.nu/archives/043369.php

50. "The Great Leap West." *Economist*, August 26, 2004. http://www.uygur.org/ wunn04/08_26.htm

51. Ibid.

Chapter 10

1. "China's Growing Pains," *Economist*, August 21, 2004.

2. "China and the Issue of Communism," Excerpts from *L' Asie et Nous,* Jean-Luc Domenach Entretien with Aimé Savard (Paris: Desclée de Brouwer, 2001). http://www.hsstudyc.org.hk/Webpage/Tripod/T134/T134_E08.htm

3. David Lynch, "Looming Pension Crisis in China Stirs Fears of Chaos." *USA Today,* April 19, 2005. http://www.usatoday.com/news/world/2005-04-19-china-social-security_x.htm

4. Ibid.

5. Ibid.

6. "Gouged," *Economist*, November 19, 2005.

7. Roberta Lipson, "Investing in China's Hospitals," *China Business Review,* November–December 2004. http://www.chinabusinessreview.com/public/0411/chindex.html

8. Peter Goodman, "Hospitals in China Find Profit in AIDS: Patients Pressured to Pay for Extra Tests, Treatments," Washingtonpost.com, November 8, 2005. http://www.washingtonpost.com/wp-dyn/content/article/2005/11/07/AR2005110701671.html

9. "Keeping China Healthy," *China Business Review,* November–December 2004.

10. Ibid.

11. "China's Health Insurance System in Transformation," *International Social Security Review* (57), March 2004.

12. "Locked Doors: The Human Rights of People Living with HIV/AIDS in China," *Human Rights Watch* (15:7c), August 2003.

13. Xiong Lei, "How SARS Could Save a Nation," *New Statesmen,* January 1, 2005. http://www.newstatesman.com/200501010018

14. See note 6 above.

15. Melinda Liu, "The Flimsy Wall of China," *Newsweek,* October 31, 2005.

16. "China's Health Care Crisis," China Challenges weblog, July 29, 2005. http://chinachallenges.blogs.com/my_weblog/2005/07/chinas_health_c.html

17. "China Focus: Poor, Rich Disparities Affect Women, Children's Health Care," People's Daily Online, April 8, 2005. http://english.people.com.cn/200504/08/eng20050408_180087.html

18. Nancy Riley, "China's Population: New Trends and Challenges," *Population Bulletin,* June 2004. http://www.findarticles.com/p/articles/mi_qa3761/is_200406/ai_n9455376/pg_2

19. Ibid.

20. Tim Johnson, "China Rising: The Boom's High Cost: China's Heavy Pollution Is Sparking Riots," *Knight Ridder,* July 20, 2005. http://www.realcities.com/mld/krwashington/12179835.htm

21. Jim Yardley, "Rivers Run Black and Chinese Die of Cancer," *New York Times*, September 12, 2004. http://www.globalpolicy.org/socecon/develop/quality/2004/0912chinapollution.htm

22. Howard French, "Anger in China Rises over Threat to Environment," *New York Times*, July 19, 2005. http://www.nytimes.com/2005/07/19/international/asia/19china.html?ex=1279425600&en=2319c5dae21c9ab8&ei=5090&partner=rssuserland&emc=rss

23. See note 21 above.

24. See note 22 above.

25. Lindsay Beck, "Violence Works Where Peace Failed for China Villages," *Reuters*, February 1, 2006. http://www.boston.com/news/world/asia/articles/2006/02/01/violence_works_where_peace_failed_for_china_villages/

26. "Entertaining or Subverting?: Chinese Television Tries to Go Global," Angry Chinese Blogger, April 10, 2006. [The Angry Chinese Blogger may be accessed at: http://angrychineseblogger.blog-city.com/]

27. Nicholas Eberstadt, "The Future of AIDS," *Foreign Affairs*, November/December 2002. http://www.foreignaffairs.org/20021101faessay9990/nicholas-eberstadt/the-future-of-aids.html

28. Ibid.

29. Ibid.

30. Ibid.

31. Ibid.

32. Ibid.

33. Ibid.

34. Lora Sabin, presentation, "Corporate Responsibility in a World of AIDS: The Economic Case for Investing Now," Socioeconomic Impact of HIV/AIDS, Center for International Health and Development, Boston University School of Public Health, November 5, 2003.

35. "People's Republic of China Continuing Abuses under a New Leadership—Summary of Human Rights Concerns," Amnesty International. http://www.amnestyusa.org/countries/china/document.do?id=566EE24E856F154280256DC8003CDDB6

36. "AIDS in China: Anatomy of an Epidemic," *Economist*, July 28, 2005. http://www.economist.com/World/asia/displayStory.cfm?story_id=4223578

37. "HIV/AIDS: China's Titanic Peril: 2001 Update of the AIDS Situation and Needs Assessment Report," UN Theme Group on HIV/AIDS in China, June 2002.

38. Alice Park, "China's Secret Plague: How One U.S. Scientist Is Struggling to Help the Government Face Up to an Exploding AIDS Crisis," *Time*, July 19, 2004. http://www.time.com/time/asia/magazine/article/0,13673,501031215-557111,00.html

39. "Blood Safety and Donation: A Global View," World Health Organization Fact Sheet 279, revised June 2005. http://www.who.int/mediacentre/factsheets/fs279/en/print.html

40. See note 37 above.

41. See note 37 above.

42. See note 12 above.

43. See note 12 above.

44. See note 12 above.

45. Joshua Kurlantzick, "China's Drug Problem and Looming HIV Epidemic," *World Policy Journal,* June 2002. http://www.worldpolicy.org/journal/articles/wpj02-2/Kurlantzick.pdf

46. See note 36 above.

47. "Life on China's Edge," *Economist,* September 14, 1996. http://www.burmalibrary.org/reg.burma/archives/199609/msg00079.html

48. Zunyou Wu, M.D. Ph.D., et al., "Community-Based Trial to Prevent Drug Use among Youths in Yunnan, China," *American Journal of Public Health* (92:12), December 2002, 1952–1957. http://www.ajph.org/cgi/content/abstract/92/12/1952

49. See note 12 above.

50. See note 12 above.

51. B. Zhang et al., "A Survey of Men Who Have Sex with Men: Mainland China," *American Journal of Public Health* (90:12), December 2000, 1949–1950. See also http://www.medicalnewstoday.com/medicalnews.php?newsid=25095.

52. Nicholas Eberstadt, "The Future of AIDS," *Foreign Affairs,* November/December 2002. http://www.foreignaffairs.org/20021101faessay9990/nicholas-eberstadt/the-future-of-aids.html

53. See note 12 above.

54. See note 36 above.

55. See note 12 above.

56. See note 38 above.

57. "Men Who Have Sex with Men in Shenzhen, China, Rarely Use Condoms to Prevent Spread of HIV," *HIV/AIDS News,* May 25, 2005. http://www.medicalnewstoday.com/medicalnews.php?newsid=25095

58. Gill Bates, Jennifer Chang, and Sarah Palmer, "China's HIV Crisis," *Foreign Affairs,* March/April 2002. http://www.brookings.edu/views/articles/gill/20020301.pdf

59. Ibid.

60. See note 45 above.

61. See note 12 above.

Chapter 11

1. This rather sobering observation was offered to me as a young graduate student at Harvard University when I interviewed Harvard's Banfield about the origins of ideology for my first book, *The Policy Game* (New York: Wiley, 1984).

2. Martin Crutsinger, "U.S. Vows to Get Tough with China on Trade Laws," *Seattle Times*, February 14, 2006.

3. Lawrence H. Summers, "The United States and the Global Adjustment Process," speech at the Third Annual Stavros S. Niarchos Lecture, Institute for International Economics, Washington, D.C., March 23, 2004. (Emphasis added) http://www.iie.com/publications/papers/paper.cfm?researchid=200

4. Jonathan Watts, "China Vows to Create 'New Socialist Countryside,'" *Guardian* (London), March 3, 2006. http://www.guardian.co.uk/guardianweekly/outlook/story/0,1721546,00.html

5. "Milestone Year for China's Economic Development," Blackwell Publishing, March 2006. http://www.blackwellpublishing.com/press/pressitem.asp?ref=693

6. "China's Parliament Endorses Major Economic Policy Changes," People's Daily Online, March 14, 2006. http://english.people.com.cn/200603/14/eng20060314_250462.html

7. "China President Hu Jintao Calls for More Sustainable Economic Growth," Xinhua Financial Network News, February 23, 2006.

8. Clifford Coonan. "China Slaps Tax on Chopsticks to Save Trees," *Independent* (London), March 23, 2006.

9. Robert Marquand, "A 'Green' Building Rises amid Beijing Smog," *Christian Science Monitor*, April 3, 2006.

10. Robert D. Kaplan, "How We Would Fight China," *Atlantic Monthly*, June 2005.

11. "Think Strategically," *Defense News*, May 29, 2006.

12. As noted by Chen Jieren, who was fired from his post as editor of China's *Public Interest Times*, "Chinese editors bow to self-censorship and assume a fawning attitude towards the government: in this way we will never manage to tell the truth." AsiaNews/SCMP, "Editors' self-censorship kills truth, says Chinese journalist," February 13, 2006.

13. For an assessment, see "China—Annual Report 2006," Reporters Without Borders for Press Freedom, undated. http://www.rsf.org/article.php3?id_article=17349

14. As noted in the *New York Times*, "To obey China's censorship laws, Google's representatives explained, the company had agreed to purge its search results of any Web sites disapproved of by the Chinese government, including Web sites promoting Falun Gong, a government-banned spiritual movement; sites promoting free speech in China; or any mention of the 1989 Tiananmen Square massacre. If you search for "Tibet" or "Falun Gong" most anywhere in the world on google.com, you'll find thousands of blog entries, news items and chat rooms on Chinese repression. Do the same search inside China on google.cn, and most, if

not all, of these links will be gone. Google will have erased them completely."
Clive Thompson, *New York Times,* "Google's China Problem (and China's
Google Problem)," April 23, 2006.

15. Center for Strategic and International Studies and Institute for International
    Economics, *China: The Balance Sheet* (New York: Public Affairs), 150. 2006.

16. "Annual Report to Congress: Military Power of the People's Republic of China
    2006." Department of Defense, Office of the Secretary of Defense, May 2006.

17. See note 15 above, page 144.

18. See note 15 above, page 146.

19. The facility was later destroyed by American bombers during the 1991 Gulf
    War. Wikipedia.

20. See note 15 above, page 126.

21. See note 11 above.

Index

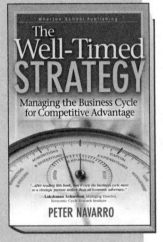

THE WELL-TIMED STRATEGY
Managing the Business Cycle for Competitive Advantage

By Peter Navarro

Most companies ignore one of their best opportunities for honing competitive advantage: the opportunity to proactively manage business cycles and macroeconomic turbulence. Despite the profound impact that the business cycle has on the fortunes and fate of so many businesses large and small—and the employees and investors that depend on them—not a single book offers a comprehensive guide to strategically and tactically managing the business cycle. *The Well-Timed Strategy* shows how to manage not just the business cycle and industry cycles but also today's unprecedented level of macroeconomic turbulence. Peter Navarro shows how to align every facet of business strategy, tactics, and operations to reflect changing business conditions.

ISBN 0131494201 ■ © 2006 ■ 272 pp. ■ $27.99 USA ■ $34.99 CAN

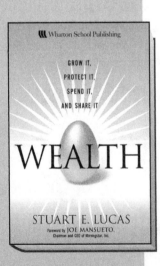

WEALTH
Grow It, Protect It, Spend It, and Share It

By Stuart E. Lucas

Here is the first book to integrate all the essential components of wealth management into a coherent whole. Generate higher, more predictable returns…identify, retain, and coordinate the right advisors…get your family to agree on goals and priorities… intelligently manage assets received through inheritances and business sales…and much more. Stuart Lucas draws on 25 years of experience managing wealth. He is Chairman of Wealth Strategist Network LLC and Principal and Investment Advisor at Cataumet Partners, his family's investment office. He is also an heir to the Carnation Company fortune after it was sold to Nestlé in 1985.

ISBN 0132366797 ■ © 2006 ■ 400 pp. ■ $25.99 USA ■ $32.99 CAN